MW01125539

THE HISTORY OF TAIWAN

Xiaobing Li

The Greenwood Histories of the Modern Nations
Frank W. Thackeray and John E. Findling, Series Editors

GREENWOOD

An Imprint of ABC-CLIO, LLC
Santa Barbara, California • Denver, Colorado

Library of Congress Cataloging-in-Publication Data

Names: Li, Xiaobing, author.
Title: The history of Taiwan / Xiaobing Li.
Description: Santa Barbara : Greenwood Publishing Group, Inc., 2019. |
    Series: Greenwood histories of the modern nations | Includes bibliographical
    references and index. |
Identifiers: LCCN 2019020661 (print) | LCCN 2019980295 (ebook) |
    ISBN 9781440861253 | ISBN 9781440861260 (ebook)
Subjects: LCSH: Taiwan—History.
Classification: LCC DS799.5 .L494 2019 (print) | LCC DS799.5 (ebook) |
    DDC 951.249—dc23
LC record available at https://lccn.loc.gov/2019020661
LC ebook record available at https://lccn.loc.gov/2019980295

ISBN: 978-1-4408-6125-3 (print)
      978-1-4408-6126-0 (ebook)

23 22 21 20 19   1 2 3 4 5

This book is also available as an eBook.

Greenwood
An Imprint of ABC-CLIO, LLC

ABC-CLIO, LLC
147 Castilian Drive
Santa Barbara, California 93117
www.abc-clio.com

This book is printed on acid-free paper ∞

Manufactured in the United States of America

Contents

Series Foreword

The Greenwood Histories of the Modern Nations series is intended to provide students and interested laypeople with up-to-date, concise, and analytical histories of many of the nations of the contemporary world. Not since the 1960s has there been a systematic attempt to publish a series of national histories, and as series editors, we believe that this series will prove to be a valuable contribution to our understanding of other countries in our increasingly interdependent world.

At the end of the 1960s, the Cold War was an accepted reality of global politics. The process of decolonization was still in progress, the idea of a unified Europe with a single currency was unheard of, the United States was mired in a war in Vietnam, and the economic boom in Asia was still years in the future. Richard Nixon was president of the United States, Mao Tse-tung (not yet Mao Zedong) ruled China, Leonid Brezhnev guided the Soviet Union, and Harold Wilson was prime minister of the United Kingdom. Authoritarian dictators still controlled most of Latin America, the Middle East was reeling in the wake of the Six-Day War, and Shah Mohammad Reza Pahlavi was at the height of his power in Iran.

Since then, the Cold War has ended, the Soviet Union has vanished, leaving 15 independent republics in its wake, the advent of the computer age has radically transformed global communications, the rising demand for oil makes the Middle East still a dangerous flashpoint, and the rise of new economic powers like the People's Republic of China (PRC) and India threatens to bring about a new world order. All of these developments have had a dramatic impact on the recent history of every nation of the world.

For this series, which was launched in 1998, we first selected nations whose political, economic, and socio-cultural affairs marked them as among the most important of our time. For each nation, we found an author who was recognized as a specialist in the history of that nation. These authors worked cooperatively with us and with Greenwood Press to produce volumes that reflected current research on their nations and that are interesting and informative to their readers. In the first decade of the series, close to 50 volumes were published, and some have now moved into second editions.

The success of the series has encouraged us to broaden our scope to include additional nations, whose histories have had significant effects on their regions, if not on the entire world. In addition, geopolitical changes have elevated other nations into positions of greater importance in world affairs and, so, we have chosen to include them in this series as well. The importance of a series such as this cannot be underestimated. As a superpower whose influence is felt all over the world, the United States can claim a "special" relationship with almost every other nation. Yet many Americans know very little about the histories of nations with which the United States relates. How did they get to be the way they are? What kind of political systems have evolved there? What kind of influence do they have on their own regions? What are the dominant political, religious, and cultural forces that move their leaders? These and many other questions are answered in the volumes of this series.

The authors who contribute to this series write comprehensive histories of their nations, dating back, in some instances, to prehistoric times. Each of them, however, has devoted a significant portion of their book to events of the past 40 years because the modern era has contributed the most to contemporary issues that have an impact on U.S. policy. Authors make every effort to be as up-to-date as possible so that readers can benefit from discussion and analysis of recent events.

In addition to the historical narrative, each volume contains an introductory chapter giving an overview of that country's geography, political institutions, economic structure, and cultural attributes. This is meant to give readers a snapshot of the nation as it exists in the contemporary world. Each history also includes supplementary information following the narrative, which may include a timeline that represents a succinct chronology of the nation's historical evolution, biographical sketches of the nation's most important historical figures, and a glossary of important terms or concepts that are usually expressed in a foreign language. Finally, each author prepares a comprehensive bibliography for readers who wish to pursue the subject further.

Readers of these volumes will find them fascinating and well written. More importantly, they will come away with a better understanding of the contemporary world and the nations that comprise it. As series editors, we hope that this series will contribute to a heightened sense of global understanding as we move through the early years of the twenty-first century.

Frank W. Thackeray and John E. Findling
Indiana University Southeast

Acknowledgments

I wish to thank the Sun Yat-sen Foundation, China Reunification Alliance, and Mainland Affairs Council, the Executive Yuan, Republic of China (ROC). They provided financial assistance for my research trips to Taiwan and arranged many interviews during my visits in 2015–2018. I am grateful to the staff of Academia Sinica at Taipei, National Palace Museum, and Taiwan National University for their assistance and advice on my research in Taiwan.

Many people at the University of Central Oklahoma (UCO) have contributed to this book and deserve recognition. First, I would like to thank Provost John F. Barthell, Dean of the College of Liberal Arts Catherine S. Webster, and Chairperson of the Department of History and Geography Katrina Lacher. They have been supportive of the project over the past years. The UCO faculty merit-credit program sponsored by the Office of Academic Affairs, as well as travel funds from the College of Liberal Arts, provided funding for my trips to conferences. The UCO Research, Creative, and Scholarly Activities grants sponsored by the Office of High-impact Practice, led by Director Michael Springer, made student research assistants available for the project during the past three years. Special thanks to Brad Watkins who drew the maps. Heidi Vaugh and her graduate assistants at UCO

Laboratory of History Museum provided archival assistance. UCO graduate student Travis Chambers copyedited several chapters. Annamaria Martucci provided secretarial assistance. This volume is also supported by the Fundamental Research Funds for the Central Universities (Project #19JNYH03), under Shao Xiao at Ji'nan University in Guangzhou, Guangdong, China.

I also wish to thank Kaitlin Ciarmiello, senior acquisitions editor at ABC-CLIO, who offered many valuable suggestions and criticism on the manuscript. She patiently guided this project in the past three years. Any remaining errors of facts, language usage, and interpretation are my own.

Timeline of Important Events

50,000–20,000 BC	First migrants arrive through a land bridge from China and create Changpin Paleolithic culture at present-day Tainan
30,000–20,000 BC	"Tsochen Man" live in south Taiwan
8000–5000 BC	Agriculture develops in the central plains
4000–1000 BC	Pottery making and Dapenkeng and Peinan Neolithic cultures
3000–500 BC	Southern Pacific Islanders, or Malayo-Polynesians and Austronesians, arrive and become the aboriginal people
200 BC–AD 200	Iron making and Shihsanhang Metal Age culture
220–280	Three Kingdoms in China
230	Wu emperor Sun Quan (Sun Chuan) sends 10,000 troops to *Yizhou* (Taiwan)
581–618	Sui dynasty
605–610	Sui Yangdi (Yang-ti) dispatches three expeditionary forces to *Liuqiu* (Taiwan)

960–1279	Song dynasty
1171	Song sets an administrative office and garrison on the Penghu (P'eng-hu, Pescadores) Islands
1271–1368	Mongol's Yuan dynasty
1292	Beijing sends 6,000 troops to attack *Little Liuqiu* (Taiwan)
1297	Fujian provincial forces attack Taiwan
1368–1644	Ming dynasty
1371	Ming emperor Hongwu issues a sea ban
1378	Ming closes the Penghu administrative office and withdraws its garrison
1430–1432	Zheng He and his fleet land on Taiwan during their overseas voyages
1553	Portuguese leases Macao (Macau) for trade
1560–1565	General Qi Jiguang leads the Ming navy to fight Japanese and Taiwanese pirates
1590	Portuguese are the first Europeans to arrive at "Formosa" (Taiwan)
1604	Dutch attacks Penghu (the "Penghu Incident")
1622–1623	Dutch fleet lands at Penghu and attacks Fujian navy at Jinmen
1624–1662	Dutch colonization of Taiwan through Dutch East India Company
1624	Governor Pieter Nuyts builds Fort Zeelandia (Anping Castle)
1626	Spanish occupies Keelung and Tamsui in north Taiwan
1628	Spanish builds Fort Santo Domingo at Tamsui
1635–1639	Dutch troops defeat Taiwanese aboriginal resistances
1635	Dutch governor Hans Putmans constructs Fort Redoubt Utrecht
1642	Putmans defeats the Spanish troops on Taiwan

1644–1911	Manchu's Qing dynasty
1652	Governor Frederick Coyett crashes a Chinese anti-Dutch rebellion
1661–1662	Zheng Chenggong defeats the Dutch forces and ends the colonization
1662–1683	Zheng's regime on Taiwan
1683	Qing navy defeats Zheng's forces and occupies Taiwan
1684–1895	Beijing establishes administrative office on Taiwan
1858	Qing opens up Taipei and Anping for European trade
1862–1865	Tamsui and other cities also are open for European trade
1874	Japan attacks Taiwan, and the Qing cedes the Penghu Islands to Japan
1875–1885	Qing officials' reform and the "Self-Strengthening Movement" on Taiwan
1886	Taiwan becomes a province of China
1894	The Qing navy and army loses the Sino-Japanese War
1895–1902	Military conquest and police-state control by arresting and executing 19,000
1895	Beijing signs the Treaty of Shimonoseki to cede Taiwan to Japan
1895	The "Taiwan Republic" lasts for months after Japan lands and kills 14,000 people
1902–1919	New colonial policy for economic reforms and urban development
1908	Cross-island railroad is completed
1919–1937	Cultural and educational assimilation
1930	Taiwanese aborigines kill 197 Japanese in the "Masha Incident"
1937–1945	Taiwan is involved in World War II and 270,000 Taiwanese serve in Japanese military

1945	The Kuomintang (KMT) troops land at Taiwan and Governor Ch'en Yi arrive at Taipei in October
1947	Armed rebellion takes place in Taiwan as the "2–28 Incident" and 28,000 are killed
1949	Mao wins the civil war, and Chiang Kai-shek moves the seat of the ROC government to Taiwan
1950	Chiang announces martial law, which lasts for 38 years in Taiwan
1950	The Korean War breaks out, and the United States sends the forces and aid to Taiwan
1953	The First Four-year Economic Plan and the Land Reform
1954	The First Taiwan Strait Crisis and the U.S.-Taiwan Mutual Defense Treaty is signed
1955	Army Chief Sun Li-jen and 300 KMT generals and officers are charged or executed
1956	Established permanent presence on the Taiping, Spratly Islands, South China Sea
1958	The Second Taiwan Strait Crisis
1965	The Fourth Four-year Economic Plan without the U.S. aid for the first time
1966	Many "Manufacturing Industrial Zones" are created
1971	Taiwan is replaced by China in the United Nations
	The announcement that the Senkaku Islands belong to Taiwan is made
1972	President Nixon visits Beijing and signs the Shanghai Communiqué
1975	Chiang Kai-shek dies on April 5
	Yen Chia-kan (Yan Jiagan, 1905–1993) becomes interim president from 1975 to 1978
1977	"Zhongli Incident"
1978	Chiang Ching-kuo becomes the president; Japan ends diplomatic relations with Taiwan

1979	The United States ends diplomatic relations with Taiwan; Congress passes the Taiwan Relations Act
	"Formosa Incident"
1986	Democratic Progressive Party (DPP) is founded
1987	Martial law is lifted
1988	Chiang Ching-kuo dies; Lee Teng-hui becomes the ROC president
1991	Constitutional reform
1992	The cross-straits talks reach an agreement known as the "1992 Consensus"
1996	Lee is elected in the first free presidential election; the Third Taiwan Strait Crisis
1998	Lee announces a "state-to-state relationship" with China and notion of "new Taiwanese"
2000	Chen Shui-bian wins the presidential election on the DPP ticket
2002	President Chen meets Colin Powell, U.S. secretary of state, in New York City
2004	Chen is reelected after surviving an assassination attempt
2006	Chen's wife and their son-in-law are indicted of corruption
2008	Ma Ying-jeou wins the presidential election on the KMT ticket; Chen is charged guilty of corruption
	ROC vice president Vincent Siew meets Hu Jintao, the PRC president, at Hainan
2009	Ma is reelected the KMT chairman
	Cross-strait agreements on direct air, sea, and mail links; visitors, tourists, and students
2010	Chen Shui-bian is sentenced to twenty years in prison
2012	Ma Ying-jeou wins the reelection
2015	Ma meets Xi Jinping, PRC president, at Singapore

TAIWAN

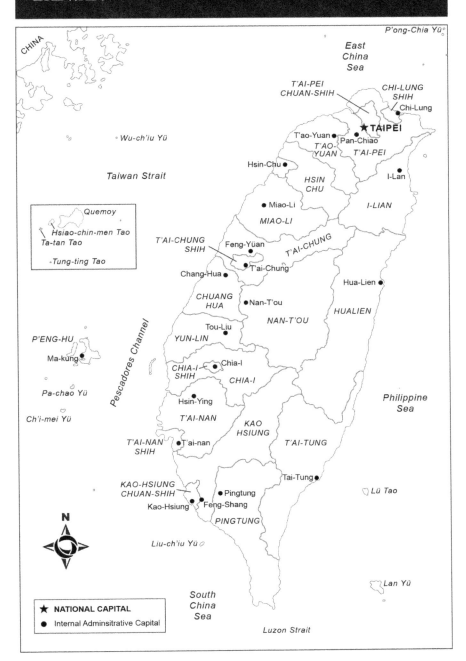

P'ong-Chia Yü

CHINA

East
China
Sea

T'AI-PEI
CHUAN-SHIH

CHI-LUNG
SHIH

Chi-Lung

Wu-ch'iu Yü

T'ao-Yuan
Pan-Chiao

★TAIPEI

T'AO-
YUAN

T'AI-PEI

Taiwan Strait

Hsin-Chu

HSIN
CHU

I-Lan

Quemoy

Hsiao-chin-men Tao
Ta-tan Tao

Tung-ting Tao

Miao-Li

MIAO-LI

I-LIAN

T'AI-CHUNG
SHIH

Feng-Yüan

T'AI-CHUNG

Chang-Hua

T'ai-Chung

Hua-Lien

CHUANG
HUA

Nan-T'ou

HUALIEN

P'ENG-HU

NAN-T'OU

Ma-kung

Tou-Liu

YUN-LIN

Pa-chao Yü

CHIA-I
SHIH

Chia-I

Ch'i-mei Yü

CHIA-I

Philippine
Sea

Hsin-Ying

T'AI-NAN

KAO
HSIUNG

T'AI-NAN
SHIH

T'ai-nan

T'AI-TUNG

Tai-Tung

Lü Tao

KAO-HSIUNG
CHUAN-SHIH

Pingtung

Kao-Hsiung

Feng-Shang

PINGTUNG

N

Liu-ch'iu Yü

Lan Yü

★ NATIONAL CAPITAL

● Internal Adminsitrative Capital

South
China
Sea

Luzon Strait

TAIWAN AND CHINA

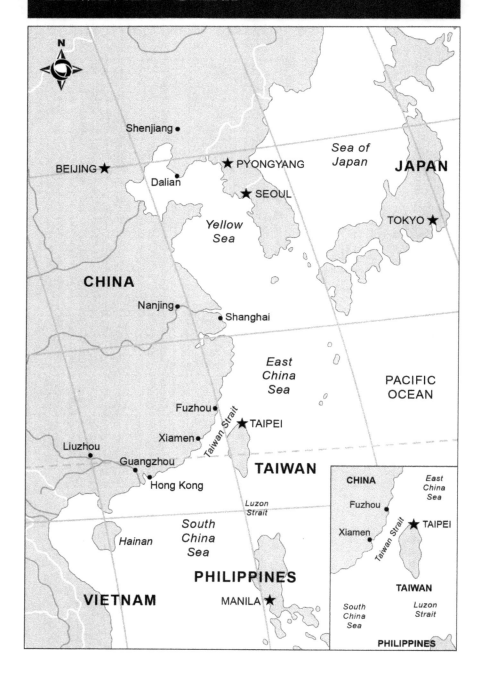

SOUTH CHINA SEA: DISPUTED ISLANDS

- ----- Philippine Claim Line
- ——— Chinese Claim Line
- --- Malaysian Claim Line

1

A Pearl in the Pacific Ocean

Few history books address the complexity of Taiwan's history because of its unique geopolitical relation to mainland China. Since the founding of the People's Republic of China (PRC) in 1949, the Chinese Communist Party (CCP) insists that Taiwan is a province of and belongs to China. As the civil war continued between the CCP and Chinese Nationalist Party (Kuomintang, KMT), Taiwan and the government of the Republic of China (ROC) also claimed one China, that was, the ROC. However, with the end of the Cold War in 1991, the Taiwanese government believed that both Taipei and Beijing should assume their own, separate sovereignties. Thereafter, the Taiwanese divided over differing views of one China, two Chinas, or one China and one Taiwan. A former president of the ROC (2008–2016) said due to Taiwan's unique historical experience, its diverse population holds different or even contradictory views on such issues.[1]

What is Taiwan's history? Chinese historians consider it a regional or provincial history since they believe Taiwan is part of China. Taiwanese scholars view it as a national history since they believe Taiwan is a state. American historians focus their narrative on U.S. policy and Taipei–Washington relations. The end of the Cold War challenged the dominant historiography with questions about the Taiwanese people's involvement, their goals, and their experience to make Taiwan what it is today.

The American public remains concerned over tensions in the Taiwan Strait, ongoing conflict over disputed islands in the South China Sea and East China Sea, and Taiwan's role in U.S.–China relations. This volume offers an accessible, but academically rigorous, general introduction to Taiwan from a new international history. It provides a comprehensive coverage of Taiwan's politics, economy, society, religion, culture, and education from about 5000 BCE to the twenty-first century. As President Ma Ying-jeou suggested, the book moves away from Chinese or Taiwanese views and instead examines Taiwan's past through an international perspective, as a global history for all peoples who can identify, relate to, and share with. This chapter provides an overview of Taiwan's geography, people, government, economy, and society.

GEOGRAPHIC SETTING AND DISPUTED ISLANDS

Taiwan is an oval-shaped island off the southeast coast of China. Geologists believe Taiwan was originally part of the mainland so its geographical features, weather, animal life, and plants are not much different from those in southern China.[2] Surrounded by the East China Sea in the north, the Pacific Ocean in the east, South China Sea in the south, and the Taiwan Strait in the west, which separates it from China (about 100 miles), its area is 13,900 square miles, slightly smaller than Maryland and Delaware combined. Taiwan is surrounded by a dozen smaller islands, and its government also controls several islands in the Taiwan Strait, including Quemoy (Jinmen) and Matsu (Mazu), as well as the Penghu (P'eng-hu or Pescadores) Islands, Orchid Island (Lan Tao), and Green Island (Lu Tao). Taiwan is 700 miles away from Japan's southernmost tip, Kyushu in the east, and is about 230 miles north of Luzon in the Philippines.[3]

As a long oval island, Taiwan is 225 miles from north to south and 85 miles wide. The Penghu, about twenty-five miles off Taiwan's eastern coast, totals forty-nine square miles. Both Taiwan and the Penghu lie on the edge of the East Asian continental shelf. The water in the Taiwan Strait is shallow, averaging about 300 feet. But the waters off its eastern coast are much deeper, about 13,000 feet deep, where they are thirty miles offshore, in the Pacific Ocean. Mountains claim nearly 65 percent of Taiwan with several north-south ranges running through the interior and rising to 13,110 feet at Yu Shan (Jade Mountain). The east side of the

Taiwan's coastline is about 980 miles with mountains in the east. In 1544, a Portuguese commercial ship passed by the island and called it "Ilha Formosa" (beautiful one). In 1624, the Dutch named their new colony "Taiwan." (Stephan Lechner/iStockPhoto.com)

mountain chain, or Central Mountain Range, is hilly, while to the west a broad, fertile plain, or Western Plains, slopes down to the shallow Taiwan Strait. There is merely 22 percent arable land. And most rivers on the island are short except the Choushui (Cho-shui) River, which runs longer than 100 miles. Taiwan's coastline is about 979 miles with three major seaports, including Kaohsiung, Tainan, and Taichung.[4]

Rugged uplands, high elevations, and prevalent mountain ranges provide a distinctive climate to Taiwan. Its subtropical weather is warm and humid with a long summer and mild winter. Taiwan's plentiful rainfall during monsoon season (June to August) delivers more than 100 inches annually, and significant sunshine allows for remarkably diverse agricultural production. Since the island lies on the northeast periphery of the tropics and is influenced by East Asian monsoon patterns, typhoons occur between June and October. During typhoon season, strong winds and heavy rain result in considerable damage, causing flooding and landslides. Other natural disasters include earthquakes, which occur more than 150 times a year.[5] Along major rivers, reservoirs and dams are built for water storage, irrigation systems, and flood control. In recent years, air, water, and industrial pollution has become political issues for local and state governments.

The island is rich in rice, but its main industrial crops are sugarcane and tea. Taiwan produces precious woods and has abundant water-power, forestry, and fishery resources. However, it lacks minerals with only small deposits of coal, silver, copper, marble, crude oil, and natural gas. Oil is by far the dominant fuel in Taiwan, meeting 44 percent of primary energy demand (PED). Coal plays an important role, accounting for more than a third of the energy market. Natural gas is the fastest-rising element of the energy mix, currently contributing just over 10 percent. The thaw in Taiwan–China relations since 2008 has heralded closer energy cooperation between the two countries.[6]

However, Taiwan, China, and several neighboring countries currently dispute the sovereignty over some islands in the Pacific. Among these disputed islands is Diaoyu/Senkaku (or *Diaoyutai* in Taiwanese) in the East China Sea.[7] UNECAFE (United Nations Economic Commission for Asia and the Far East) indicated potential crude oil and natural gas reserves in the East China Sea and estimated the area to contain approximately seven trillion cubic feet of natural gas and up to 100 billion barrels of oil.[8] It is strategically important among the surrounding states, including South Korea, Japan, Taiwan, and China. The ROC government asserted sovereignty of the Diaoyu/Senkaku. Its Executive Yuan (cabinet, as the State Department in the United States) announced in 1971 that these islands belonged to Yilan County of Taiwan. Since 2010, military tensions have mounted between China and Japan in the East China Sea. Both deployed naval or coast guard vessels to the disputed waters and sent aircraft to patrol the areas. In early 2012, Beijing invited Taipei to work together to resolve the territorial dispute in the East China Sea, with Japan. In April, Lai Shin-yuan, minister of the ROC Mainland Affairs Council (MAC), declined the invitation, and announced, "The ROC and Mainland China will not deal together with the disputes."[9] Nevertheless, President Ma Ying-jeou continued to claim ROC's sovereignty of the Senkaku Islands. He has published three books on the legal status of the disputed islands in the East China Sea from an international maritime legal perspective.[10]

Taiwan, China, Vietnam, the Philippines, and Malaysia also claim the Spratly Islands (*Nansha* in Chinese, *Quan Dao Truong Sa* in Vietnamese, and *Kalayaan* in Filipinos) and Paracel Islands (*Xisha* in Chinese and *Quan Dao Hoang Sa* in Vietnamese) in the South China Sea. The South China Sea is strategically important because it is the second most used sea lane in the world, with one-third of the world's shipping transit passing through its waters. Beneath its seabed are crude oil reserves of 7.7 billion barrels, about 20 percent of the total in the Asia-Pacific region. It has estimated natural gas reserves of 266 trillion cubic feet, about 45 percent of the total in the Asia-Pacific region. In the 1980s, as oil and gas shifted to deep-water explorations, international tensions rose among some of the surrounding countries over sovereignty of islands in the South China Sea.[11]

The Spratly Islands, the largest group in the South China Sea, covers a water area of 61,755 square miles and includes approximately 100 small islands. Although most of these are rocky, small, and uninhabited, the competing claims reflect the interests in oil and gas reserves beneath these islands. Among the countries occupying some of the islands, the PRC controls seven islands, Vietnam twenty-nine, the Philippines nine, Malaysia nine, and the ROC has one, the Taiping Island (also known as Itu Aba Island).[12] The Taiwanese established a permanent presence in the Spratly Islands in 1956. In December 2007, the Taiping Island Airport was completed.[13] On February 2, 2008, President Chen Shui-bian (2000–2008), accompanied by a large naval force, visited the island. On January 28, 2016, President Ma Ying-jeou led an official Taiwanese government delegation to the largest island (about 110 acres) in the Spratly Island Group, the ROC-controlled Taiping Island. The Paracel Islands are the second-largest group in the South China Sea, including about fifteen to thirty small islands. Since 1974, China has controlled the major islands in the center of the archipelago, deploying military forces, building airstrip, and establishing communication facilities.

PEOPLE AND LANGUAGES

Taiwan has a total population of 23.55 million (2018) with a median age of 41.3 years. According to Taiwan's census, its population grew from 5.8 million in 1940, 13.5 million in 1966, and to 20.4 million by 1990 with a high annual growth rate of 2–3.1 percent. Since the 1980s, the government encouraged two children per married couple so its population growth rate slowed down. After the 1990s, the birthrate of Taiwan has lowered than the world's average. Beginning in 2000, the birthrate was lowered to 0.8 percent, 0.6 percent in 2001, and in the 2010s, a merely 0.15 percent, significantly lower than the world average.[14]

There are numerous reasons for Taiwan's population decline, primarily the limited farmland that discouraged traditionally large, rural families as seen in mainland China. Second, the government sponsored birth-control programs. Third, after the 1990s, about one million Taiwanese businessmen moved to China and more than 400,000 of them lived in Shanghai.[15] While participating in trade, investment, and joint adventures, many of them settled there; found first, second, and even third wives there; and had children in China. Fourth, social institutions were evolving along the course taken by other industrialized nations. For example, more education meant later marriages and fewer children for women. The educated couples were more willing to accept a two-child ideal. The last but not the least was an increasing cost of living in Taiwan, especially in the urban areas, where children became increasingly expensive and contributed little in economic terms.

Because of declining population and birthrate, Taiwan became one of the fastest-aging societies in the world. In the 1960s, Taiwanese society was very young with 45 percent of its population under age 15 and only 2.6 percent over 65. In the 1990s, however, about 25 percent of the population was still under 15, and 6.8 percent over the age of 65. In 2015, only 12 percent of the population was under age of 15 and more than 14 percent was over 65. That year, dependency ratio increased to 35.2 percent, the highest in Taiwan's modern history. By 2018, estimated median age was 41.3 years. The government faces new demographic problems, including youth unemployment, job security, social welfare and retirement, and labor shortages. Since Taiwan has the lowest fertility rate in the world (about one child per woman), shortage of labor, declining tax revenue, and an aging population, as serious economic and social problems, have emerged. It is estimated that by 2025 senior Taiwanese over 65 will make up nearly 20 percent of the total population.[16]

The majority of Taiwanese live in urban areas as a result of recent urbanization. In 1952, only 47 percent of the population lived in cities. By 1980, more than 78 percent of Taiwanese lived in cities. Among today's largest cities in Taiwan are New Taipei City (4.3 million), the capital Taipei (2.7 million), Taoyuan (2.19 million), Kaohsiung (1.53 million), and Taichung (1.28 million). Coincidently, overpopulated cities face many issues, including overpriced housing, public safety, traffic jams, lack of public transportation, and urban pollution. Since the 2000s, urbanization has slowed down because of these problems. About 99 percent of Taiwanese live on the main island. The adjacent Penghu Islands (a handful of small islands within the Taiwan Strait) has 90,000 permanent residents, Quemoy 50,000, and Matsu only 8,000. The numbers do not include large garrisons of the ROC military stationed on these islands for defense purposes. In Quemoy, for example, there were about 16,000 troops stationed on the island in 2000.[17]

Han Chinese comprise the largest ethnicity, making up 95 percent of Taiwan's total population. Several Chinese groups linguistically identify with three different categories, the first being Southern Min (*Min*

Nan) or early Fujianese-speaking migrants from Southeast China's Fujian (Fukien) Province. They call themselves *pen ti jen* (natives) or *pen sheng jen* (local Taiwanese) and comprise about 73.3 percent of the total population. The second group are Hakka (or *Hejia*) from Guangdong (Canton) Province in south China. They speak Hakka Cantonese, reference themselves as *ke chia jen* (guest people), and constitute about 12 percent of the population. The third group, which accounts for 13 percent of Taiwan's ethno-linguistic demography, speak Mandarin, and are called *wai sheng jen* (people from other provinces).[18] Former ROC presidents Chiang Kai-shek (Jiang Jieshi, 1950–1975) and Chiang Ching-kuo (Jiang Jingguo, 1978–1988) were *wai sheng jen*. President Lee Teng-hui (Li Denghui, 1990–2000) is Hakka. From this breakdown, we can see that almost all Taiwanese (except 1.7 percent of speakers of Austronesian languages) linguistically relate to the Chinese-Tibet language family. Although the official language is Mandarin Chinese, each ethnic group has its own dialect.

ABORIGINES AND ETHNIC MINORITIES

Taiwan is a multiethnic and multilingual island. There are sixteen indigenous groups recognized by the Taiwanese government. This suggests that Taiwanese people are not homogeneous; they have different cultures and languages. Aborigines totals 450,000 and consist of 2–3 percent of the population. Aboriginal groups dominated Taiwan before the seventeenth century.[19] The ancestors of most aborigines lived in remote, isolated mountainous areas, separate from the majority of the population. While Chinese islanders transitioned to modern Taiwanese after the seventeenth century, aboriginal people maintained their own traditional culture, tribal communities, and spoken languages.

The ancestors of the aborigines came from the southern islands in the Pacific Ocean. They are Austronesian, or Malayo-Polynesian people, who developed their own speaking language system, or the Southern Island language. Indigenous Southern Island language is widely used and spoken as far as Easter Island in the Pacific, in Madagascar along Africa's eastern coast, in New Zealand and New Guinea to the south, and Taiwan to the north. Some scholars suggest that Southeast Asia was the birthplace of the Southern Island language.[20] The Southern Island linguistic system is the only world language on the island and peninsular countries, including Malaysia, Indonesia, the Philippines, Melanesia, Micronesia, and Polynesia. Although anthropologists, archeologists, and linguists have not yet discovered any written form of the Southern Island language, Taiwanese aborigines and Austronesians maintain rich cultural, economic, and social resources since the ancient age.

Among the aborigines are two officially identifiable ethnic minorities. These include the *Gaoshan* (mountain) aboriginal people from the mountainous areas and *Pengpu* (Pingpu) aboriginal people from the central and southern plains. Traditionally, mountain aborigines were divided into nine ethnic groups, Atayal, Paiwan, Rukai, Puyuma, Bunnun, Tsou, Ami, Yami, and Saisiyat. Since 2001, five more ethnic groups have been identified by the government, Sediq, Kavalan, Thao, Truku, and Sakizaya.[21] Currently, fourteen groups exist as Gaoshan aborigines, totaling 320,000 people. Among the large Gaoshan groups are Ami (174,361), Paiwan (84,058), Atayal (82,084), Bunnun (49,343), and Truku (23,819). Among the small groups are Sakizaya (243), Thao (631), and Kavalan (1,107).[22]

The Gaoshan people lived in central Taiwan for centuries. With increased immigration and continuous cultivation, they migrated into remote, primeval forests in the mountains to preserve their culture and tradition. Today, they inhabit only eight counties, primarily in less populous mountainous regions between 1,000 and 4,500 feet above sea level. Rukai group, for example, lives on the hills of the eastern mountains between 1,500 and 4,000 feet. Atayal, the third-largest group of the Gaoshan, live in central high mountainous areas above 4,500 feet. Farming, hunting, and handcrafts are among their main industries.[23]

Gaoshan nationalities have maintained some of their traditions, rituals, and customs for intimate associations, weddings, and post-nuptial rules. Each Gaoshan village has two chiefs. One is a religious leader, a male priest (*rahan*), who performs religious and social ceremonies like weddings and funerals. Another is a political elder (*ayawan*), who makes decisions and settles disputes. Many Gaoshan girls marry early, typically around the age of fourteen. Parents arrange marriages for their children according to family status, economic condition, and kinship relations. In most cases, they cannot marry to a family with the same last name. Pre-marriage sex is prohibited in most groups, and brides move in with the groom's family after marriage. Women's rights and dignity are respected as equally as men within marital relations between bride and groom.

The second group of Taiwanese aborigines are of Pengpu ethnicity, who live in central plains. Since they interacted with Han Chinese through agriculture, trade, and interracial marriage, it is difficult for Pengpu aborigines to preserve their own racial and cultural identities. Conversely, since the seventeenth century, the Pengpu assimilated with the Chinese. According to historical records and relics, the Pengpu aborigines consisted of nine ethnic minority groups in the

1660s, Siraya, Hoanya, Babuza, Papora, Thao, Taokas, Ketagalan, Kavalan, and Pazeh.[24] Today some of these groups have been identified as Taiwanese aborigines totaling 100,000.

After the Dutch established a colonial government on Taiwan in 1642, the Dutch administration conducted nine population surveys on Taiwan for colonial control and taxation purposes between 1644 and 1657. Their surveys showed that there were more than 50,000 aborigines of Pengpu descents.[25] They lived in more than 300 villages all over the island and engaged in farming, hunting, fishing, and pottery making. Among their main crops were rice and millet. Women were the prime hands in the rice paddy. Men engaged in hunting and fishing. They primarily hunted deer, fox, mountain pigs, and wild boar.

The Pengpu people had their own religions, traditions, and languages. Before the seventeenth century, many of their clans lived in a matriarchal society with female leaders in both political and spiritual realms. One of the reasons for the matriarchal communes of the Pengpu aborigines was that women engaged in farming and produced more stable food supplies than hunting and fishing by men. Female spiritual leaders (*inibs*, or witch) were very powerful in Siraya and other aboriginal groups. With their heavenly communicative abilities, they helped tribal members with ailments, difficulties, funerals, and weddings. Later, *inibs* became major obstacles for European Catholic priests. In their marital systems, all of the Pengpu people keep their own special ritual formalities, disciplines, and family practices of the group. In most cases, after weddings, men moved into the wife's house, and a daughter rather than a son was entitled to family assets.

Moreover, there is one thing in common and identical to all the Pengpu groups; young people marry for true, free love. Couples can freely and intimately associate with each other, enjoy freedom of communication, choose their own beloved, and gain permission from both families after they make their decision for marriage. There are no strict rules against premarital sexual relations or outside the marriage. All young men (*mada*) of the Pengpu carried a knife for family security and village protection. After the seventeenth century, more Chinese arrived in Taiwan, and Pengpu groups interacted with them assimilating with Chinese culture. In recent years, however, some villages in southern and eastern Taiwan revived some of the Pengpu aboriginal tradition, including folk music, clothes, and religious ceremonies.

GOVERNMENT AND POLITICAL PARTIES

The ROC Constitution of 1947 divides the government into legislative, executive, and judicial branches, or respectively, Legislative Yuan,

Executive Yuan, and Supreme Court. The Legislative Yuan is a uni-
cameral parliament with 113 representatives. Among them seventy-
three are directly elected in their constituencies by simple, majority,
popular vote; thirty-four are directly elected in a single, island-wide
constituency by proportional, representative vote; the remaining six
are directly elected in multiseat aboriginal constituencies by proportional, representative vote. The last representative election was held
on January 16, 2016. All elected members serve four-year terms. Currently, between the two major parties, the Democratic Progressive
Party (DPP) has sixty-eight seats in the Legislative Yuan, and KMT has
thirty-five. Among other political parties, NPP (New Power Party) has
five, PFP (People First Party) three, and the others two. This is the first
non-KMT-led legislature in Taiwan's history. The next election will be
held in January 2020.

KMT is also known as the "Pan-Blue Party" in Taiwan. It was
founded by Sun Yat-sen in August 1912, after the 1911 Revolution, and
ended Qing rule, thereby establishing the ROC. After Sun died in 1925,
Chiang Kai-shek became KMT leader and ROC president in 1927. Chiang and KMT lost the Chinese Civil War to the CCP in 1949. He moved
the seat of government from mainland China to Taiwan along with
two million troops, officials, and their families.[26] From 1950, the ROC
government ruled Taiwan as a state with its first priority to return to
mainland China. After Chiang issued martial law in 1950, KMT had
been the only political party, controlling the government, military, and
media in Taiwan.

After Chiang Kai-shek died in 1975, his son Chiang Ching-kuo became ROC president (1978–1988) and began political and social reforms. During his tenure, Chiang Ching-kuo addressed Taiwanese
(*pen sheng jen*) interests and promoted local political participation. He
appointed Taiwanese Lee Teng-hui his successor, and lifted martial
law and party bans on other political organizations, including opposition parties. A retired general of the KMT army told the author that
Taiwan's economic growth and educational reform in the 1960s–1970s
prepared a democratic transformation in the 1980s–1990s.[27]

When Chiang Ching-kuo died in 1988, Lee Teng-hui became the
first ROC president who was born on Taiwan. Lee carried political reform much farther in the 1990s, including constitutional amendments,
representative reelection, and Taiwanization of political power. Soon
KMT split in 1993 between the "old guards" and "new reformers,"
who denounced political domination, power abuse, corruption, and
scandals in the party. Thereafter, KMT lost political power to DPP.
During the legislative elections, KMT shared 53 percent of votes in

1992, but it decreased to 31.3 percent votes in 2001, and 26.9 percent in 2016. KMT's current chairman is Wu Den-yih (since 2017).[28]

DPP, also known as the "Pan-Green Party," was founded in 1986 and ended Taiwan's thirty-six-year pattern of one-party politics. Many of its early members were victims, their families, and defense lawyers against KMT authoritarian government. Although a young party, it soon gained popular support in the 1990s from local Taiwanese, or *pen sheng jen*, against dominant KMT. In 2000, DPP presidential candidate Chen Shui-bian won the election and ended KMT domination in Taiwan. Then, DPP built up its political support steadily during the legislative elections from 29 percent in 1998 to 36 percent in 2001, and up to 44 percent in 2016, and it became the largest party in the Legislative Yuan. In the 2016 presidential election, DPP candidate Tsai Ing-wen defeated other candidates and retook the presidency from KMT. Since 2016, DPP under the leadership of Lin Yu-chang (acting chairman) and Hung Yao-fu (secretary general since 2016) controlled both the presidency and legislative branch of the Taiwanese government.[29]

Taiwan is a presidential republic, and all Taiwanese citizens, twenty years and older, can vote for both the president and their representatives. The Taiwanese government recognizes dual citizenship, only barring the PRC. The presidential election takes place every four years by direct, popular vote. It was not until 1996 that the first free presidential election was held in Taiwan after nearly fifty years of KMT political control.

The election of 2000 ended KMT domination when DPP candidate Chen Shui-bian won the election and managed the first peaceful transfer of power in Taiwan. President Chen won his reelection in 2004, and the politics of Taiwan entered a new era of multiparty democracy. KMT candidate Ma Ying-jeou defeated the DDP candidates and won back the presidency in the election of 2008 and reelection of 2012. On January 16, 2016, DPP's candidate Tsai Ing-wen won the election with Chen Chien-jen as her vice president (2016–2020). These closely contested elections between the two major parties suggest considerable division in Taiwan's political future.

As the first female chief of state, President Tsai appointed Lai Ching-te as premier of the Executive Yuan. As the head of the executive branch, Premier Lai recommended ministers for his cabinet at President Tsai's approval. The Executive Yuan is the governmental cabinet under the leadership of the premier. The executive branch is a semi-presidential system, in which the president and the premier share the executive power as heads of government. Then, the premier selects his or her own ministers for the administration. Nevertheless, the Legislative Yuan can pass regulations without regard for executive power because neither the president nor the premier has veto power. Local governments include thirteen counties, three cities, and six special municipalities directly under the jurisdiction of the Executive Yuan with Taipei as its capital. The three cities are Hsinchu, Keelung, and Chiayi. The special municipalities include Taipei, Kaohsiung, Taichung, Tainan, Taoyuan, and New Taipei.

The president also appoints justices to the highest courts, including the Supreme Court and Constitutional Court. The Supreme Court has a court president, vice president, and about one hundred justices, who organize eight civil and twelve criminal divisions. Supreme Court justices serve for life. The Constitutional Court also has a court president, vice president, and thirteen justices. They serve for eight-year terms with half the justices renewed every four years. Under the Supreme Court, there are local high courts, district courts, and administrative courts.

ECONOMY AND TRADE

In 1975, when Chiang Kai-shek died, successful KMT rule had made Taiwan more prosperous than it had ever been. Over the next two decades, Taiwan's economy took off and enjoyed one of the world's fastest-growing economies, with an increasing export of electronics, machinery, and petrochemicals. In 1980, Taiwan's gross domestic product (GDP) was $61.9 billion, and its GDP per capita was $3,463. Through the 1980s, the economy grew at an annual rate of 7–11 percent, and had a trade surplus with many countries, including the United States and China. In 1990, its GDP increased to $205 billion with $10,048 per capita. In 2000, Taiwan's GDP doubled and reached $481 billion with $21,590 per capita. In 2010, its GDP almost doubled again to $894 billion, the twenty-fourth largest economy in the world, with $38,593 per capita.[30]

Taiwan's success is described as an "economic miracle" and made it one of the four "economic dragons" (South Korea, Singapore, and Hong Kong) in East Asia after Japan. The leading industries include electronics, communications and information technology products, petroleum refining, chemicals, textiles, iron and steel, and machinery. Industry composes about 36 percent of the GDP, agriculture about 1.8 percent, and services more than 62 percent.

Among Taiwan's successful growth policies are its export-led trade policy, a key in its economic development in the 1970s–2000s. Its major trading partners include Japan, the United States, Europe, and later China. Taiwan had a favorable trade surplus with all these countries except Japan, which had 15 percent of Taiwan's international trade. For example, Taiwan enjoyed an annual trade surplus of $16 billion with the United States in 1987 and up to $24 billion in 2005. Taiwan played an important role in the global economy as the world's seventeenth-largest exporter and the eighteenth-largest importer at the beginning of the 2010s. After the 1990s, China became the largest trading partner of Taiwan. In 1994, Taiwan had a total of $2 billion trade with China.

In 2004, Taiwan's trade with China increased to $53.1 billion, about 15.1 percent of its trade total and exports of $36.3 billion to China. In 2006, China became the second-largest importer of Taiwan's manufacturing goods after Japan. By 2014, Taiwan's cross-strait trade reached $130.2 billion, more than 22 percent of its global trade, including its exports of $82.1 billion to China.[31] Its exports and natural resources became more dependent on China, its largest trading partner with 27.1 percent of Taiwan's total exports in 2012, while their political differences and territorial conflicts continue.

In 2010, Taiwan's GDP grew 10.7 percent, but its growth slowed down to 4 percent in 2011, and fell to 1.3 percent in 2012 when its GDP totaled $918.3 billion and per capita GDP was $39,400. In 2017, Taiwan's GDP reached $1,185 billion with an annual growth rate of 2.9 percent and ranking 22 in the world. Its GDP per capita was $50,500 in 2017, ranking 28 in the world. Taiwan also had the fifth-largest foreign reserves in the world of $456 billion by the end of 2017. Currently, Taiwan is the largest foreign investor in China. In 1994, Taiwan invested $1 billion in China. In 2004, its annual FDI (foreign direct investment) in China increased to $6.9 billion. In 2014, it reached $10.3 billion, about 58.5 percent of all Taiwan's investment in the world. Its cumulative FDI in China had totaled $150 billion in 2015.[32] More than two-thirds of Taiwanese companies reported some level of investment or cooperation in China.

In 2017, Taiwan's exports reached $349.8 billion. Among the major exports were semiconductors, petrochemicals, auto parts, ships, wireless communication equipment, electronics, and computers. In the same year, its imports were $269 billion, mainly crude oil, natural gas, coal, and steel. Taiwan imported 846,400 barrels of crude oil a day in 2015, ranking the thirteenth-largest oil importer in the world. Most of Taiwan's crude oil imports come from the Persian Gulf and West African countries. Refining capacity is at a slight surplus, equal to around 1.2 million barrels a day. Taiwan imported 16.31 billion cubic meters of liquefied natural gas (LNG) in 2011, with Indonesia and Malaysia being the country's top two suppliers. Gas consumption is rising rapidly, as Taiwan consumed 15.5 billion cubic meters of natural gas in 2011, up by 10.1 percent year-on-year and up by 36.8 percent compared with 2009. Taiwan imported 22.14 billion cubic meters of LNG in 2017, ranking the fifteenth-largest natural gas importer in the world.

Among its five major seaports are Kaohsiung, Keelung, Taichung, Hualien, and Suao. Kaohsiung is the fourth-largest container port in the world after Shanghai, Hong Kong, and Singapore. Taiwan has approximately 1,500 miles of railway track and 12,000 miles of highway and main roads. Because of the completion of several major freeways and expressways, privately owned vehicles rapidly increased in recent years. Taipei and Kaohsiung have some of the best public transportation networks in the world. Of course, due to urban traffic jam, motorcycles remain popular as local transportation increased from five million in 1980 to ten million in 1999.

Beside the challenging cross-strait relationship, Tsai's government faces new economic problems, including youth unemployment and job security. Another issue is the employment rate, which is much lower than in other developed countries, around 45 percent for more than ten years with no indication of increasing. This shows a clear discrimination against women in hiring requirements and processes. There are many restrictions for interviews and hiring procedures. It is easy to find in newspaper advertisements "reserved leading position for man," "office worker for woman." Despite women holding the same administrative level as men, they received only about 66.92 percent of salary of their male contemporaries. Promotion opportunities and upward mobility are more difficult for women than it is for men. The percentage of women at leading positions is 9.24 percent, a very low figure compared to women's test scores for these positions. Taiwan has established an economic protection system, which proved advantageous for working males, knotted by weft of social security for work insurance and warp of medical insurance for public health care and the backup plan of social aid system especially for aged women.

RELIGION, EDUCATION, AND SOCIAL PROBLEMS

Taiwanese society is influenced by different cultures and religions, predominantly China. Chinese culture is composed of numerous philosophical and spiritual systems like Confucianism, Taoism (Dao-ism), and Buddhism. In 2017, the Buddhists accounted for 35.3 percent of the total population in Taiwan, Taoists were 33.2 percent, Confucians 10 percent, and Christians about 3.9 percent. Among these, Confucianism has been the most influential in Chinese society. Confucian beliefs are used to organize educational programs and processes.

Taiwanese enjoy religious freedom and practice Christianity and Buddhism. Foreigners are struck by the omnipresence of Buddhism in Taiwanese society. On streets everywhere, stores sell Buddhist goods of all types, people wear Buddhist objects, and Buddhism exists in every facet of Taiwanese life. It is estimated that almost an half of Taiwan's population in Taiwan is Buddhist believers congregating around one of the four dominant masters who lead four independent groups. Some people refer to these four masters as representative of different schools or factions of Buddhism. In fact, there are no conflicts among the four groups, and they differ only slightly. These Buddhist organizations all preach and practice similar basic Buddhist ideas. When asked if there were any differences among the four groups, respondents identified the following: the four groups stationed in different areas, with different influential figures (or what they call Buddhist Masters) and different constituents, and emphasize different aspects in their practices.

Perhaps, the most influential Buddhist organization is called Ci-Ji Gongde Hui (Ciji Society of Charitable Deeds), based in Hualien in the east. It is the only Buddhist organization headed by a nun named of Master Zhengyan. Ci-Ji's congregation consists of mostly people from middle and upper classes, with the largest group of women as its active participants. Followers are estimated to be approximately four million. Established in 1966, Ci-Ji focuses on charities, medical care, education, and cultural activities. In the past twenty years, Ci-Ji has set up hospitals, nursing schools, medical schools, and a TV station by the name of Da-Ai (Big Love). Fo-Guang Shan, stationed in Kaohsiung in the south of Taiwan, is well known for what its leader, Master Xingyun, does to promote Buddhist education and internationalize Taiwan-style Buddhism. Since 1964, Master Xingyun and Fo-Guang have established, both in Taiwan and overseas, six Buddhist colleges and four universities; Nanhua Management College, built in Chiayi in 1996, is one of the four universities. It is said that Fo-Guang has set up over one hundred branches in other places in Asia, Africa, Latin America, North America, and Europe.

The Taiwanese government carried out educational reform in the 1990s and spent massive amounts on public education. In 2017,

Taiwan had 10,884 public schools, including 6,323 pre-schools (kindergartens), 2,630 primary (elementary) schools, 732 junior high (middle) schools, 511 senior secondary (high) schools, 13 junior colleges, 15 four-year colleges, 129 universities, 5 religious colleges, 28 special education schools, 93 continuing education colleges, and 405 supplementary schools. These public schools and colleges had 294,000 teachers and enrolled more than 4.4 million students.[33] In 2010, more than 98 percent of the population was literate, and Taiwan's colleges and universities had world-class professors in all disciplines.

As part of its reform, the Ministry of Education opened up the textbook market to the private sector, and separated the process of editorship and assessment to provide more freedom of curriculum development and liberal arts education. In July 2002, Taiwan's Ministry of Education officially adopted Tongyong Pinyin as the standard transliteration system. The Taiwan public faced the situation where Tongyong Pinyin and several other systems coexist. Among the parallel systems is the Hanyu Pinyin system (HP), adopted in 1958 by the first People's Congress in Beijing. Hanyu Pinyin has since gained the status of the most popular Chinese romanization worldwide. The system was adopted by the Library of Congress in the United States and by the International Organization for Standardization as the standard romanization for modern Chinese.

Although Taiwan has a high living standard, it still faces some serious social problems, including gender issues, population aging, crime, and suicide. As for women's political status and social position and as the tradition they inherited, their concerns and demands have not yet become hot issues in today's Taiwan. Some gender discrimination reflects political issues and social problems in Taiwan as exemplified by the public health insurance system. It needs many improvements, including oversight to ensure women's needs are addressed. Women have no positive choice of their own in the current system, and there is unequal distribution of money between males and females. Therefore, lacking a public support system and having limited private resources to take long-term responsibility, women sacrifice their own health, social contact, and life quality.

In recent years, along with social inequality and unemployment, suicide and divorce rates have reached a record-high level. *People's Daily* reported that the divorce rate is reaching a new high.[34] For every 2.9 marriage couples, one ended their relationship with divorce in 2001, compared to an average of one in every 3.5 couples in 2000.[35] The divorce rate has increased fivefold in the past three decades.[36] In the meantime, unemployment reached a record 5 percent in late 2001.[37]

Risk factors for suicide have long been understood as associated with society and culture. Long-term suicide trends for Taiwanese men and women correlate with long-term trends like marriage, divorce, and unemployment rates from 1959 to 2001.[38] However, women and men's suicides vary significantly relating to birth, unemployment and employment, divorce, marriage, and secondary education rates.

Since the early twenty-first century, Taiwan has witnessed tremendous political, economic, and social changes, which seem quite different from its experience in the Cold War. The world was surprised when U.S. president Donald Trump talked to Taiwanese president Tsai Ing-wen on the phone in early 2017, an unprecedented shift between Washington and Taipei since the United States broke diplomatic relations with the ROC nearly forty years ago. Theoretically, Taiwan remains engaged in the civil war with China. A former ROC president told the author in the summer of 2017 that Taiwan faces a historical moment, which will determine the future of the island for many years to come.[39] To grasp this historical moment, we need to have a better understanding of the history of Taiwan.

NOTES

1. A former president of the Republic of China in Taiwan, meeting with the author and other scholars in Taipei on June 8, 2017.

2. Gregory Veeck, Clifton W. Pannell, Christopher J. Smith, and Youqin Huang, *China's Geography: Globalization and the Dynamics of Political, Economic, and Social Change*, 2nd edition (Lanham, MD: Rowman & Littlefield, 2011), 345–46.

3. John F. Copper, *Taiwan: Nation-state or Province?* 4th edition (Boulder, CO: Westview, 2003), 4.

4. Shelley Rigger, *Why Taiwan Matters: Small Island, Global Powerhouse*, updated edition (Lanham, MD: Rowman & Littlefield, 2014), 11.

5. Chiao-min Hsieh, *Taiwan-Ilha Formosa: A Geographical Perspective* (Washington, DC: Butterworths, 1964), 20.

6. Xiaobing Li and Michael Molina, "Taiwan (the Republic of China)," in *Oil: A Cultural and Geographic Encyclopedia of Black Gold*, eds. Xiaobing Li and Michael Molina (Santa Barbara, CA: ABC-CLIO, 2014), 2: 672–73.

7. The Chinese government published the names of seventy-one geological formations of the Diaoyu group in March 2010. See Chinese State Oceanic Administration, *Zhongguo Diaoyudao dimingce* [Geographic manual of China's Diaoyu Islands] (Beijing: Haiyang chubanshe [Oceanic Publishing House], 2012), 29–32.

8. BBC, "Questions and Answers: China-Japan Islands Row," *BBC News* (UK), September 11, 2012, www.bbc.co.uk/news/wrold-asia-pacific-11341139. Assessed on August 24, 2016.

9. Radio Taiwan International, "Taipei Declines Beijing's Invitation to Solve Disputed Territory Issues Together," *Radio Taiwan International*, April 26, 2012.

10. Among his books are Ma Ying-jeou, *Diaoyutai lieyu zhuquan zhengyi: huigu yu zhanwang* [Disputed sovereignty of Diaoyu Islands: The past and future] (Taipei: ROC Government Printing, 1996); *Cong xin haiyangfa lun Diaoyutai lieyu yu Donghai huajie wenti* [New oceanic regulations: Issues of the Diaoyu Islands and border of the East China Sea] (Taipei: Zhengzhong Books, 1986).

11. Xiaobing Li, "South China Sea," in *Modern China: Understanding Modern Nation*, ed. Li (Santa Barbara, CA: ABC-CLIO, 2016), 20–22.

12. Sarah Raine and Christian Miere, *Regional Disorder: The South China Sea Disputes* (London: Routledge, 2013), 17–19, 42–43.

13. Ministry of National Defense, ROC, "MND Admits Strategic Value of Spratly Airstrip," *Taipei Times*, January 6, 2006.

14. ROC Government Information Office, *The Republic of China Year Book: Taiwan 2002* (Taipei: Government Information Office, 2002), 23.

15. ROC Directorate General of Budget, *Statistical Yearbook of the Republic of China 2001* (Taipei: Accounting and Statistics, Executive Yuan, 2001), 22.

16. Gregory Veeck, Clifton W. Pannell, Christopher J. Smith, and You-qin Huang, "Taiwan: Enduring East Asian 'Economic Miracle,'" in *China's Geography: Globalization and the Dynamics of Political, Economic, and Social Changes*, eds. Gregory Veeck, Clifton W. Pannell, Christopher J. Smith, and Youqin Huang (Lanham, MD: Rowman & Littlefield Publishers, 2011), 355–56.

17. For the garrison on Jinmen, see Michael Szonyi, *Cold War Island: Quemoy on the Front Line* (New York: Cambridge University Press, 2008), appendix, 257–58.

18. Feng-fu Tsao, "Preserving Taiwan's Indigenous Languages and Cultures: A Discussion in Sociolinguistic Perspective," http://www.kokugakuin.ac.jp/ijcc/wp/global/07tsao.html, 2001.

19. Michael Stainton, "The Politics of Taiwan Aboriginal Origins," in *Taiwan: A New History*, expanded edition, ed. Murray A. Rubinstein (London: Routledge, 2015), xv.

20. Gao Min-shi, ed., *Taiwan shi* [History of Taiwan], 2nd edition (Taipei: Wunan tushu [Wunan Books], 2015), 18, 30.

21. Taiwanese government recognized the Truku group as an ethnic group of the Gaoshan nationalities in 2004, Sediq in 2004, and Sakizaya in 2007.

22. Committee of Aborigines in Taiwan, Executive Yuan, ROC, *Taiwan yuanzhu minzu gezu renkou tongji* [Statistics of all ethnic minorities in Taiwan] (Taipei: Government Printing Office, 2008).

23. Rigger, *Why Taiwan Matters*, 13–14.

24. Y. R. Gong Ben and G. B. Wei, *Native Ethnic Groups in Taiwan* (Taiwan: Cheng Xin Publishing Company, 2001), 3–5, 42.

25. Gao, *Taiwan shi* [History of Taiwan], 35–36, 37–38.

26. Xiaobing Li, *A History of the Modern Chinese Army* (Lexington: University Press of Kentucky, 2007), 76–78.

27. A retired KMT army general met with the author and other scholars at Rongzong (Glory General Hospital), Taipei, Taiwan, during May 27–28, 1994.

28. Jason C. Hu (Chi-chiang Hu), vice chairman of KMT (2014–2017), meeting with the author and other scholars on June 2, 2017, in Taipei, Taiwan.

29. Dr. Chiu Chui-Cheng (DPP), deputy minister of the Mainland Affairs Council, the Executive Yuan, ROC, meeting with the author and other scholars on June 1, 2017, in Taipei, Taiwan.

30. Veeck, Pannell, Smith, and Huang, "Taiwan: Enduring East Asian 'Economic Miracle,'" 343.

31. Syaru Shirley Lin, *Taiwan's China Dilemma: Contested Identities and Multiple Interests in Taiwan's Cross-Strait Economic Policy* (Stanford, CA: Stanford University Press, 2016), 5.

32. Scott L. Kastner, *Political Conflict and Economic Interdependence across the Taiwan Strait and Beyond* (Stanford, CA: Stanford University Press, 2009), 76–78, 83.

33. Ministry of Education, Republic of China (Taiwan), "2018 Education Statistical Indicators," https://englilsh.moe.gov.tw/cp-27-14504-9E20A-1.html.

34. *People's Daily*, "Taiwan Marriage Rate Hits 10-Year High," www.english.peopledaily.com.cn, 2001.

35. Chang-chieh Hsieh, "Comments Made in Regard to Suicide," interview by Li Liying at the headquarters of the People's First Party (PFP) in Taipei in 2001.

36. Mei-ling Lee, "Divorce Rate Skyrockets in Taiwan," *China Post*, www.chinapost.com.tw, 2000.

37. "Jobless Rate Predicted to Hit 5 Percent," *Taipei Times*, www.taipeitimes.com/news/archives, 2001.

38. Li Li-ying, "Suicide in Taiwan," in *Taiwan in the 21st Century*, eds. Xiaobing Li and Zuohong Pan (New York: University Press of America, 2003), 98.

39. A former president of the ROC, meeting with the author and other scholars in Taipei on June 8, 2017.

2

Prehistory and Aboriginal
Cultures to 1100

Centrally located in the Asia-Pacific region, Taiwan became a "cross-roads" for Southeast Asian trade and was accessible for oceanic migrations. The ancestors of Taiwanese aborigines came from different parts of East and Southeast Asia and brought with them different languages and cultures. Since written records were not available in Taiwan until 400 years ago, discovery of Taiwanese prehistory depends on geological, archeological, and anthropological data. This chapter examines its early settlements and cultural exchanges with surrounding countries from 20000 BCE to AD 1000. It consults official records and archival collections in Taiwan, China, and Japan. A global perspective provides Asia-Pacific regional context and historical background of Taiwanese origins.

According to archeological and anthropological evidence, including fossils, tools, and other artifacts, the earliest migrants came from Continental China, about 50,000 years ago (Paleolithic Age), via a land bridge. Other migrants arrived around 5,000–2,500 years ago (Neolithic Age), from the Southern Pacific Islands in today's Philippines,

New Guinea, Solomon, and Iwo Jima. As Austronesian or Malayo-Polynesian people, they settled and survived by hunting, gathering, and fishing around the island. Beginning around 200 BCE–AD 200 (Bronze Age), they engaged in agriculture, primarily growing rice; domesticated animals; and made bronze and iron tools and weapons.

From AD 200 to 1000, Chinese migrants along the Taiwanese coast and Penghu islands developed trade and maintained interactions with Han Chinese from the mainland. Despite their minority standing during Taiwan's prehistory, Chinese migrants gained a majority presence and assimilated into modern Taiwanese after the seventeenth century. Coincidentally, migrants from Chinese ethnic minorities and from the Southern Pacific Islands continued living in remote, isolated mountainous areas. Oceanic migrants existed as the majority of Taiwan's population early on and adapted to the environment, established tribal communities, and maintained their indigenous languages and cultures. Although some of them assimilated with Chinese and continental cultures, others maintained their cultural and racial identities throughout history. They became the aboriginal people who dominated Taiwan until the seventeenth century and European arrivals on the island.

LAND CONNECTION AND PALEOLITHIC CHANGPIN CULTURE

According to Taiwanese geologists, Taiwan was part of mainland China during the glacial age (between 10,000 and one million years ago), when cold weather dominated the earth, and ice and snow covered most of Asia. During the Ice Age, ocean levels were low (about 140 meters lower than present levels), the floor of the Taiwan Strait was exposed, and Taiwan connected to present-day China. Archaeological evidence suggests that the earliest migrant groups likely traveled from China to Taiwan across the land bridge, searching for warmer weather and food sources.[1]

In 1968, Taiwanese anthropologists and archeologists unearthed a considerable cache of small tools, stone weapons made by humans, who lived in the eastern coast of Taiwan dated from 20,000 to 50,000 years ago, at Baxian Cave of Changpin (Changbin), Taitung County. The Baxian site, existent during the Paleolithic Age, is evidence of Taiwan's oldest settlement and was described as the "Changpin Culture." During 1971–1972, several Taiwanese scholars and a Japanese biologist discovered human remains, including three cranial fragments and a tooth, in Tsochen (Zuozhen), Tainan County. "Tsochen Man," the earliest evidence of human habitation, was a descendent of Changpin culture and lived in south Taiwan about 20,000–30,000 years ago. More human remains were discovered on the adjacent Penghu, the island groups between China and Taiwan. Described as the "Land Bridge Man" (*Luqiao jen*), he lived along the present-day oceanic trench about 10,000–30,000 years ago. In 1982, Taiwanese government passed the National Cultural Relics Preservation Act to protect these sites. By the 2010s, over one thousand archeological sites were protected, and eleven were designated as national historical sites (four first-class, two second-class, and five third-class).[2] Relics showing similar human remains and cultural artifacts have been found in many parts of southern China.[3]

Taiwanese Han groups share similar biology with southern Han groups, including Hakka and Hoklo of China. It is likely that Hakka and Hoklo populations in Taiwan and China are descended from southern Chinese migrants. Biological data, including human lymphocyte antigen, thalassemia mutants, microsatellite, mitochondria DNA, and other biological studies, indicate that Taiwan's earliest inhabitants originated from South Chinese.[4] Immunoglobulin analysis has shown that Hakka and Hoklo populations in Taiwan are closely related to southern minorities of China. Based on immunoglobulin haplotypes gene frequencies, it is estimated that 20–25 percent of current Chinese Hakka or Hoklo genes came from northern Han Chinese and 75–80 percent from southern Chinese groups. Most ancestors (65–70 percent) likely came from southern China, and the other 15 percent are descended from Taiwanese aborigines.[5] All this suggests that Han Chinese people in Taiwan and Continental China came from the same ancestors in southern and southeastern China. The native Taiwanese residents mainly belong to Yue and Miao nationalities, who used to live in southwestern areas of mainland China and moved to Taiwan some 10,000 years ago.[6]

When glaciers melted during the last Ice Age, the land link submerged under water, separating Taiwan and its inhabitants from the mainland. The ancestors of Taiwanese became islanders and adapted to the changing environment by engaging in hunting, fishing, and stone-tool making. Many animals like tigers, elephants, bears, and deer from the mainland also survived and continue to populate the island. Warmer climate changes, improved tools, and domestication of animals between 7,000 and 10,000 years ago led to significant agricultural development and an expanding population from coastal to inland areas.[7] Gradually, Taiwanese ancestors progressed from living as small, isolated groups to joining other groups into tribes. Skill specialization from different groups allowed them to acquire pottery-making, clothing, and bow and arrow production for daily needs, hunting, and protection. Later, clans from Changpin culture developed a patriarchal society, which continued until 5,000 years ago (3000 BCE) before replacement by aboriginal culture.

SOUTHERN ISLANDERS AND ABORIGINAL LANGUAGES

After Taiwan was separated from the mainland, new migrants arrived by boat. The first group came from mainland China by crossing the narrow Taiwan Strait around 5000 BCE. They settled and began farming the island.[8] Thereafter, more migrants crossed the ocean and arrived at Taiwan. Some of them, with their successful sailing skills and improved boats, continued their oceanic journey by island-hopping across the southern Pacific. Therefore, the ancestors of the Taiwanese aborigines came from different parts of East and Southeast Asia. Anthropologists and ethnologists both agree that Atayal people are identical to the Yueh (Yue) and Miao ethnic minorities of present-day China, and that Yami people came from the northern islands of the Philippines. After martial law was lifted on Taiwan in 1987, the government began to encourage and promote the revival of many aboriginal cultures and languages.

Among the Southern Islanders were Austronesian people from the Pacific islands, including today's Philippines, New Guinea, Solomon, and Iwo Jima.[9] They are known as the Southern Island Peoples who diversified the Taiwanese population and continue their own spoken languages and cultures, separate from the Chinese. Some scholars believe they are similar "to the present-day Malay people who inhabit Malaysia and Indonesia."[10] Some of them speak early Austronesian or later Malayo-Polynesian languages, which are found across the Pacific, from Madagascar to Hawaii. Since they brought no written language, their origins and experience in Taiwan depend on unearthed artifacts and oral, folk legends. As they continued their tradition and culture until today, they became the aboriginal people of Taiwan.

One academic argument suggests that Taiwan may be the birthplace of the Austronesian (Malayo-Polynesian) language. Other scholars disagree and point to Southeast Asian countries like Indonesia and the Philippines as the cradle of Southern Island Languages given their rich prehistory. Among Western scientists who believed Southeast Asia was the origin of humanity, Dutch physician Eugene Dubois discovered a partial, human skeleton in 1891. Dubois unearthed the bones at Java, Indonesia, and the specimen was popularly known as the "Java Man," who lived about 1.5 to 2 million years ago. In 2004, a group of scientists discovered bones of a three-foot tall human known as the "Hobbit" on the islands of Flores. The "Hobbit" lived in Indonesia about one million years ago and used stone tools that were equally as sophisticated as those produced by modern humans. The "Hobbit" people survived and continued to live on the Indonesian islands until 18,000 years ago, when anatomically modern humans inhabited much of Indonesia. In Java, for example, early people built temples, palaces, and tombs around the fourth millennium BCE.

Some might have migrated from Indonesia to Southeast Asia and Taiwan on rafts made of plants and powered by tsunamis. The earliest humans who appeared in the Philippine islands came from the Malayan Archipelago about 250,000 years ago. Later, during the Ice Age (25,000 years ago), Mongoloid people came from the north over a land bridge. The largest migrations to islands occurred in approximately 200 BCE from the Malay Peninsula. Migrants brought iron tools and trade contacts from Arabia, India, and China. By the fifth century CE, a new Filipino civilization emerged from the mixture of Negrito, Indonesian, and Malay cultures.[11]

THE NEOLITHIC DAPENKENG CULTURE

About 4,000–7,000 years ago, Chinese and Southern Island migrants used Neolithic tools and developed new cultures, which were more advanced than Paleolithic Changpin culture. They learned to polish the stones and sharpen stone arrowheads and axes. Since unearthed artifactual evidence was discovered at the Dapenkeng (Dafenkang) site near Bali Village (Bali xiang), Taipei County, it is named as the "Dapenkeng Culture" and dated between 5000 and 2000 BCE. The Dapenkeng people were pioneers of oceanic migration to Taiwan. Unearthed evidence revealed no connection between the Changpin and the Dapenkeng cultures.[12]

Agriculture was central to Dapenkeng culture and featured pottery-making technology as pottery containers, cooking ware, and decorative pieces were found. Similar pottery unearthed at Kaohsiung, Tainan, and adjacent Penghu also had code marks, pecked pebbles, and artistic patterns with polished stone adzes. Although the Dapenkeng culture was more advanced than Changpin culture was, the latter continued its coexistence with the former for another 2,000 years. The Changpin culture eventually disappeared around 3000 BC, and pottery culture became the leading cultural development on Taiwan from 2500 to 1500 BC. Among other historical sites, Taichung, Nantou, Tainan, Kaohsiung, Pending, Hualien, and Taitung all feature red-painted pottery and red, cord-painted pottery (*shengwen hongtao*). Although pottery-making and painting came from China, Shengwen Hongtao culture indicates that Taiwan entered the Neolithic Age with improved agriculture, rice and millet farming, advanced stone tools and weapons, and settled communities inland.[13] After Changpin culture disappeared, Dapenkeng culture expanded to many different cultures, up to modern times.

Thereafter, Dapenkeng culture continued and expanded into many places on the island, including the Tahu, Yingpu, and Yuanshan cultures. In 1897, one Japanese scholar discovered more sharpened stone tools and weapons at Yuanshan in Taipei. Following that discovery, the site was named the Yuanshan culture. Yuanshan people knew how to grow rice on the flat land along the Tamsui (Danshui) River in the northern Taiwan. Rice farming provided a more stable food supply than other grains. They also fished nearby lakes and consumed shellfish daily. The Yuanshan women made needles from animal bone for clothing production and domesticated dogs.[14]

Among relics found from the Southern Island Peoples, two unique cultures, the "Peinan" and "Qilin" (or Large Stone culture), were evident in eastern Taiwan. Both cultures existed during the late Neolithic age (1500–100 BCE) and are noted for their use of stone and having pottery technology different from that of the Chinese.[15] In the 1980s, during the construction of a new railway station at Peinan, rail engineering crews uncovered some remains on the construction site. For the next ten years, Taiwanese scholars discovered large numbers of stone coffins, stone statues, and huge stone pillars along the Peinan Mountain and at Chenggong town, Taitung County. At the site of Peinan, archeologists unearthed nearly 2,000 stone coffins. Varying styles, sizes, and decorations on the stone coffins indicated separate social classes within Peinan culture. Most stone coffins pointed in a northeast direction toward the Dulan Mountains, where the Peinan people believed they were reborn.[16]

Beginning around two millennia ago, Taiwan entered the Metal Age, when they learned how to make iron tools and weapons from the Chinese. Artifacts discovered in north, central, and south Taiwan include metal materials and iron-making technology. Among these sites is Shihsanhang site near present-day New Taipei City. During 1988–1989, anthropologists unearthed iron tools and glassware dating from 100 BC–AD 200. There were rich deposits of iron ore in the nearby mountains, and Taiwanese ancestors learned how to make iron axes, knifes, and nails.[17] They used local bloomeries to produce wrought iron around AD 400, an iron-making technology introduced from the Philippines. At the same site, scholars also unearthed trade items from overseas, including more advanced porcelain, tools, and weapons from China. This indicates Taiwan had developed trade with China and the surrounding South Pacific islands.

TAIWAN IN ANCIENT CHINESE RECORDS

Chinese historical records held different names for Taiwan. Chinese scholars of the Xia and Shang dynasties referred to Taiwan as *Daoyi*. However, no solid contemporaneous evidence exists to corroborate Chinese relations with the island prior to the Zhou (1027–221 BCE) dynasty. The Xia dynasty was reportedly established by the Great Yu (*Dayu*) and lasted from 2205 to 1766 BCE. Xia emperor Yu led people to dredge rivers and build irrigation projects. Thereafter, Chinese rice production along the Yellow River and Yangzi (Yangtze) River generated enough wealth and food to support a growing population.[18]

Then, Xia began to expand its territory into the mountainous and forested southwest, today's Guizhou Province in China. Tribes in Guizhou organized strong defenses and protected their farm land. Although later Confucian scholars theorized that Xia emperors developed a bureaucratic government with a large army, they imagined that resistance and revolt toppled the Xia Empire, leading to the ascension of a new dynasty. Ch'eng Tang established the Shang dynasty (1766–1027 BC). Under Shang, China grew economically and militarily. Relics discovered in the Yin ruins suggest a structured government and well-organized army. Walled cities appeared, along with bronze weapons. Inscriptions were discovered on some early bronzes, but most Shang writing was incised on "dragon bones," in actuality tortoise shells, cattle shoulder-blades, and other flat bones.[19]

Shang emperor Ch'eng Tang continued territorial expansion and waged war against the Guizhou barbarians. In 1740 BC, he launched a large-scale attack and drove the tribesmen out of the southern hills, forests, and mountains. According to Chinese historians, however, the tribesmen did not surrender, but instead migrated southeast and later to offshore islands, including Taiwan. Since its early history, Taiwan became a place for mainlanders seeking refuge from government attacks or pressures. They were the ancestors of people now known as the Yueh and Miao, who are large minorities in southeastern China, and the Atayal people on Taiwan.[20] Atayal men continue to make facial tattoos to ward off evil spirits. While Chinese anthropologists and historians argue that early Taiwanese aboriginal people came from China, other scholars, including some Western scientists, contend that the Atayal came from Japan and the Southern Pacific Islands. Yet it is very possible that Taiwanese aborigines were mixed peoples from various, surrounding countries. By the late Shang, continuous military expeditions, aristocratic factions and corruption, and hard punishment weakened the dynasty. Vassal or even rival states emerged, and Shang control diminished.

Taiwan was also recorded as *Daoyi* (tribal islands) in *Shang Shu* (*Book of Prehistory Documents*), one of the earliest Chinese official history books written about 1000–500 BCE during the Zhou dynasty.[21] After the Shang dynasty (1600–1046 BCE) declined, the state of Zhou, one of the Shang's subordinate states in the west (modern Shaanxi Province), rose rapidly. By 1027 BCE, Zhou defeated remaining Shang loyalists and established its own dynasty. The Zhou dynasty (1027–221 BCE) is historically divided into two periods: the Western Zhou (1027–771 BCE) with its capital in Hao (Xi'an, Shaanxi Province) and the Eastern Zhou (771–256 BCE) with its capital in Luoyi (Luoyang, Henan Province).

During the Zhou dynasty, *Daoyi* (Taiwan) was under the Yangzhou state government. The Zhou government divided its territory into nine states, including the eastern state of Yangzhou. In 771 BCE, the reigning king was killed by an alliance of Zhou vassals and people from regions to the west of the capital of Hao. Though one of the king's sons was established as the new ruler and a new capital established further east, the Zhou never again exercised its political dominance. Instead, Zhou kings became figureheads and their territory divided among *de facto* independent kingdoms. This period of division in the Eastern Zhou can be further divided into two historical periods: the Spring and Autumn Period (722–481 BCE) and the Warring States Period (403–221 BCE). During the latter phase, the king of Qin embarked upon a dramatic conquest of ancient China's seven separate kingdoms. In 221 BCE, China was unified under Qin, from which emerged the nation's Westernized name: China. The Qin dynasty (221–206 BCE) built a highly centralized regime, the first of its kind in Chinese history. With all political power at his disposal, Qin Shi Huangdi (the first emperor of Qin who reigned during 221–210 BCE) headed a massive bureaucracy.[22] Though Qin Shi Huangdi was frequently remembered as a totalitarian emperor, aspects of his legal, military, administrative, and bureaucratic procedures remained key features of the Chinese imperial system through the end of the Qing dynasty (AD 1644–1911).

According to governmental records, the first official delegation sent by a Chinese emperor to Taiwan was during the Era of Division between the Han (206 BCE–AD 220) and Sui (581–618) dynasties. In the late Qin dynasty, peasant leader Liu Bang (256–195 BCE) overthrew the Qin and established the Han dynasty, thus beginning a continuous cycle of dynastic changes in China for the next two thousand years. Military successes and land expansion during the Han dynasty convinced the Chinese people of their superiority in civilization and institutions. The Chinese began to call themselves the "Han people" (*Hanzu*, or Han nationals, have historically constituted the demographic majority in China, and are 90 percent of its population today). Han emperors believed that China (*Zhongguo*) was the "Central Kingdom," and thus superior to any other nation, occupying a central position among countries in Asia. Nevertheless, overseas expeditionary efforts to invade Korea and Vietnam drained its national sources and added heavy taxes to Chinese peasants. In late Han, large-scale peasant rebellions and minority uprisings eventually led to the collapse of the dynasty in 220 CE.[23] Then, China entered a period of political uncertainty and instability known as the "Era of Division" (AD 220–589), during which several dynasties rose and fell in rapid succession.

After the fall of the Han dynasty, China divided into Three Kingdoms (220–280) led by three military leaders turned territorial magnates. Among the warlords were Cao Cao (T'sao T'sao, 155–220), who controlled northern China; Liu Bei (161–223), who claimed provinces in the southwest; and Sun Quan (Sun Chuan, 182–252), who controlled central and southeastern parts of China along the Yangzi River. The Three Kingdoms they established were known, respectively, as Wei (220–265) with its capital at Luoyang; Shu (221–263) with its capital at Chengdu; and Wu (229–280) with its capital at Nanjing (Nanking). Each "kingdom waged war against the others over territory, population, and economic resources."[24]

According to *Sanguo zhi* (*History of the Three Kingdoms*), Taiwan was called *Yizhou* (or *I Chou*), meaning "a barbarous region to the east," through the third century AD. Following the Three Kingdoms era, Sui emperor Wendi (Wen-ti, r. 581–604) reunified the country and the court records described Taiwan as *Liuqiu* (or *Liu Chiu*) during the sixth century. The Chinese pronunciation was close to Ryukyu, a Japanese island chain in the East China Sea. Then, in the seventh century, Sui changed the name of Taiwan to *Xiao Liuqiu* (or *Little Liu Chiu*). Some Sui generals described it as a "Precious Round Stone." During the Sui dynasty (581–618), books included maps and people of Taiwan as well as recorded commercial exchanges and military expeditions to the island.[25] The Tang dynasty (618–907) continued Taiwan's designation of "Little Liu Chiu" as governmental records indicated the island was under the administration of the District of Lingnan.

CHINESE EXPLORATIONS AND EXPEDITIONS

During the Three Kingdoms Period (220–280), Chinese emperors showed interest in Taiwan and other offshore islands as court records began to include more information on "barbarian territory." To win the civil war, Wu emperor Sun Quan sent Generals Wei Wen and Zhuge Zhi to Taiwan for recruitments and war materials. Wu state record details an imperial debate in 230 about cross-strait expeditions to *Yizhou* (or I Chou, "a barbarous region to the east"). Although most state officials opposed such a large-scale amphibious operation, which included 10,000 men and sailors, Sun Quan launched the mission. Despite successfully traveling to Taiwan and bringing back several thousand Taiwanese, Generals Wei and Zhuge lost more than half their troops as mainland Han soldiers were susceptible to tropical diseases like malaria and small pox.[26] Although military reports exaggerated the difficulties of the island's living environment, Sun's failure did not dissuade later Chinese emperors from exploring Taiwan.

In 581, after reunified the country, Emperor Wendi tried to restore China's dominant position in East Asia. Sui attempted to reconquer Korea three times, drafting "several million peasants as soldiers and laborers for the military expeditions." Then, after Wendi's reign in 605, Sui Yangdi (Yang-ti, r. 605–617) sent his representative Zhu Kuan (Chu K'uan) to *Liuqiu* (Taiwan) for negotiations. According to Sui's records, Captain Zhu and his fleet arrived at Taiwan but could not communicate with the native people. He returned to the mainland with several captured natives. Two years later, Zhu made his second expedition with one thousand troops under the command of General Chen Ling.[27]

The expeditionary force crossed the Taiwan Strait in 607 "to explore the new land" and asked for Taiwan's submission to the Sui dynasty.[28] With translation aid from captured natives, Captain Zhu negotiated with the Taiwanese for a tributary relationship and acknowledgment of the sovereignty of Emperor Yangdi. However, Zhu failed again as the natives refused the recognition of Sui authority. General Chen Ling threatened war, and the Taiwanese willingly accepted the Chinese expeditionary force's challenge. Zhu and Chen departed from Taiwan without a tributary agreement from local leaders.[29]

In 610, Emperor Sui Yangdi sent another expeditionary force to Taiwan, numbering more than 10,000 troops and commanded by

During the Sui dynasty, both Emperors Wendi and Yangdi, pictured above, tried to restore China's dominant position in East Asia. In 610, Yangdi sent a large expeditionary force to attack Taiwan and defeated the aborigines. (Burstein Collection/Corbis/Getty Images)

Generals Chen Ling and Zhang Zhenzhou. The aborigines organized under the experienced command of Ke Cidou, who previously fought three defensive battles against the Sui army. Unfortunately, for Ke, aboriginal defenses crumbled before the invading army. Sui troops broke through native defense lines and took over Ke's headquarters, killing him in the battle. After their offensive expedition, Generals Chen and Zhang returned victorious with several thousand Taiwanese prisoners.[30] Nevertheless, the Sui army suffered heavy casualties on Taiwan. Emperor Yangdi's generals convinced him that controlling a backward island was not worth another large-scale landing, amphibious assault. Thereafter, the Sui court lost interest in Taiwan and did not pursue further political, military, or commercial establishment on offshore islands.

Although successful in its campaigns on Taiwan and into Vietnam, Sui's forces encountered fierce resistance in Korea against the Goguryeo (one of the Three Korean Kingdoms of Korea at the time). Each of the four, failed, offensive campaigns into Korea required a force of one million men, which eventually bankrupted the Sui Empire and forced its people to revolt.[31] As a result of overseas expeditionary efforts, Sui peasants and its treasury alike were exhausted. With unbearable burdens upon them, the farmers rebelled and dealt a fatal blow to the Sui regime. Li Yuan, one of the rebel leaders, and his son Li Shimin started a revolt, quickly occupying the Sui capital of Chang'an in 617. One year later, the Sui emperor was murdered by one of his own bodyguards, marking the end of the Sui dynasty. Li Yuan assumed the imperial title at Chang'an (present-day Xi'an) and established the Tang dynasty (618–907).[32]

TANG-SONG TRANSITION AND THE PENGHU

The Tang became one of the most successful dynasties as it recentered Chinese power in Asia. After Li Yuan, his son Li Shimin became Emperor Tang Taizong (T'ai-Tsung, r. 627–649). Regarded as one of the greatest Chinese emperors, Taizong expanded China's borders far west- and eastward. He fought Turkic nomads in the west and defeated those in the east. In addition, Emperor Taizong cultivated Chinese–Tibetan relations. He also initiated sovereignty over western kingdoms along the Silk Road. To meet military expeditionary needs, Tang emperors established a peasant-soldier reserve system to secure manpower and economic resources. The land-service system recruited peacetime farmers as wartime soldiers under the command of local city mayors and provincial governors. Local military and political power increased through the Tang dynasty. Taizong's successor, Gaozong (Kao-Tsung, r. 650–683) married one of his father's concubines, an extremely ambitious woman known as Empress Wuhou. She was the power behind the throne, and when Gaozong died in 683, she seized power and became the only empress (684–794) in Chinese history. She ruled with an iron hand and enjoyed some success in foreign policy.

Due to lack of commercial incentives, Tang emperors showed no renewed interest in Taiwan. Among other reasons were the following: First, Tang merchants traded with the world along the Silk Road and Southeast Asian countries along the Rice Road. Taiwan was not on their sea routes for overseas trade. Second, Taiwan did not offer spices, ivory, and other trading items Chinese merchants were looking for. Third, Chinese fishermen sailed beyond Taiwan into the Pacific, for their catch. During the Tang dynasty, the Penghu Islands, rather than Taiwan, became popular for refuge, shipwreck rescues, and new Chinese immigration. Chinese fishermen used the Penghu as a midway point between the mainland and the Pacific Ocean. Moreover, after a well-known Tang poet, Shi Jianwu (Shih Jian-wu), moved to the Penghu with his family around 806,[33] his poems depicted a positive image of Penghu landscapes and fishermen's life. The Tang dynasty was a golden age of poetry, literature, art, and architecture.

After eighty-year-old Empress Wu's death in 705, a succession of weak leaders followed. Border wars continued against Tibetans in the west and with Khitan Mongols in the north. Warfare became a constant, inciting rebellion in the second half of the eighth century. Rapid decentralization of political and military power provided provincial governors, local warlords, and army generals the opportunities to dominate the next century. The Tang remained, in name, until 907 when the last emperor ceded rule to one of his generals.

Zhao Kuangyin (Chao Kuang-yin), known as Taizu (T'ai-tsu, r. 960–976), founded the Song dynasty (960–1279) and established a new capital in the northern city of Kaifeng. To stymie the turmoil and prevent re-emerging local regimes, Song Taizu centralized the military and created a palace army. The Song government assumed "authority hitherto belonging to the military [governor] general and only civil officials could be appointed heads of military and administrative affairs at the local level. This civil-military relationship became another part of Chinese military tradition." Some Chinese historians argue, however, that civilian bureaucracy's superior place in military affairs resulted in one of the least successful militaries of any Chinese dynasty.[34]

Song Taizu's reign was followed by that of his son and grandson, respectively, Emperors Taizong (T'ai-tsung, r. 976–997) and Zhenzong (Chen-tsung, r. 998–1022). Both continued Taizu's policy of political centralization and transitioning from domestic trade to national and international markets. The Song dynasty brought with it a span of economic progress, specifically in the areas of commerce and manufacturing. Innovations in the production of iron and steel led to increased agricultural capability and stronger, suspension bridge construction. The period brought advancements in iron and steel production used for agriculture and suspended bridge constructions. Metallurgic innovations propelled Song shipbuilders to be the most advanced in the world, highlighted by the creation of airtight ship compartments and rudders placed behind a ship's stern, for advanced navigation. Trade and commerce flourished within growing cities, bolstered by coined currency and newly created waterways.

During the early Song dynasty, Chinese fishermen continued to arrive and settle at the Penghu. Many of them came from Fujian Province and some from Guangdong (Canton) Province. Soon these provincial governments began to send troops as paid protection for their fishermen against pirates, barbarians, and settlement disputes. Song troops began arriving in the Penghu regularly, coming in the spring during the fishing seasons and leaving in the fall after rice harvest. They built roads, defensive works, warehouses, and living quarters with more than 200 rooms.[35] Eventually, the Song government established a local administrative office on the Penghu in the 1100s.

NOTES

1. Wang Yufeng, *Taiwan shi* [History of Taiwan], 3rd edition (Taichung, Taiwan: Haodu chuban [How-Do Publishing], 2017), 7–9.

2. Hong Li-wan, "Pre-History Era of Taiwan," Chapter 1 in *Taiwan shi* [History of Taiwan], 2nd edition, ed. Gao Min-shi (Taipei: Wunan tushu [Wunan Books], 2015), 20–21.

3. John K. Fairbank and Merle Goldman, *China: A New History*, enlarged edition (Cambridge, MA: Harvard University Press, 1998), 31–32.

4. Jen-yih Chu, "Biological Relationships of Ethnic Groups in Taiwan," www.hoklo.org/YuetCulture/Articles/?item=1#1.

5. Ibid.

6. David Barber, "DNA Shows Maoris Came from Taiwan, Says Scientist," *South China Morning Post*, August 11, 1998; Xiaobing Li and Patrick Fuliang Shan, "Beijing's Dream and Ethnic Reality," in *Ethnic China: Identity, Assimilation, and Resistance*, eds. Xiaobing Li and Patrick Fuliang Shan (Lanham, MD: Lexington Books, 2015), xiii–xvii.

7. Compilation Committee, National Palace Museum, ROC, *A Chronological Table of Chinese and World Cultures* (Taipei: National Palace Museum, 1985), 5–7.

8. Yueh-ting Lee and Da-you Wang, "Aboriginal People in Taiwan, Continental China and the Americas: Ethnic Inquiry into Common Root and Ancestral Connection," in *Taiwan in the Twenty-First Century*, eds. Xiaobing Li and Zuohong Pan (New York: University Press of America, 2003), 67–68.

9. Wang, *Taiwan shi* [History of Taiwan], 11–12.

10. Copper, *Taiwan*, 30.

11. Xiaobing Li and Michael Molina, "The Philippines," in *Oil: A Cultural and Geographic Encyclopedia of Black Gold*, eds. Xiaobing Li and Michael Molina (Santa Barbara, CA: ABC-CLIO, 2014), 2: 615.

12. Gregory Veeck, Clifton W. Pannell, Christopher J. Smith, and Youqin Huang, *China's Geography: Globalization and the Dynamics of Political, Economic, and Social Change*, 2nd edition (Lanham, MD: Rowman & Littlefield, 2011), 348.

13. Wang, *Taiwan shi* [History of Taiwan], 14–15.

14. Hong, "Pre-History Era of Taiwan," 25.

15. Compilation Committee, National Palace Museum, *A Chronological Table of Chinese and World Cultures*, 16–17.

16. Hong, "Pre-History Era of Taiwan," 26.

17. Wang, *Taiwan shi* [History of Taiwan], 19–20.

18. Kim Draggoo, "Xia Dynasty (Hsia)," in *China at War: An Encyclopedia*, ed. Xiaobing Li (Santa Barbara, CA: ABC-CLIO, 2012), 495–96.

19. Xiaobing Li, Yi Sun, and Wynn Gadkar-Wilcox, *East Asia and the West: An Entangled History* (San Diego: Cognella, 2019), 8–9.

20. W. G. Goddard, *Formosa: A Study in Chinese History* (London: Macmillan, 1996), 16.

21. *Shang Shu* [Book of pre-history documents] (Beijing: Qinghua University Collection), https://baidu.com/item/Shangshu/6297?fromtitle.

22. Edward L. Dreyer, "Continuity and Chang," in *A Military History of China*, updated edition, eds. David A. Graff and Robin Higham (Lexington: University Press of Kentucky, 2012), 23.

23. John K. Fairbank and Merle Goldman, *China: A New History*, enlarged edition (Cambridge, MA: Harvard University Press, 1998), 72–73.

24. Xiaobing Li, "Three Kingdoms," in *China at War: An Encyclopedia*, ed. Li (Santa Barbara, CA: ABC-CLIO, 2012), 453–55.

25. Jonathan Manthorpe, *Forbidden Nation: A History of Taiwan* (New York: Palgrave Macmillan, 2005), 22, 38.

26. Hong Li-wan, "Era of Sea Powers in the Sixteenth and Seventeenth Centuries," Chapter 2 in *Taiwan shi* [History of Taiwan], 2nd edition, ed. Gao Min-shi (Taipei: Wunan tushu [Wunan Books], 2015), 61.

27. Wang, *Taiwan shi* [History of Taiwan], 29.

28. Cen Zhongmian, *Sui Tang shi* [History of Sui and Tang dynasties] (Beijing: Zhonghua shuju [China Books], 1982), 41–42.

29. Manthorpe, *Forbidden Nation*, 36.

30. Su Ge, *Meiguo duihua zhengce yu Taiwan wenti* [U.S. China policy and the issue of Taiwan] (Beijing: Shijie zhishi chubanshe [World Knowledge Publishing], 1998), 5.

31. Hong, "Era of Sea Powers in the Sixteenth and Seventeenth Centuries," 64.

32. Xiaobing Li, *A History of the Modern Chinese Army* (Lexington: University Press of Kentucky, 2007), 18.

33. Manthorpe, *Forbidden Nation*, 38.

34. Michael S. Neiberg, *Warfare in World History* (London: Routledge, 2001), 23.

35. Wang, *Taiwan shi* [History of Taiwan], 31–32.

3

Emperors, Immigrants, and Pirates, 1100–1624

Tang dynasty (618–907) lacked strategic and commercial interests on Taiwan. The island did not offer trade items like spices, sugar, tobacco, and silver that China wanted. Moreover, Taiwan did not have organized government agencies to deal with the mainland. In addition, Tang emperors endured enough domestic problems and had no desire to explore or develop Taiwan. Successors to the Tang, like the Song (960–1279), Yuan (1279–1368), and Ming (1368–1644) dynasties, showed increased concern over Taiwan and the Penghu in terms of population growth and mainland security.

As a result of economic reforms under Song Shenzong (Shen-tsung, r. 1068–1085) and his premier Wang Anshi (1021–1086), Song China experienced a commercial revolution. The country also developed international trade through its tributary system, which was established during the Han dynasty. It allowed the empire to conduct diplomacy and trade from the first to nineteenth centuries. Under this system, gift exchanges between foreign rulers and the Chinese emperor were commonplace. Foreigners sent representatives to the

Chinese capital to present tributes (exotic luxury goods, local special products, or people) to the Chinese emperors. In return, they were rewarded with promises and gifts from the Chinese emperor, such as political recognition, nonaggression agreement, and gifts like porcelain and silk.[1] China's tributary system ensured that the Chinese emperor enjoyed a superior position among trading partners. The Chinese emperor recognized foreigner's authority and sovereignty, confirming their legitimacy only after they had adopted a subjugated posture and recognized the supremacy of the Middle Kingdom. China's tributary system not only helped establish diplomatic relations with other countries but also promoted large-scale commerce.

Therefore, all diplomatic and trade missions were construed in the context of a tributary relationship. There were many tribute states to the empire throughout Chinese history, including Japan, Korea, Vietnam, Cambodia, Borneo, Indonesia, and countries in South and central Asia. Under such a system, hierarchies developed, in which Korea and Vietnam were placed higher than others like Japan, the Ryukyus, Siam, the Burmese kingdoms, and other Indochinese kingdoms that also gave tribute. During the Song, the court received more than 300 tribute missions from other countries.[2] As such, the Song was the longest-lasting dynasty with 300 years of history.

SONG'S IMMIGRATION AND MILITARY ADMINISTRATION

Despite commercial success with the tribute system, the Song dynasty faced continuous military threats from northern nomads like the Mongols and Jurchen (State of Jin). The Song army frequently engaged nomadic forces in the steppes but eventually lost half of China, north of the Yangzi River. As Song military strength waned, China was unable to control distant colonies like Vietnam, which had remained under Chinese administration since 101 BCE. Song commanders, who governed China's colonial localities, exerted control over their respective areas, thereby filling power vacuums left by the Chinese and established quasi-independent regimes. In the intervening 960s, powers vied for control of the north and various local rulers vied for power in Vietnam. Many short-lived rulers took power in the tenth century and maintained tributary relations with the Song court. After Vietnam became an independent state to the southwest, Song emperors also recognized Silla (later Korea) as an independent Korean government to the northeast.

According to Song records, one of the most important tributary items from Vietnam was a new kind of rice, historically known as *Zhancheng*, which required a very short productive cycle of fifty days for each harvest. It could achieve three to four harvest seasons within one year.[3] *Zhancheng* produced much more than traditional China rice, which yielded one harvest a year. Rice was and still remains a Chinese dietary staple. In 1011, Emperor Song Zhenzong (Chen-tsung, r. 998–1022) introduced the fine *Zhancheng* seeds to southern farmers along the Yangzi River and Fujian, Zhejiang, and Guangdong Provinces along the southeast coast. As a result, peasants enjoyed a "green revolution" while rice production increased and rectified the heavily populated regions' food shortages.[4]

The *Zhancheng* rice became so famous that Zheng He, a well-known Ming explorer, visited the Vietnamese town 400 years later. According to Ming records, Zheng He arrived at Zhancheng (Zhan city) in 1405 during his first journey to the Indian Ocean (*Xiyang*). He explained that the name of Zhan (Cham) city usually dated back to the kingdom of Champa and referred to its capital (near present-day Quy Nhon, Binh Dinh Province). Zhancheng was the first regular stop for Zheng He's fleet on all seven voyages from 1405 to 1432. Records indicate that with a favorable wind, Zhancheng could be reached from Fujian in ten days and, with headwind, about fifteen or sixteen days. Zheng He's last visit to Zhancheng was on February 12, 1432.[5]

Improved food production resulted in population increase during the Song dynasty. China's population more than doubled, from 53 million during the Tang dynasty (754) to 120 million during the Song dynasty (1110). Song became the first dynasty in Chinese history to reach a population over 100 million. All of the southern provinces experienced rapid population increase, including Fujian and Guangdong. Fujian Province had a total population of 1.6 million, ranking the sixth most populated province in the country. Soon its cities, towns, and villages became crowded.

Urbanization began as more and more farmers moved from rural areas to cities with their families. During the Northern Song period (960–1127), the capital city Kaifeng had a population of 1.5 million, Shaoxing 1.3 million, and Lin'an 1.2 million, all three existed as the most populous cities in the world. In addition, migrations increased on a large scale, away from the war-torn, unproductive north toward the peaceful and abundant south. Coinciding with migrations to southern China, there was also increased immigration to the offshore islands of the Penghu and Taiwan.

During the 1120s, Chinese farmers and fishermen, along with their families, immigrated from overpopulated provinces like Guangdong and Fujian to Taiwan, Penghu, and other offshore islands, seeking new land opportunity and more living space.[6] Immigrants from Guangdong were Hakka, an ethnic minority in southern China. Those who came from Fujian were Hoklos or Hokkien-speakers (Fujianese) from Quanzhou and Zhangzhou. They became the vanguard of a long-term migration and ancestors of the great majority of modern Taiwanese.

In 1171, Emperor Xiaozong (Hsiao-tsung, r. 1163–1189) formally included the Penghu Islands into the Song Empire and put them under the Quanzhou District government of Fujian. According to government records, about 1,300 Chinese, both Hakka and Hoklo people, lived on the Penghu Islands and engaged in fishing and regularly traded with Taiwanese aborigines. Song Chinese coins unearthed in Taiwan indicate increased exchanges and trade between the two islands.[7] The provincial government sent troops to Penghu to protect Chinese fishermen and settlers on the island. The Song army also fought against Japanese "dwarf pirates" (*Wakou*), who actively interrupted tributary trade in the Taiwan Strait and East China Sea.

According to a report sent by Wang Dayu (Wang Ta-yu), an officer of the Song army, the Penghu Chinese were attacked "regularly by island barbarians" from Taiwan. During one of the Song army's defensive battles, Commander Wang described a large-scale invasion with more than one thousand Taiwanese aborigines. They were armed with bows, spears, and knives. The invading force, however, was no match against the better-trained Song army, which defeated the aboriginal invaders, killed their chief, and captured four hundred Taiwanese.[8] According to Song records, Taiwanese attacks were common along the southeastern coastal areas in Fujian Province from 1174 to 1189.[9]

Song sent more reinforcements to the Penghu Islands. Troops arrived in spring during the rice-sowing season and returned to the mainland in fall after the harvest. Eventually, Chinese troops stayed and built military posts, command offices, living quarters, warehouses, and supply depots. In 1225, the district records showed "the Quanzhou administered the offshore islands, including the Penghu (Pescadores) and other islands."[10]

Song naval development was pivot for China's increased oceangoing activities around Taiwan and Penghu. Before the Song dynasty, China focused internally and interacted with nations accessible by land. Song was the first Chinese dynasty to establish a standing navy. Even after the Song retreated south in the wake of devastating territorial losses to the Jurchen, the navy maintained a valuable position.

Rather than remaining adjunct to the army, the Song navy was placed under the command of the Imperial Commissioner's Office for the Control and Organization of the Coastal Areas in 1132, and grew from approximately three thousand men to more than fifty thousand later.[11]

Nevertheless, from the 1100s to 1200s, Song faced direct threats from Jurchens and Mongols of the northern steppe. In 1125, the northern Jin dynasty or Jurchens (1115–1234) attacked Song China. Two years later, the Jurchens captured the Song emperor Qinzong (Chin-tsung, r. 1126–1127) and ended the Northern Song dynasty. Anti-Jin Chinese supported the Song Qinzong's brother to move the imperial capital to the south. Historically, the Song dynasty is divided into the Northern Song dynasty (960 to 1127) and Southern Song dynasty (1127 to 1279). To an extent, the Southern Song was an exile dynasty, having been pushed out of the north by the Jurchens. The Southern Song never gave up hope to recapture their former territory and re-establish the first Song Empire of Taizu (T'ai-tsu, r. 960–976).

In 1211, the Mongols attacked the Jin dynasty, which controlled north China, including the Hebei (Hopei) and Shandong (Shantung) Provinces. In the 1220s, the Mongols negotiated with Southern Song to attack Jin together; the Mongols planned an attack from the north, while Song attacked from the south. The Mongols promised Song a return of the territories south of the Yellow River after their victory. In 1234, the Jin dynasty was defeated by a joint attack of the Mongols and Southern Song. When the Southern Song army tried to return to north China in 1234, they were attacked by the Mongol army.

The Song-Mongol War began. The Southern Song army failed to re-cover the Mongol-occupied northern territories. The Southern Song army withdrew to the south for several reasons. Since the Southern Song had a completely defensive mind-set, they did not frequently engage in offensive campaigns. Although it also took what might be considered extreme steps to prevent the rise of powerful military leaders, they did put into place fairly effective offensive measures. In 1231, the Mongol army invaded Korea and took over the capital.

YUAN'S ATTACK ON TAIWAN

By the 1200s, the Mongol-Song War moved into the south and more southern Chinese migrated to Taiwan. Since Fujian settlers outnumbered the Hakka from Guangdong, the former occupied better farmland on the plains. Due to the imminent, foreign, barbarian takeover by Mongols, Chinese immigrants to Taiwan held no intentions of return to the mainland; they considered Taiwan a refuge from war.

During the thirteenth century, various peoples inhabited Taiwan. Initially, aborigines occupied the central region and maintained control of most of the island. Then, Chinese immigrants extended their farmland to the southwest, coastal plain area. Among others, the Hakka and Hoklo were the majority of Chinese immigrants, who wrested more farmland from the aboriginal Taiwanese. Eventually, Japanese pirates and immigrants controlled some northern coastal areas.[12] Aside from the Japanese pirates, all of these groups survived through the seventeenth century.

In 1251, the Mongol army launched new offensive campaigns against the Southern Song in three directions from the north. The Mongol army relied on the speed and mobility of their cavalry and existed as one of the most formidable, medieval military systems in the world.[13] Military service was mandatory for Mongol males during wartime. Trained in the steppes, Mongolia's skilled horsemen and hunters possessed tremendous stamina and speed that dazzled their Chinese opponents. They also used ferocious terror tactics, sparring compliant cities and often massacring all inhabitants of non-compliant ones. They elected tribal chiefs for courage, military prowess, judgment, and leadership.[14]

In 1260, Kublai Khan (Khubilai Khan, 1215–1294) became the Mongol leader. In 1271, Kublai Khan was proclaimed the emperor of Yuan and formally established the Yuan dynasty. The Yuan capital moved to Dadu (Beijing) in 1272. Eventually, Southern Song defenses could not keep Mongol invaders out. Southern Song strategy was self-defeating for it institutionalized a weak army and relied on relatively static defenses. Obvious weakness revealed itself when Kublai broke through those defenses and conquered the Southern Song. In 1279, the Mongols destroyed the Chinese army, ended the Song dynasty, and established the Yuan dynasty.

The Yuan dynasty lasted officially from 1279 to 1368 and is considered both as a division or continuation of the Mongol Empire and as an imperial dynasty of China. Although Khubilai Khan established the dynasty, he placed his grandfather Genghis Khan (Chinggis Khan or Chengiz Khan, 1162–1227) as its founder, Yuan Taizu, in official record. Besides the emperor of China, Khubilai Khan also claimed the title of Great Khan or supreme ruler of Mongol khanates (Chagatai Khanate, Golden Horde, Il-khanate). The Yuan dynasty is occasionally referred to as the Empire of the Great Khan as Mongol emperors presided over Mongol khanates.

The Yuan dynasty restored China to its central role in Asian economics and politics. Yuan power extended to Xinjiang (Hsin-Kiang) in the northwest and Tibet (Xizang) in the west, for the first time in Chinese

history. Moreover, Yuan control strengthened over Taiwan and the Penghu Islands. While the Yuan government continued dispatching troops to Penghu, it also sent administrative officials and opened an "Inspection and Administrative Office." Yuan officials allowed local administration to collect annually about 1,025 taels (16,400 oz.) of silver as a salt sales tax from Chinese-Penghu residents.[15]

In 1260, Kublai Khan became the Mongol leader. This painting shows him in a war chariot atop four armored elephants. In 1279, he defeated the Song dynasty and established the Yuan dynasty in China. In 1291, his attacking fleet encountered a strong resistance and failed to conquer Taiwan. (Library of Congress)

In 1274, Kublai Khan launched a large-scale attack on Japan with more than 40,000 troops and 900 vessels. However, the landing campaign failed due to military miscalculations and weather conditions. More than 200 ships were destroyed in the Tsushima Strait between Korea and Japan by a typhoon.[16] The Japanese reverently referred to the typhoon as *Kamikaze* (the divine wind). After the loss of 13,000 soldiers, the Mongol generals withdrew. Nevertheless, Peter Lorge states, "Peace proved difficult for the Yuan dynasty, since it retained the military orientation of Khubilai and the Mongol war machine."[17]

The Mongols launched their second invasion of Japan with a larger force in 1281. The Mongol fleet included 4,400 ships and carried 140,000 men. Kublai Khan changed his offensive strategy from landing on major islands to attacking surrounding small islands first. In late June, the first fleet of his invading force arrived at Hakata Bay in Kyushu. The Mongols were unsuccessful as they faced a strong resistance from local Japanese samurai and armed peasants. The second fleet came in August, and it again faced a strong typhoon in the Gulf of Imari. Many Mongol ships crashed into one another due to strong winds. More than half of the soldiers were killed or drowned in the storm.[18] The second Mongol landing campaign failed.

In 1291, Admiral Yang Xiang (Yang Tsiang) proposed an attack on Taiwan with 6,000 troops as a primary step for an invasion of Okinawa. The Yuan emperor approved his plan and appointed two more officials, Wu Zhidou and Ruan Jian, to join his expeditionary army. In 1292, the expeditionary fleet arrived at Penghu, and then sailed toward Taiwan. Yang encountered a strong Taiwanese resistance after landing and had to pull back to Penghu. He engaged in a fierce argument with Wu about another attack on Taiwan, and the latter disappeared next day. Yang and Ruan were jailed for Wu's disappearance, and the Yuan expedition ended without victory or control of Taiwan.[19]

Nevertheless, during the Yuan expedition, Chinese Hakka and Hoklo migrants took over more farmland from the aboriginal tribes. The Hakka extended their domains on the western plains by driving the aborigines into the mountainous areas. They built fortified villages, and some moved to easily defendable, mountainous areas. The Fujian Hoklo soon outnumbered the Hakka and moved even deeper into aboriginal territory. Both Chinese groups frequently clashed with the Austronesian people. Beginning in the fourteenth century, the two Chinese migrant groups disputed and clashed over influence and power, which has continued into contemporary Taiwanese politics and society.

Meanwhile, Taiwanese raids on the mainland continued and intensified. Fujian governor Gao Xing (Kao Hsing) reported to Emperor Chengzong (Ch'eng-tsung, r. 1295–1307) in 1297 that frequent attacks on the coastal areas required retaliation against Taiwan to solve their security problem. Although Chengzong agreed, he asked the governor to mobilize his own provincial troops for the new expedition. Governor Gao appointed General Zhang Hao (Chang Hao) to command the Fujian invasion. Despite the lack of central government support, General Zhang's amphibious landing went well. Many aborigines retreated into the mountains to avoid Yuan attacks. From a defensive position in the mountains, they harassed Zhang's troops while they protected their own population. After a few months of jungle war, exhausted and depleted, General Zhang pulled his troops out of Taiwan.[20]

The Mongol Yuan emperors relied heavily upon their military to maintain stability. Retrospectively, Yuan military administration and centralized authority insufficiently addressed the empire's social instabilities and racial discriminations. To sow discord, Yuan rulers divided the various nationalities into four classes. Mongols were placed at the top; followed by Semu, Xia, and Uygur people from northwest and central Asia; Han Chinese, and finally Southern Chinese. This division was intended to prevent other nationalities from joining together against the Mongols. Cruel Mongol oppression led to mass resistance of all peoples. "In 1351, 'the Red Turban Army,' rose in Ying-zhou, Anhui, and peasants in many other areas responded favorably. One of the peasant forces captured Dadu and overthrew the Mongol regime."[21]

MING'S SEA BAN AND ZHENG HE'S VOYAGES

The leader of the rebellion, Zhu Yuanzhang (Chu Yuan-chang), was a former Buddhist novice and became the first emperor of the newly established Ming dynasty (1368–1644). Zhu began his ascent to power and established himself as a military leader who held his forces to-gether; loyalty extended from him to his commanders and to their men in the ranks. Zhu, called the Hongwu (Hung-wu, r. 1368–1398) emperor, confirmed Nanjing (Nanking) as the dynasty's capital in January 1368. Though trained as a Buddhist, he was a merciless leader who pushed for a return to Chinese tradition after the period of Mongol rule. He also reestablished China's sovereignty over its neighbors. Within ten years, the Chinese court received tribute from and negoti-ated trade contacts with Okinawa, Borneo, the Malay Peninsula, Java, the Indian coast, and Japan. The Ming dynasty is the most studied of all Chinese history as their historical records remained intact and not only recorded Chinese history, but history of the surrounding coun-tries. Ming records were the first to use "Taiwan" to identify the ac-curate location and people on the island. Under Ming power, China's overseas exploration grew tremendously.[22]

Under the Ming dynasty, countries that attempted to establish po-litical, economic, and cultural relations with the powerful Chinese em-pire had to enter the tribute system. Thus, tribute was often paid for practical objective, instead of only as devotion to the Chinese emperor. Many tributes consisted of native products, such as elephants from Siam (Thailand) and eunuchs and virgin girls from Korea, Vietnam, or the Ryukyu Islands.

To keep it official, for a short period, tribute existed as the only ele-ment of foreign trade for China. Emperor Hongwu, the first Ming em-peror, prohibited any private foreign trade in 1371. In fact, the emperor closed the coast by enforcing a "sea ban." The imperial ban stopped Chinese fishermen from offshore fishing. Simultaneously, Chinese set-tlers on the Penghu Islands had to leave and return to the mainland. Many Hakka refused to follow the order and moved to Taiwan. The Inspection and Administration Office on Penghu was closed down. In 1387, the Ming emperor withdrew the military garrison from Penghu and established a naval base intended to fight active pirating raids.[23] Aside from a few government tributary agencies, the sea ban stopped overseas trade between China and other Asian countries.

To increase the number of tribute states, Emperor Yongle (Yung-lo, r. 1403–1424) expanded the tribute system and dispatched massive overseas missions to the South Seas in the early fifteenth century. Zheng He's (Cheng Ho, 1371–1435) expeditions carried goods to build tribute relationships between the Ming and newly discovered kingdoms in Southeast Asia, South Asia, and Eastern Africa.[24] Between 1405 and 1433, as an imperial official, naval admiral, diplomat, and eunuch of the Ming dynasty, Zheng He made seven voyages to the Western seas. After the Yongle emperor gained the throne in 1402, Zheng He was promoted to Grand Director of the Directorate of Palace Servants, the highest position of all eunuchs. Zheng was also appointed as admiral in charge of a huge fleet, armed forces, and shipyards near Nanjing for the emperor's overseas expeditions.[25] Over 2,000 vessels were built under Zheng He's command during 1404–1419, including a hundred big "treasure ships," approximately 370 to 440 feet in length and 150 to 180 feet abeam. The average loading capacity is estimated to have been about 3,000 tons, with as many as fifty cabins capable of carrying 450 to 500 men each.[26]

In June 1405, Admiral Zheng He embarked on his first voyage with over 200 vessels, of which 62 were treasure ships, carrying silk, porcelain, gold, and 26,800 men. His fleet sailed west to Vietnam, Java, Bengal, and India. Some sources mention that a few of Zheng He's ships reached Taiwan during the first voyage. Their reports found the island a worthless place with tropical diseases and "inhabited by headhunting savages."[27] Between 1407 and 1411, Zheng made two more voyages to central and West Asian countries. One of the principal functions of his expeditions was to carry tribute envoys to China and back home. His fourth voyage from 1413 to 1415 reached many ports on the east coast of Africa, as far south as Malindi (near modern-day Mombasa, Kenya). From 1417 to 1422, he made two more voyages, visiting and revisiting thirty countries in East Africa, the Persian Gulf, Arabia, and the Red Sea. A year after Yongle died in 1424, his son Emperor Hongxi (Hung-hsi, r. 1425) discontinued the oversea voyages, but his reign lasted only one year.[28]

Emperor Xuande (Hsuan-te, r. 1426–1435) resumed the expedition and ordered Zheng He to his seventh voyage. This trip was described as *Xia Xiyang* (Down to the Western Ocean, or the Indian Ocean) in Ming sources.[29] During his seventh and final voyage from 1430 to 1433, Zheng He landed on the western coast of Taiwan. According to

Ming records, he contacted Taiwanese aborigines and traded with the natives. On his way back from Southeast Asia, the fleet had a shipwreck and Zheng landed on Taiwan. His fleet received supplies and herbal medicine from the aborigines. All details appeared in his report to Emperor Xuande. Zheng He died in 1435.[30] It would be another thirty-seven years before Portuguese explorers on the west coast of Africa sailed south to the Gold Coast, and fifty-nine years before Christopher Columbus set sail.

The Ming dynasty's remarkable shipbuilding played a pivotal role in China's increased ocean-faring diplomacy and activity around Taiwan and Penghu. There was a transition during the Yuan dynasty, which dealt with outsiders both by land and by sea. Globalized environments forced the Chinese government and people to develop and grow. During the early Ming, the Chinese navy had over 3,500 vessels and dozens of naval bases. The court deployed 2,700 warships along the coast line to keep the seas, tributary diplomacy, and commercial trade safe against pirate attacks. After the 1500s, the Ming navy declined.

WAR AGAINST PIRATES

The tribute system was challenged and interrupted from time to time. During the Ming dynasty, active pirate attacks threatened tributary sea routes along Chinese coasts. Hongwu, the first Ming emperor, prohibited any private foreign trade in 1371. Soon many private merchants engaged in smuggling and shipped their goods to offshore islands and small coastal towns in Guangdong, Fujian, and Zhejiang. Smuggling provided opportunities for pirates, especially after the Ming navy's decline in the 1520s–1580s and Japanese pirates, or *Wakou*, flourished in East and South China Seas. The Japanese called Taiwan "Takasago," named after a seaport. Most Japanese *Wakous* were armed merchant pirates who conducted their own smuggling and attacked other commercial ships in their way. Some pirates were samurai, who did not find any opportunity to serve as such since the Tokugawa Shogunate (1603–1868) maintained a long peace in Japan. For almost two centuries during the Ming dynasty, Japanese pirates frequently raided China's southeastern coast, killing and plundering. They sometimes attacked and captured coastal villages and cities and brought about enormous damages from the 1500s to the 1700s. Since it was beyond Ming rule, many Taiwanese and Chinese fishermen joined Japanese pirates and made Taiwan their refuge. Some historians point out after the 1550s Chinese pirates outnumbered Japanese.[31]

According to Ming court records, Taiwan served as a base area for many pirates since it was not far from Chinese ports and trade routes. The Ming also had no military presence on the island. During the reign of Emperor Jiajing (Chia-ching, r. 1522–1566), there were at least a dozen pirate armies on Taiwan. They did not only prey mercilessly on commercial shipping but also attacked coastal villages and towns. Among others were several major groups under the command of Lin Daohan (Lin Tao-hen), Lin Feng, Zeng Yiben (Cheng Chi-ben), and Li Zhong (Li Chong). In 1557, Emperor Jiajing made major efforts to reduce, if not stop, pirating activities along the Chinese coast. In 1560, the court sent a large naval force commanded by Admiral Yu Dayu (Yu Ta-yu) to the southeastern coastal areas to suppress Lin Daohan's pirate army.[32]

Lin Daohan was a fisherman in Fujian. After the Ming sea ban, offshore fishing was prohibited along the coast. Lin Daohan organized thousands of angry fishermen to attack and rob commercial cargo ships off the coast. His fleet made both Taiwan and Penghu bases. Having established new bases and growth in numbers, Lin expanded his pirating from the Chinese coast to the coasts of Southeastern Asian countries like Vietnam, Cambodia, and Thailand. In 1562, the Ming navy traced Lin's pirates off the Fujian coast. Admiral Yu Dayu engaged Lin's fleet in the open sea and forced him to engage the powerful Ming armada. Lin's pirate fleet was no match for Yu's disciplined naval force. After five hours of heated battle, Lin was routed and fled with his pirates to Taiwan.

Admiral Yu did not follow Lin to Taiwan, but instead landed on Penghu to destroy Lin's base there. At Lin's suggestion, the Ming court established a garrison and sent a governor to the island, thereby officially including Penghu in the Ming territory. While in retreat on Taiwan, Lin Daohan's forces found it impossible to regroup under constant attack by aborigines. Lin ordered the surrounding aboriginal villages be attacked. The aborigines, however, withdrew into the forests and mountains to avoid a frontal assault and imminent slaughter. After Lin retreated, they returned to their villages and continued harassing the pirate bases. After Lin built new bases in Southeast Asia, he moved his headquarters to Thailand and died there.[33]

Another pirate leader, Lin Feng, also organized Chinese fishermen into a pirate army and frequently attacked Chinese and foreign cargo ships along the coast. He and his pirates learned that Spanish commercial ships carried more valuable trading items than the Chinese ships, including gold, silver, and tobacco. Lin planned a large attack on Spanish warehouses at Manila, the capital of the Spanish colony in the Philippines. In 1574, Lin led his pirate army with more than 3,500 men and women to attack Manila. Although they landed successfully and broke through Spanish defenses, they could not return to their ships after they robbed the warehouses. Lin and his pirates were encircled and blocked by Spanish troops outside Manila. After four months of fighting, Lin broke through the Spanish encirclement and returned to Taiwan with only thirty ships.[34]

Ming suppression of Chinese pirates was not very successful. To reduce Chinese participation in pirating, Emperor Jiajing lifted the sea ban in 1557. He opened the Yuegang seaport, Zhangzhou, Fujian Province, and legalized incoming and outgoing foreign trade to China. As a result, many Fujian people left China for trade and immigration in Taiwan, Japan, the Philippines, Malaya, and Indonesia. They became the pioneers of Chinese immigrants to Southeast Asian countries.[35] In the meantime, Emperor Jiajing also reinforced anti-piracy efforts and appointed Qi Jiguang (Ch'i Ji-guang, 1528–1587) in charge of the war against Japanese pirates. With the support of the local authorities and coastal villagers, General Qi repeatedly defeated these pirates in Zhejiang, Fujian, and Guangdong during 1561–1565 and improved the coastal defense situation.

In 1592, however, Japan's overlord Toyotomo Hideyoshi (1536–1598) launched a large-scale landing, with more than 150,000 Japanese troops, on the Korean Peninsula and the Ming court resumed its sea ban. Known as the Imjin War (1592–1598), Peter Lorge points out Hideyoshi's "invasion of Korea with the avowed intention of then conquering China."[36] The Japanese took the capital, Seoul, in April and captured Pyongyang in May. In June, Hideyoshi ordered his main strength to advance further north toward the Yalu River and the Korean king took refuge there. Emperor Wanli (Wan-li, r. 1573–1620), after procuring funds for Korea's defense, sent an expeditionary force of 45,000 troops under the command of frontier generals Li Rusong and Song Yingchang.[37] In February 1593, General Li attacked Pyongyang, taking over the surrounding hills where his troops could move their heavy cannons and fire directly on the city walls. After breaching the walls, the allied troops, including 43,000 Chinese, 10,000 Koreans, and 5,000 warrior monks, engaged in hand-to-hand combat with the Japanese and forced them to retreat.[38] The war resumed in March 1597 when Hideyoshi launched new attacks with 140,000 troops on southern Korea. Upon new requests sent by the Korean king, the Ming court again sent an expeditionary force of 80,000 Chinese troops to Korea in July under the command of Xing Jie.[39] Hideyoshi's new offensives faced a strong Chinese-Korean defense in central Korea. After the Battles of Seoul and Chiksan (Jiksan) in the fall, the invading Japanese could not launch another major attack. The

Battle of Chin Island in November was the decisive battle at sea, where the Japanese navy lost 133 ships.[40] Lorge concludes, "The Koreans were saved by their navy, and that of the Ming."[41]

Meanwhile, the Ming emperors also tried to stop Japanese merchant-pirates along the Chinese coast. The court sent several letters to the Japanese shogun, demanding an end to pirating and smuggling. Certainly, there was no response or reduction of Japanese pirating in the 1500s. In response, the Ming government issued several orders to Chinese merchants banning any trade, exchange, or contact with Japan. Any Japanese on Chinese soil or any Chinese returning from Japan were arrested. Although Japanese record shows no official communication between the Ming court and Japan, the Japanese Bakufu (the shogun of all the shoguns) had interests in Taiwan in the late 1500s and early 1600s. For example, in 1591, Harada Magoshichiro led an armed diplomatic delegation to Manila for a trade agreement. As part of his mission, he also had a letter from the shogun asking for tributary relations between Taiwan and Japan. On his way back to Japan, Harada stopped at Takasago on Taiwan. However, he found no leaders or authority on the island to which he could deliver the letter, and returned home with it. In 1603, the new *Bakufu*, Ieyasu Tokugawa, also showed interest in Taiwan. In 1609, he sent a senior lord Arima Harunobu to Taiwan to survey land, people, and resources for possible colonization and organization of the Japanese merchant-pirate groups into a Japanese federation. Arima completed Taiwan's resources evaluation but failed to bring all Japanese on the island into a coherent organization.[42]

While the Japanese held interests in Taiwan, later Ming rulers proved less capable of controlling Taiwan and the offshore islands along the southeastern coast. In 1602, another Ming armada sailed to attack pirate bases on Taiwan and Penghu under the command of Generals Shen Yourong and Chen Di. After their expedition, Chen Di compiled his journals into a book, *Dongfan Ji* [Records of Dongfan Experience] (the Ming officials called Taiwan "Dongfan" at that time). It became the first comprehensive book about Taiwan published in China. It was not until 1636 when the Tokugawa government issued a Japanese sea ban that *Wakou* piracy declined.

Soon the growing power of Jurchen and Manchu tribes in the northeast threatened Chinese frontiers while peasant uprisings in the northwest occupied the Ming army. Moreover, the Imjin War of 1592–1598 against Japan further weakened the Ming. Peasant taxpayers refused to pay, leaving a war debt, and Ming power deteriorated. The Ming dynasty fell less than fifty years after the war as it overexerted itself to protect tributary states like Korea.[43] George Elison states, "The drain on its public treasury and its military manpower seriously weakened a Chinese regime that was already burdened with an enormity of external and internal problems and made it sink deeper into the dynastic decline that was to overcome it a half century later."[44] The Manchus from northeast China (Manchuria) capitalized on the Ming dynasty's frail state and attacked the Great Wall. Before Emperor Jiajing, more than 890,000 Ming troops guarded the Great Wall. After Wanli, less than 390,000 Chinese troops stationed along the wall to defend the northern border due to insufficient financial resources.[45] Eventually, the Manchus entered the Great Wall and replaced Ming with the Qing dynasty.

NOTES

1. David C. Kang, *East Asia before the West: Five Centuries of Trade and Tribute* (New York: Columbia University Press, 2012), Chapters 1 and 2.

2. Curtis Andressen, *A Short History of Japan: From Samurai to Sony* (Canberra, Australia: Allen & Unwin, 2002), 62–63.

3. History Research Institute, China Academy of Social Sciences (CASS), *Jianming zhongguo lishi duben* [Concise history of China] (Beijing: Zhongguo shehui kexueyuan chubanshe [China Academy of Social Sciences Press], 2012), 295.

4. Kim Draggoo, "Song Dynasty (960–1279)," in *China at War: An Encyclopedia*, ed. Xiaobing Li (Santa Barbara, CA: ABC-CLIO, 2012), 416–17.

5. Edward L. Dreyer, *Zheng He: China and the Oceans in the Early Ming Dynasty, 1405–1433* (New York: Pearson/Longman, 2007), 151–52.

6. U.S. State Department, *Area Handbook for the Republic of China* (Washington, DC: U.S. Government Printing Office, 1969), 22.

7. Hong Li-wan, "Era of Sea Powers in the Sixteenth and Seventeenth Centuries," Chapter 2 in *Taiwan shi* [History of Taiwan], 2nd edition, ed. Gao Min-shi (Taipei: Wunan tushu [Wunan Books], 2015), 64.

8. The quote from Jonathan Manthorpe, *Forbidden Nation: A History of Taiwan* (New York: Palgrave Macmillan, 2005), 36.

9. W. G. Goddard, *Formosa: A Study in Chinese History* (London: Macmillan, 1996), 26.

10. Zhao Rushi, *Zhufan Zhi* [Records of offshore territories] (Shanghai: Zhonghua shuju [China Books], 1985), 1: 26–27.

11. Jung-Pang Lo, "The Emergence of China as a Sea Power in the Late Sung and Early Yuan Periods," *The Far Eastern Quarterly* 14, no. 4 (August 1955), 490–91.

12. John F. Copper, *Taiwan: Nation-state or Province?* 4th edition (Boulder, CO: Westview, 2003), 32.

13. Michael S. Neiberg, *Warfare in World History* (London: Routledge, 2001), 30.

14. Albert M. Craig, *The Heritage of Chinese Civilization* (Upper Saddle, NJ: Pearson Education, 2007), 88.

15. History Research Institute, CASS, *Jianming zhongguo lishi duben* [Concise history of China], 325.

16. John K. Fairbank and Merle Goldman, *China: A New History,* enlarged edition (Cambridge, MA: Harvard University Press, 1998), 167, 298.

17. Peter Lorge, *War, Politics and Society in Early Modern China, 900–1795* (London: Routledge, 2005), 91.

18. Thomas Conlan, however, believes historians overemphasized the notion of the "divine winds" and ignored military miscalculations of the Mongol generals. Conlan, *In Little Need of Divine Intervention: Scrolls of the Mongol Invasions of Japan* (Ithaca, NY: Cornell University Press, 2001), 259.

19. Wang Yufeng, *Taiwan shi* [History of Taiwan], 3rd edition (Taichung, Taiwan: Haodu chubanshe [How-Do Publishing], 2017), 32–34.

20. Hong, "Era of Sea Powers in the Sixteenth and Seventeenth Centuries," 62.

21. History Research Institute, CASS, *Jianming zhongguo lishi duben* [Concise history of China], 344.

22. Xiaobing Li, Yi Sun, and Wynn Gadkar-Wilcox, *East Asia and the West: An Entangled History* (San Diego: Cognella, 2019), 22–23.

23. Wang, *Taiwan shi* [History of Taiwan], 34.

24. Gavin Menzies, *1421: The Year China Discovered America* (New York: Perennial, 2003), 64–65, 105–6.

25. Xiaobing Li, *Modern China: Understanding the Modern Nation* (Santa Barbara, CA: ABC-CLIO, 2015), history chapters.

26. Dreyer, *Zheng He,* 28–34.

27. Manthorpe, *Forbidden Nation,* 41.

28. Fairbank and Goldman, *China: A New History,* 137–38, 193.

29. Dreyer, *Zheng He,* 150.

30. Gavin Menzies, *1421: The Year China Discovered America* (New York: Perennial, 2003), 64–65, 105–106, 455–56.

31. Manthorpe, *Forbidden Nation,* 22.

32. History Research Institute, CASS, *Jianming zhongguo lishi duben* [Concise history of China], 361.

33. Manthorpe, *Forbidden Nation,* 44–45.

34. Wang, *Taiwan shi* [History of Taiwan], 35.

35. Hong, "Era of Sea Powers in the Sixteenth and Seventeenth Centuries," 59–60.

36. Peter Lorge, *War, Politics and Society in Early Modern China, 900–1795* (London: Routledge, 2005), 131.

37. Kenneth M. Swope, *A Dragon's Head and a Serpent's Tail: Ming China and the First Great East Asian War, 1592–1598* (Norman: University of Oklahoma Press, 2009), 110–12.

38. Morgan Deane, *Decisive Battles in Chinese History* (Yardley, PA: Westholme Publishing, 2018), 112–14.

39. Zhang Xiuping, *Yingxiang zhongguo de 100 ci zhanzheng* [One hundred decisive battles in Chinese history] (Nanning, Guangxi: Guangxi renmin chubanshe [Guangxi People's Press], 2003), 279.

40. Swope, *A Dragon's Head and a Serpent's Tail*, 251.

41. Peter Lorge, "Water Forces and Naval Operations," in *A Military History of China*, ed. David A. Graff and Robin Higham, extended ed. (Lexington: University Press of Kentucky, 2012), 93.

42. Manthorpe, *Forbidden Nation*, 45.

43. Samuel Hawley, *The Imjin War: Japan's Sixteenth-Century Invasion of Korea and Attempt to Conquer China* (Seoul, Korea: Royal Asiatic Society, 2005), 565–67.

44. George Elison, "The Inseparable Trinity: Japan's Relations with China and Korea," in *Cambridge History of Japan Volume 4: Early Modern Japan*, ed. John Whitney Hall (Cambridge, UK: Cambridge University Press, 1991), 290.

45. China National Military Museum, comp., *Zhongguo zhanzheng fazhanshi* [History of Chinese warfare] (Beijing: Renmin chubanshe [People's Press], 2001), 1: 395.

4

Formosa: The Dutch Colony, 1624–1662

In the sixteenth century, European countries engaged in exploration, conquest, and colonization. The Portuguese were the first Europeans who arrived in East and Southeast Asia. In 1511, they conquered Malacca and, in 1517, began raids around coastal Guangdong Province in attempts to open up trade with China. The foreign Portuguese were not in China's tributary sphere and as such were repulsed by Ming troops and local peasants. In 1519, Portuguese captain Ferdinand Magellan led five ships on a circumnavigation mission by way of the South American straits bearing his namesake, across the Pacific Ocean, and finally reached the Philippines. Magellan was killed in a conflict with Visayan natives upon arrival. Only eighteen men in one ship returned home and completed the first circumnavigation of the world in 1522. Thereafter, Portuguese rushed eastward fueled by spirits of adventure and lucrative trade opportunities, and Spain, Holland, and Britain followed. Coupled with economic opportunity, proselytizing zeal to spread Christianity to the "heathen" world motivated European colonizers. Therefore, early exploration and colonization of East

Asia became a commercial and evangelical pursuit for Europeans and a political and economic test for Asians.

When Europeans arrived, East Asia and Southeast Asia were politically weak and divided. Dynastic problems and parochial jealousies consumed the energies of petty isolated emperors, while the peasants eked out their burdensome existence. No Asian power challenged Western expansion. China, India, and Japan were factionalized and isolationist, while China and India were actually the primary focuses of European expansion and influence. Simultaneously, Ming China (1368–1644) underwent a rapid decline as an old dynasty. Ignorant, overconfident, and unwilling to make major institutional reforms, Ming government was ill-prepared to fend off Western incursions. When the Dutch demanded open relations, the Central Kingdom was not only unprepared for Western "barbarian" encroachment but was also unable to fully comprehend the gravity of this global development. Ming emperors did not understand that the intruders were decades ahead of China in science and technology.

Ming isolationist policy proved tragic for Taiwan, which became the first European colony in East Asia. As one of the major sea powers in the world, the Dutch established themselves in Taiwan in 1624 and expelled the Spanish from the island. The Dutch named their new colony "Tayowan" (or Taijouwan, a coastal sandbank near present-day Anping, Tainan County, where the Dutch built their military post) until 1662 when Chinese troops commanded by Zheng Chenggong (Cheng Ch'eng-kung) landed.

EARLY EUROPEAN CONTACT AND CONFLICT

In 1544, a Portuguese commercial ship passed by Taiwan and called it "Iiha Formosa" (one beautiful island).[1] In 1553, the Portuguese, in order to obtain a lease and trade rights, bribed local Chinese officials and occupied part of Macao (Macau). In 1557, they enlarged their holdings in Macao and established administrative offices and fortified garrisons.[2] Despite Ming administration of Macao, the Portuguese regarded Macao as their colony and claimed sovereignty over it. Meanwhile, private or illegal trade between European and Chinese merchants thrived in Macao and brought in surplus 60,000 lbs. of silver annually. Since Formosa was on their trade routes, the Portuguese were the first Europeans arrived there in 1590.[3]

In the wake of Portuguese arrivals came the Spanish and Dutch, who also pushed into East Asia in search of trade. In 1565, Spain established its first settlement in the Philippines, and in 1571 it conquered

Manila, turning the Philippines into a Spanish colony. Under Spanish rule, the Philippines became the only Asian country with a majority Christian population. The Spanish were also rejected trade rights by the Ming court, despite their offer of Mexican silver dollars, which the Chinese government used and needed for official foreign exchanges.[4] In 1626, the Spanish landed on Taiwan, occupying Keelung and Tamsoya (present-day Tamsui) on the northeastern coast.

During Portugal and Spain's colonial rival, Holland emerged as a major sea power. Thanks to its shipbuilding capacity, Dutch owned 16,000 out of 20,000 of the total European merchant ships. In 1602, it established the "United Dutch East India Company" (VOC) headquartered at Batavia (present-day Jakarta, the capital of Indonesia). The Dutch East India Company soon dominated the European trade in the East and established trading offices in nineteen Asian countries, including Japan. In 1619, the Dutch colonized Indonesia, while Portuguese holdings shrunk to one Indonesian island, Timor. The Taiwan Strait became an important trading route between Java and Japan. Soon the Dutch arrived in China and were intent on establishing their own trade and military posts along the Chinese coast, including Macao.[5]

In 1602, the Dutch attacked Macao and attempted to seize it and drive the Portuguese out of China. However, with the aid of local Chinese, the Portuguese defeated Dutch forces. The Dutch commander did not give up after Macao and attacked the nearby Penghu islands in 1604, known as the "Penghu Incident" (Pescadores Incident) for the purpose of establishing trade posts in China.[6] That summer the Dutch fleet under the command of Wybrand van Warwyk (Wijbrand van Waerwijk) landed at Penghu. Captain van Warwyk built the trade offices and military bases to monitor traffic in the Taiwan Strait and intercept Portuguese and Spanish ships.[7]

When news of the Dutch military establishment on Penghu reached the provincial government of Fujian, the Chinese governor ordered administrative chief of Jinmen (Quemoy) Shen Yourong to stop Dutch attempts for permanent occupation of Penghu. Shen prepared for military confrontation and concentrated the Fujian fleet around Jinmen. He visited Warwyk with some Chinese troops at Penghu and warned the Dutch captain that any foreign occupation of the island would lead to war. Warwyk realized his small fleet had no chance against the Fujian navy and agreed to withdraw his troops from Penghu a few days later.[8]

It happened again in 1622 when another Dutch expeditionary fleet attacked Macao. After his unsuccessful attack on Macao, Commander Cornelius Reijersen (or Reyerszoon) landed at Penghu. That fall, the Dutch commander prepared for winter and built houses on the northern island. Again, Fujian governor Nan Juyi warned the Dutch and sent his representative, along with the Fujian fleet, to Penghu. Commander Reijersen, however, persisted in gaining a trade deal and even prepared for possible confrontation until Chinese signed one. While Governor Nan asked for an immediate withdrawal before any trade negotiations, Commander Reijersen demanded a trade agreement before he would leave the island. In early 1623, the Dutch fleet attacked the Fujian navy at Jinmen.[9] Although Nan agreed to talks thereafter, the governor had no intention for a trade deal with the Dutch. The Chinese governor knew he did not have authority to make a trade deal since the central government continued their century-long isolationist policy, barring any diplomatic and commercial relationship with the West. When Dutch negotiators arrived at Fuzhou, Governor Nan arrested them and executed several of them. Then, he ordered the Fujian fleet to attack the Dutch and destroyed several ships.

After their setback, the Dutch government reinforced its navy at Penghu, and replaced Reijersne with Martinus Sonck in the summer of 1624. As an experienced naval officer, Commander Sonck engaged the Chinese fleet, while he looked for an opportunity to reach a trade deal with China.[10] Eventually, both sides accepted Chinese merchant Li Dan (Li Tan) as a mediator for a cease-fire between the Dutch and Fujian government.[11]

Li Dan, also known as Yan Siqi (Yen Ssu-chi), grew up in Fujian and became a smuggler, traded illegally on Taiwan, and also headed a group of Chinese pirates along the Fujian coast. In addition, he became a Christian in Manila and took a new European name, Andrea Dittis. He provided European traders with Chinese and Japanese goods unavailable for Europeans. Chinese trade items included porcelain, silk, and tea. As non-official traders, Li and company became a major supplier to the Dutch-China trade.[12] "Captain China," as Europeans referred to him, became popular among Westerners. By 1624, Li Dan established his merchant-pirate empire on Taiwan.

Although the Dutch knew "Captain China," they were suspicious of his intentions during the Chinese-Dutch dispute. Li suggested a compromise that the Dutch fleet leave Penghu, and the Fujian government allow the Dutch to use "Tayowan" (Taiwan) for trade with China. Li Dan also offered his own transportation depot at Peikang (present-day's Northport) for Dutch use to engage in trade with

China. Exhausted from their naval confrontation, both sides agreed to Li's compromise.[13]

DUTCH CONQUEST

In 1624, the Dutch fleet arrived at Taiwan. The Dutch established their trading post and military base at Anping near present-day Tainan, and began a thirty-eight-year colonization of Taiwan. The real authority over the island was the Dutch East India Company, which dealt mostly with Chinese smugglers and Li's pirates since the Ming government maintained its sea ban. Li Dan, or "Captain China," dominated European trade between Taiwan, China, and Japan.[14]

Li's business skyrocketed, and he needed more workers. When Fujian faced serious famine during 1624–1625, Li Dan capitalized on it and recruited many hungry peasants. It was the first organized, large-scale immigration from mainland China to Taiwan. Thereby, Li is memorialized as a pioneer in Taiwanese history. A monument of "Yan Siqi's Exploration of Taiwan" stands in the city center of today's Peikang.[15] After Li died, his young associate twenty-one-year-old Zheng Zhilong (Cheng Chih-lung) took over the business and large pirate army on Taiwan. Zheng continued supplying the Dutch with Chinese trade items and built more than ten pirate bases and a naval force in northern Taiwan. During his stay in Japan, he married a local woman. In 1624, their first son Zheng Chenggong (Cheng Cheng-kung, or Koxinga) was born in Japan. He later became a Chinese national hero in the anti-colonial war against Dutch.[16]

After Li's death in 1625, tensions mounted between Zheng Zhilong and the Dutch. Zheng had a fleet of more than one thousand vessels and continued to attack other Chinese and Japanese commercial ships in East and South China Seas. Soon, his pirate fleet attacked and captured Dutch, Portuguese, Spanish, and English ships.[17] The Dutch disliked Zheng's dominance in East Asian waters or his trade alliance with Japan in Southeast Asia. The Dutch East India Company tried to squeeze Zheng out of Taiwan and reinforced its garrison there. Under pressure, Zheng moved his entire fleet from Taiwan to Xiamen, a seaport city in Fujian Province. Then, the Dutch attempted to end Zheng's control of Chinese trade. In 1628, the Dutch East India Company sent eight warships commanded by de With to the Taiwan Strait. Commander de With mistakenly attacked the fortified city of Xiamen in June rather than engaging Zheng's junks at sea. The Dutch fleet faced well-organized defensive fire at Xiamen. After the Dutch suffered heavy casualties and lost six out of eight warships, de With returned to Batavia.[18]

The conflict between Zheng and Dutch continued from 1628 to 1635 as Zheng controlled Xiamen and Dutch governor Hans Putmans controlled Taiwan. The Ming court looked favorably on Zheng's fight against European influence in the south as it freed up the Ming army to defend against Manchu threats in the north. Zheng enjoyed the support of both the Ming navy and Ming emperor. In 1629, the Ming emperor commissioned Zheng Zhilong as a naval commodore of the imperial fleet, commanding essentially his own pirate fleet about three thousand ships.[19] In 1630, Zheng was promoted admiral.

In August 1633, Dutch governor Hans Putmans launched another attack from Taiwan on Zheng's fleet in Quanzhou Bay in Fujian. Putmans had initial success and demanded free trade along the Chinese coast. Zheng refused and both sides continued conflict for two months. Then, in October, Zheng launched a counterattack at night and destroyed several of Putmans's warships. The Dutch governor returned to Taiwan with the remaining ships.

Eventually, Dutch forces conceded to Zheng's pirate dominance of the Taiwan Strait and desired to end hostilities. In 1636, the Dutch governor visited Xiamen and reached an agreement with Zheng. According to the agreement, Zheng would collect tariffs from all commercial ships along the southeast coast of China. In return, he recognized Dutch control of Taiwan. After the Battle of the Taiwan Strait, the Dutch shifted their policy toward Taiwan, from a Chinese trade post to a colonization.[20]

The Dutch East India Company appointed Pieter Nuyts as the first Dutch governor to Taiwan. In 1624, Governor Nuyts built Fort Zeelandia (present-day Anping Castle) at Tayowan, which included administrative offices, military command, living quarters, warehouses, and service facilities. Soon it became the colonial center of Taiwan. Several streets around the fort created an international commercial center and included trade markets, company offices, bars, restaurants, and churches. One of the streets, Yanping Street, became known as the First Street of Taiwan. In 1625, Nuyts constructed another business center, Provintia, for Chinese merchants. After Hans Putmans replaced Pieter Nuyts, the new governor built another fort nearby in 1635 to protect Fort Zeelandia. Governor Putmans completed Fort Redoubt Utrecht, south of Tayowan, in 1640. The Dutch continued the construction of military forts in the 1650s. They built another fort at Provintia, which is known as Provintia Castle today. In 1641, the Dutch captured Malacca from Portugal and continued taking major portions of the Malayan world.

The Dutch colonized Taiwan from 1624 to 1662. The first Dutch governor Pieter Nuyts built Fort Zeelandia (present-day Anping Castle) in 1624 and used it as an administrative office, military headquarters, and residence. (Thomson, J., *The Straits of Malacca, Indo-China and China*, 1875)

Dutch colonization of Taiwan faced rivalry from Spain, which conquered the Philippines as their military and commercial center in the East. Spain challenged Dutch domination of Taiwan from its onset, since the former had seized Keelung and Tamsui on the northeastern island. The Spanish considered Dutch occupation of Taiwan as a direct threat to their trade routes between Manila and Japan. The Spanish reinforced more troops on Taiwan and built Fort San Salvador at Keelung in 1626 and Santo Domingo (also known as the "Red Hair Fort" in Chinese) at Tamsui in 1628, both were military bases near Keelung in the north opposed to Dutch fortifications in the south. Coincidently, over thirty Spanish missionaries established themselves and erected four Catholic churches and two schools at Keelung and Tamsui.[21]

In 1627, the Spanish sent troops from Manila and Keelung to attack the Dutch on Taiwan, but failed. In the 1630s, Spanish forces on Taiwan left for the Philippines, where there were large-scale anti-Spanish riots. Fewer than 400 Spanish troops guarded San Salvador and Santo Domingo. In 1642, Governor Putmans ordered his troops to attack the Spanish garrison around Keelung and destroyed the two forts, burning all the Catholic churches and schools during the offense.[22] The defeat of Keelung ended a sixteen-year Spanish presence on Taiwan, and the Dutch East India Company established its domination over the island.

Japan also established a trading depot in Taiwan before the Dutch. After their conquest in 1626, the Dutch collected all tariffs from international cargo ships through Taiwan. Japanese merchants were displeased and organized a plot against the Dutch. In 1634, the Japanese asked for a meeting with the Dutch. During the meeting, they kidnapped Dutch officials and took them to Japan. Simultaneously, the Japanese government closed all the Dutch trading offices and agents in Japan. The Dutch East India Company at Batavia eventually agreed to stop taxation on Japanese goods through Taiwan in exchange for Japan's re-opening trade and releasing the hostages. Ten years of hostility between the Dutch and Japan ended in 1636.

COLONIAL CONTROL AND DEVELOPMENT

After the Dutch established a colonial government in Taiwan, there were about 3,100 Dutch officials, merchants, missionaries, and their families in Taiwan from 1624 to 1634. The colonial government and military command headquarters were in Fort Zeelandia, where there were trade markets, foreign offices, schools, and churches. It became the colonial center for Europeans in Taiwan. There were more than 2,000 Dutch soldiers garrisoned at Fort Zeelandia. Then, the Dutch built Fort Provintia, in present-day Tainan. It became the second-largest town for Chinese in Taiwan with numerous shops, restaurants, warehouses, and hospitals. There were more than 500 Dutch troops in Fort Provintia.

To secure colonial rule in Taiwan, the Dutch East India Company adopted a divide-and-conquer strategy, using different policies toward the aborigines, Chinese, and ethnic groups on the island. The aborigines, who had dominated Taiwan since the early ages until the seventeenth century, included the Pengpu people. Most Pengpu aborigines lived in small, isolated, tribal villages. To conquer the aboriginal peoples, the Dutch launched military attacks on their fortified, mountain villages. Although the aborigines overwhelmingly outnumbered the Dutch, the latter were confident in their naval superiority and advanced military technology. Dutch matchlock muskets, for example, were the first practical and portable firearms. Their unwavering musket volleys produced fearsome noises and clouds of smoke that terrified the aboriginal peoples.

In 1635, more than 500 Dutch troops attacked four Pengpu villages in the southern mountains. The aborigines engaged in fierce combat armed only with spearhead and arrows. Most of the aborigines, including women and children, were killed during the attacks. The East India Company sent reinforcements and more attacks followed. According to a Batavia headquarters' report, 405 aborigines were killed, 697 captured, 197 sent to Batavia as slaves, and 482 were relocated by the Dutch military from 1635 to 1639.[23] Beginning in 1641, the Dutch commenced attacks on the aborigines in the central region. After a few more years of conquest, the Dutch controlled the southern region of the island.

After defeating the aborigines in the 1640s, the Dutch reorganized them into four federate regions: the central federate region, southern region, Pi'nan (eastern) region, and Tamsui (northern) region. Each village elected a representative, who created a tribal leadership and accepted the federation administration including local leaders, Dutch officials, and priests. Local leaders, including the aborigines, Chinese, and Dutch, provided effective leadership in the colonial government with the support of the Dutch garrison. They collected local taxes, supervised trade, and enforced Dutch East India Company regulations. Catholic priests also established Christian congregations in each federate regions. Despite the first, seemingly efficient administration on Taiwan, there were complaints, protests, and even uprisings against the Dutch colonizers.

Dutch missionaries built the first Christian church on Taiwan in 1627. Schools soon followed and introduced the Western spelling language to the aboriginal inhabitants. The missionaries translated the pronunciations of aboriginal language into writing alphabets, and created a new romanized written language for the aborigines. Taiwanese Chinese called it *Hongmao ch'i* (Red-hair characters). The Dutch used the new writing in all legal documents, contracts, and educational curriculum. By the 1640s, the Dutch had established a youth school, adult male school, and girl school, totaling 526 students. More than fifty aborigines worked in the schools as instructors or staff members, who converted to Christianity.

The Dutch colonial policy toward Chinese was different from that toward the aborigines. Most Chinese were rice farmers in northern areas of the island as contract laborers for Zheng Zhilong as his tenants. After Zheng left Taiwan for Xiamen, many of them completed their labor contract and purchased small parcels from the Dutch for subsistence farming.

Dutch colonization of Taiwan aimed to expand trade with China. Given the Ming court's sea ban and Chinese piracy, Dutch–Chinese trade relations developed slowly between the 1620s and the 1640s. Conventional smuggling in the 1620s was not successful, and the Dutch navy was unsuccessful against Zheng Zhilong at Jinmen and Xiamen in the 1630s. The Dutch shifted their gunboat strategy to diplomacy, accordingly. In the 1640s, the Dutch negotiated a secret trade deal with Zheng. Per the agreement, Dutch ships paid taxes to Zheng, who promised provision of Chinese trade items and acknowledgment of the Japanese-Dutch trade. Chinese trade items included silk, tea, sugar, and fur, while the Dutch paid in silver.

To balance the China trade, the colonial government in Taiwan began to develop commercial agriculture, including tropical cash crops like sugarcane for international markets in Persia, Japan, and Europe. Before Dutch colonization, aborigines and migrant Chinese farmers grew rice for subsistence. Following traditional farming methods, they used no animal assistance, improved farming tools, or irrigation systems.

Dutch commercial development required a system of indentured servitude to supply laborers. The Dutch sought aid from then Ming admiral Zheng Zhilong and Fujian governor Hsiung Wen-tsan as Fujian peasants were land-starved and famine-stricken. The Fujian governor commissioned Zheng transport landless peasants to Taiwan. By the 1650s, more than 20,000 Chinese peasants immigrated from Fujian to Taiwan with the help of Zheng's fleet. He is described as the father of Chinese colonization on Taiwan.[24] Most Chinese came from the Quanzhou and Zhangzhou regions of Fujian. As contracted laborers, they rented land and borrowed money from the Dutch East India Company in the spring, and paid their rentals and taxes against their fall harvest. The Dutch provided water buffaloes, horses, and improved farming tools. They introduced sugarcane and other tropical and semi-tropical cash crops like tobacco, pineapple, snow peas, and tomatoes. The Fujian Chinese peasants built irrigation systems that brought water from rivers to newly cultivated farmland at higher elevations. Cooper states, "Dutch East India Company rule led to an expansion of commerce on the island and trade with merchants in China, Japan, and elsewhere in the region."[25]

Since south China was war-torn between the remnants of the Ming dynasty and Manchu Qing army, most immigrant peasants settled in Taiwan after the completion of their labor contracts. Many rented or purchased small plots and became independent farmers. However, there was occasional conflict between Chinese and Dutch colonists.

In 1650, Chinese farmers enjoyed an abundant rice and sugarcane harvest. The unexpected agricultural surplus surpassed Dutch trade and transportation capacities. Surplus stock soon lowered the price of cash crops while the Dutch East India Company raised farmers' taxes based on productivity rather than their sale. Many Chinese farmers joined an armed uprising under the leadership of Guo Huaiyi (Kuo Huai-yi) against colonial taxation. Guo Huaiyi, from

Smeer, a small village north of Chikan, disliked Dutch discriminatory policies toward Chinese. While the aborigines experienced no tax imposition, the Dutch taxed the Chinese on almost everything, including farming, fishing, trading, and hunting. The Chinese were required to have hunting permits and were also taxed on the sale of buckskin, antlers, and velvets. Taiwan reported an annual export of 200,000 buckskin. All of these factors compelled Guo to respond, and he organized an armed, open rebellion against oppressive Dutch taxes.[26]

In the fall of 1652, Dutch governor Frederick Coyett learned of the rebellion from Chinese sources. On September 7, he sent troops to Smeer and tried to arrest Guo and other leaders. The Dutch did not realize that Guo had organized more than 5,000 farmers for the uprising; the Dutch withdrew immediately. On September 8, Guo launched the armed rebellion and attacked the Dutch stronghold at Provintia. They reached the city center, burned East India Company's offices, and destroyed its warehouses. The Dutch sent their main force from Tayowan and defeated the inexperienced Chinese farmers. After Guo died in battle, the rebellion collapsed and suffered more than 3,000 casualties. Also known as the "Guo Huiyi Incident," it was the largest anti-Dutch resistance in Taiwanese history.[27]

MING'S FALL AND ZHENG'S TAKEOVER

During the Dutch colonization of Taiwan, a tremendous change took place in China. The Ming dynasty ended in 1644, as the Northern Manchus usurped power and established the Qing dynasty. As peasant uprisings increased in the northwest, Jurchen and Manchus threatened the northern frontiers, and Ming rulers proved less and less capable in defense. The Japanese invasion of Korea in the 1590s brought Chinese armies into Manchuria, where despite forcing a Japanese withdrawal, they were weakened.[28] Costs of war could not be paid due to peasant taxpayers' revolting, and thus Ming power diminished. Because Ming officials were increasingly preoccupied with Manchu threats in the northeast, they ignored the conditions of Shaanxi (Shensi) and other northwestern provinces. Neglect bred a lack of faith in government, and deepening regional depression led to increased bandit uprisings.

In 1627, northern Shaanxi Province experienced a severe drought. Yet, the government continued to demand peasant taxes. As thousands of peasants starved, survivors fomented rebellion. By 1631, in Shaanxi and Shanxi (Shansi) Provinces, there were more than thirty-six outlaw bands comprised of some 200,000 men. Li Zicheng (Li

Tzu-ch'eng, 1605–1645) became the leader of the peasant rebellion. In 1643, he assigned himself the rank of generalissimo and reorganized his followers to march on Beijing. Promising a new era of peace and prosperity, Li and his army moved across north and central China. The Ming army had no adequate defense for their capital and as Li approached, courtiers and royal family members fled the city to their substantial, country estates. Li and his forces met no major resistance when they entered Beijing on April 25, 1644. The last Ming emperor Chongzhen (Ch'ung-cheng, r. 1628–1644) hung himself from a tree.[29]

With the Ming deposed, Manchu troops entered the Great Wall from the north, defeated Li's army, and established the Qing dynasty (1644–1911) in June 1644. The Manchu state, which occupied northeast China (Manchuria), fought the Ming army over the Great Wall and surrounding territories for decades. Manchu leaders recognized the Ming's collapse as an opportunity to usurp power and rule China. Despite the power shift, many southern Ming officials and military leaders, loyal to the Ming emperor, refused to accept "foreign rulers" from the north and organized a resistance. After 1644, Ming loyalists supported a young Ming emperor in Nanjing. As a result, the Qing army launched a large-scale southern campaign against Ming remnants.

Among the former Ming officers was Admiral Zheng Zhilong, naval fleet commander of Fujian. Zheng joined others in re-establishing a new Ming government in the south and supported Longwu as emperor in 1645. Zheng Zhilong intended to maintain his power in Fujian and protect his established interests in overseas trade. However, not enough Ming forces rallied behind Emperor Longwu to oppose the Qing army.

The Qing government made offers to Longwu's supporters in exchange for their loyalty to the Manchu rulers. In 1646, Beijing offered Zheng Zhilong a governorship of Fujian and Guangdong Provinces. With such an unexpected, lucrative offer and the realization of Qing supremacy over the decayed Ming, Zheng defected from Nanjing to Beijing. However, the Qing court never trusted Zheng. Shortly after he arrived at Beijing, he was captured and jailed for fifteen years. In October 1661, Zheng Zhilong was executed for his refusal to persuade his son to surrender to the Manchu. After his father's death, Zheng Chenggong assumed leadership of the anti-Qing resistance war.[30]

Zheng Chenggong was born in Japan as Zheng San. His Japanese mother cared for Zheng Zhilong's two sons in Japan after he left home for Taiwan. During the seventeenth century, the Japanese Bakufu government also enforced sea ban and did not allow any Japanese to leave the country. After Zheng Zhilong became a Ming admiral, he began negotiations with the Japanese government for reunion with his family. Finally, when Zheng Chenggong was seven years old, the Tokugawa government allowed Zheng Zhilong's wife and two young sons to rejoin him in China. After their arrival, Zheng Zhilong sent his two sons to private schools with Confucian-Mencian curriculums. As a classical philosophy and ruling ideology, Confucianism urges all people to become "elevated persons" and act as moral, societal leaders. "A gentleman should cultivate himself morally, show loyalty where these are due, and cultivate humanity." When Zheng Chenggong was twenty-one, he enrolled in the Nanjing Academy, one of the top Chinese institutes in the country.

When Longwu was crowned in Nanjing, Zheng Zhilong presented his son to the emperor, who bestowed upon his son a new name, "Chenggong" (success). Zheng Chenggong was also granted the honor to use the imperial surname Zhu (Chu). Then, Zheng Chenggong became *Kuoxingye* (Koxinga in Fujian dialect), "Lord of the Imperial Surnam."[31] When Zheng Zhilong surrendered to the Qing in 1646, the family split. Zheng Chenggong opposed his father's surrender to the Qing and publicly criticized his father's betrayal to the Ming. Young Zheng fled from Fuzhou to Xiamen and took over the command of his father's forces, reorganizing the troops and making Xiamen his command headquarters.[32] Zheng Chenggong also controlled trade along China's southeastern coast. The Dutch continued their trade with Zheng Chenggong from 1648 to 1662.

In 1647, at Xiamen, Zheng Chenggong proclaimed his leadership over the remnant Ming army and navy. Historians divide his military career into three phases. The first phase, from 1647 to 1651, Zheng prepared a northern expedition against the Qing by rearming and training his troops. The second phase, 1651–1660, he launched three northern expeditions, landed near Shanghai, took several major cities in southeast China, and reached Nanjing. By 1655, he had about 50,000 cavalry, 70,000 infantry troops, and 3,000 war junks.[33] The Manchu sent an armada of eight hundred war junks and attacked Zheng's fleet at Xiamen. The Manchu amphibious assault ended in failure against Zheng's seasoned navy. However, the Manchu Banner Army succeeded on land. From 1658 to 1659, Zheng Chenggong had more than 170,000 troops and aimed for a decisive battle against the Manchu at Nanjing. He made several strategic mistakes, resulting in heavy losses, and he failed to establish a foothold in China.[34]

In the third phase, from 1660 to 1662, Zheng shifted his strategy from the north to the south by utilizing his naval force. He successfully attacked the Dutch on Taiwan and drove them out, ending their thirty-eight-year colonization of Taiwan.[35]

Even before his Taiwan offensive, the Dutch East India Company considered Zheng a nuisance as he controlled trade along China's southeastern coast. After founding the Qing dynasty, the Manchu emperor instituted new sea bans, which still outlawed Dutch trade in China. Dutch governor Frederick Coyett turned to Zheng and sent his envoy He Bin (Ho Pin) to Xiamen to negotiate a deal in 1657. The agreement allowed Zheng to collect taxes from Taiwanese ships involved in Chinese trade. In exchange, Zheng agreed to allow Dutch commercial ships trade rights in southeast China. Later that year, Zheng opened a tariff office at Tayowan and authorized He Bin to collect taxes for him in Taiwan. In early 1659, the Dutch East India Company, uninformed of the deal between Zheng and Coyett, arrested He Bin and shut his office down. In April, He escaped from jail and fled to Xiamen.[36]

In 1660, Zheng reconsidered his military strategy. His disastrous northern expeditions indicated the Qing army was a superior ground force with firepower, cavalry, and a well-organized Banner System. Northward offensives into central China had no chance to win against the Qing. Moreover, Qing sea bans forced fishing villages to evacuate southeastern coastal areas and isolated Zheng's army. Nevertheless, he had an experienced, battle-hardened navy, which had engaged numerous, foreign sea powers. With that in consideration, Zheng shifted his strategic focus from a northward, land war to a southward, naval war. Therefore, Taiwan became strategically important since it "offered the most secure prospect for a haven from which to relaunch the Ming cause."[37] As he shifted strategically, the army around Xiamen expected new attacks from the strong Qing army. Since the Qing did not have a strong navy, Zheng convinced his Fujian generals to make Taiwan their new military base for the resistance war against the nomadic Manchu army.

On April 21, 1661, Zheng Chenggong led his attack force, with 400 war junks and 25,000 troops, across the Taiwan Strait. His main force landed at Penghu first. Then, on the morning of April 30, Zheng's landing force reached the northern beaches between Forts Zeelandia and Provintia with the knowledge that 1,140 Dutch troops were concentrated in the southern part of Taiwan. Chinese settlers at Luerhman, a town near Fort Zeelandia, rushed to the beaches and helped the landing troops. Next, Zheng's army attacked Provintia and defeated the Dutch garrison.[38] On May 1, Governor Coyett sent four Dutch warships to halt the Chinese amphibious advance, but they instead engaged with Zheng's war junks off Luerhman. Although Zheng lost more than ten junks, the Chinese sunk the most formidable Dutch warship, the *Hector*.

However, the Chinese attack on Fort Zeelandia faced a strong Dutch defense. Governor Coyett launched counterattacks against the Chinese troops. The Dutch were overly confident in their advanced military technology and victories against the aborigines. They assumed a similar victory was imminent as Chinese soldiers were armed only with crossbows, swords, and pikes against the Dutch matchlock muskets and heavy cannons. However, Zheng's soldiers were well-trained veterans, battle-tested against the Manchu army for many years and much different from the aborigines and farmers. When 240 Dutch troops attacked the Chinese, they faced a rain of arrows in front and from behind. Jonathan Manthorpe believes, "Many Dutch died in the first few minutes of the engagement. Others threw down their cumbersome muskets and fled back to Fort Zeelandia or ran into the sea."[39]

Despite the initial success, Zheng considered the Dutch defenses' superior firepower and besieged the fort to avoid heavy casualties of a frontal attack. In July 1661, the Dutch India Company sent a rescue fleet of ten warships with 700 soldiers commanded by Jacob Caeuw. The fleet failed to land at Fort Zeelandia after their arrival on August 12 due to bad weather. Then, Caeuw sailed back to Batavia after witnessing the besieged fort and realized his reinforcements would not save Governor Coyett. After his return in November, Caeuw was charged with neglect of duty for his desertion. On January 25, 1662, Zheng launched the final attack and fired more than 2,500 shells in one day. After the Chinese attack broke through Dutch defenses from the north, Governor Coyett surrendered to Zheng on February 1 and ended thirty-eight years of Dutch colonization.[40]

After his takeover, Zheng became the hero of Taiwan. However, he died on May 8, 1662, of sickness at the age of thirty-eight. Thereafter, Taiwanese people built many temples and memorials to commemorate their hero. After 1681, when the Qing empire conquered Taiwan, the new administration banned Zheng's memorialization. Despite the ban, Taiwanese people secretly erected tombstones and shrines to commemorate Zheng Chenggong. Local people used pseudonyms like "King of Taiwan" or the "Founder of the Mountain" for Zheng's epitaphs. It was not until 1847, 185 years after Zheng's death, that the Qing government lifted the ban and allowed Taiwanese people to build one formal temple in commemoration of Zheng Chenggong. After the death of Zheng Chenggong, his brother Zheng Jing assumed command and continued their Taiwan-based struggle against the Qing from 1662 to 1681.

NOTES

1. Shelley Rigger, *Why Taiwan Matters: Small Island, Global Powerhouse*, updated edition (Lanham, MD: Rowman & Littlefield, 2014), 14.

2. History Department, Tianjin Normal College, comp., *Zhongguo jianshi* [A concise history of China] (Beijing: Renmin jiaoyu chubanshe [People's Education Press], 1980), 278.

3. Shen Fuwei, *Zhongxi wenhua jiaoliushi* [History of the cultural exchanges between the East and West] (Shanghai: Shanghai renmin chubanshe [Shanghai People's Press], 1985), 362–63.

4. Su Ge, *Meiguo duihua zhengce yu Taiwan wenti* [U.S. China policy and the issue of Taiwan] (Beijing: Shijie zhishi chubanshe [World Knowledge Publishing], 1998), 9–10.

5. History Research Institute, China Academy of Social Sciences (CASS), *Jianming zhongguo lishi duben* [Concise history of China] (Beijing: Zhongguo shehui kexueyuan chubanshe [China Academy of Social Sciences Press], 2012), 381.

6. Wang Yufeng, *Taiwan shi* [History of Taiwan], 3rd edition (Taichung, Taiwan: Haodu chuban [How-Do Publishing], 2017), 39–40.

7. Jonathan Manthorpe, *Forbidden Nation: A History of Taiwan* (New York: Palgrave Macmillan, 2005), 48.

8. George Beckmann, "Brief Episodes—Dutch and Spanish Rule," in *Taiwan in Modern Times*, ed. Paul K. T. Sih (New York: St. John's University Press, 1973), 32–37.

9. Manthorpe, *Forbidden Nation*, 48.

10. John F. Copper, *Taiwan: Nation-State or Province?* 4th edition (Boulder, CO: Westview, 2003), 33.

11. Manthorpe, *Forbidden Nation*, 48.

12. Wang, *Taiwan shi* [History of Taiwan], 40–41.

13. Hong Li-wan, "Era of Sea Powers in the Sixteenth and Seventeenth Centuries," Chapter 2 in *Taiwan shi* [History of Taiwan], 2nd edition, ed. Gao Min-shi (Taipei: Wunan tushu [Wunan Books], 2015), 74.

14. Copper, *Taiwan*, 33.

15. Wang, *Taiwan shi* [History of Taiwan], 42.

16. Hong, "Era of Sea Powers in the Sixteenth and Seventeenth Centuries," 83.

17. Manthorpe, *Forbidden Nation*, 52.

18. Hong, "Era of Sea Powers in the Sixteenth and Seventeenth Centuries," 76.

19. Manthorpe, *Forbidden Nation*, 54.

20. History Research Institute, CASS, *Jianming zhongguo lishi duben* [Concise history of China], 381.

21. Rigger, *Why Taiwan Matters*, 14.

22. Su, *Meiguo duihua zhengce yu Taiwan wenti* [U.S. China policy and the issue of Taiwan], 10.

23. Hong, "Era of Sea Powers in the Sixteenth and Seventeenth Centuries," 78–79.

24. Hung Chein-chao, *A History of Taiwan* (Rimini, Italy: Cerchio Iniziative Editoriali, 2000), 31.

25. Copper, *Taiwan*, 33.

26. Simon Long, *Taiwan: China's Last Frontier* (New York: St. Martin's, 1991), 10–11.

27. History Department, Tianjin Normal College, comp., *Zhongguo jianshi* [A concise history of China], 300.

28. Kenneth M. Swope, *A Dragon's Head and a Serpent's Tail: Ming China and the First Great East Asian War, 1592–1598* (Norman: University of Oklahoma Press, 2009), 294–95.

29. Xiaobing Li, *A History of the Modern Chinese Army* (Lexington: University Press of Kentucky, 2007), 22–23.

30. Jonathan D. Spence, *The Search for Modern China*, 3rd edition (New York: W. W. Norton, 2013), 41.

31. History Department, Tianjin Normal College, comp., *Zhongguo jianshi* [A concise history of China], 300.

32. Spence, *The Search for Modern China*, 53.

33. Manthorpe, *Forbidden Nation*, 80.

34. Hong, "Era of Sea Powers in the Sixteenth and Seventeenth Centuries," 84.

35. History Research Institute, CASS, *Jianming zhongguo lishi duben* [Concise history of China], 393.

36. Jiang Renjie, *Jiegou Cheng Chenggong* [Revisit Cheng Chenggong] (Taipei: Sanmin chubanshe [Three Peoples Publishing], 2006), 58–59.

37. Manthorpe, *Forbidden Nation*, 82.

38. History Department, Tianjin Normal College, comp., *Zhongguo jianshi* [A concise history of China], 300.

39. Manthorpe, *Forbidden Nation*, 89.

40. Spence, *The Search for Modern China*, 53.

5

Zheng's Control and the Qing's Administration, 1662–1894

Zheng Chenggong died on May 8, 1662, only three months after he took over Taiwan from the Dutch colonial government. Thereafter, his sons began to govern the island from 1662 to 1683. They focused on agricultural development to establish a self-sustained economy to maintain the last military base of the Ming against the Qing dynasty for twenty-one years. They also launched large-scale offensive campaigns on the mainland to fight against the Manchu army. However, the power struggle and isolated efforts undermined Zheng's regime on Taiwan.

In 1683, the Qing army crossed the Taiwan Strait and defeated Zheng's forces. From 1683 to 1894, the Qing government administrated Taiwan for more than 211 years. Nevertheless, after its taking-over, the Qing was preoccupied by its military territorial expansions into China's southwest and northwest such as Tibet and Xinjiang (meaning "new territory"). Qing was not interested in investment and development of Taiwan. From 1683 to 1858, Beijing continued an inactive, preventive, and incomplete policy toward Taiwan even with many restrictions like no cross-strait contact, no immigration to Taiwan, sealing its mountainous areas against cultivation, banning Taiwanese from serving in military and local governments, and even prohibiting iron making without government permission. The isolationist policies had negative impact and caused mismanagement, corruption, population imbalance, hostility, and frequent ethnic and mass riots. Some Taiwanese rebellions were armed and violent.

Nevertheless, as Qing experienced a population explosion during 1685–1858, more and more Chinese immigrants took the risk and crossed the strait at night illegally. In 1685, China's population was about 100 million. It increased to 142 million in 1741, 268 million in 1776, 301 million in 1790, and to 350 million in 1800. When Taiwan became one of the nineteen provinces of China in 1886, the Qing Empire had a population of 432 million.[1] The Taiwanese Chinese totaled 400,000 during the Kangxi (K'ang-hsi, r. 1662–1722) period, and reached one million by the Qianlong (Ch'ien-lung, r. 1736–1795). During this period, the Chinese replaced the aborigines and became the dominant people on the island. The Chinese occupied most farmland; developed irrigation and transportation; established urban society and culture; and promoted trade, education, religion, and local administration.

Taiwan became part of China not only territorially but also commercially, socially, and culturally. In 1811, the total population of Taiwan was 1.9 million. In 1893, before the Japanese colonization, its population reached 2.5 million.[2] After 1858, the Qing court realized the strategic importance of Taiwan in its resistance against European expansion and influence and shifted its isolationist, inactive policy to an active, progressive policy by appointing Minister Shen Baozhen (Shen Bao-ch'en) as the new governor. Shen engaged the island in the Self-Strengthening Movement and launched economic and cultural reforms. Taiwan began to build modern factories, shipyards, railroads, postal service, and schools. In 1886, the Qing government proclaimed Taiwan as the nineteenth province of China.

ZHENG'S ECONOMY, POLITICS, AND MILITARY

During 1662–1683, the anti-Qing force under the command of Zheng's family-controlled Taiwan. Zheng Jing (Cheng Ching) was the most important and influential leader in his family. Nevertheless, Zheng Jing's succession from his father Zheng Chenggong was not a natural transition. When Zheng Chenggong landed at Taiwan and fought against the Dutch colonial garrison, he appointed his elder son Zheng Jing as the commander of his troops in Xiamen to defend their stronghold on the mainland. After he was told Zheng Jing had a baby with his younger brother's nanny, Zheng Chenggong was so upset of his son's adultery and sent his treasury minister to Xiamen to execute Zheng Jing. The generals of Zheng Jing asked for Zheng's patron and detained his minister at Xiamen. Thereafter, tension and hostility mounted between Taiwan and Xiamen. Some historians believe that it was one of the reasons for Zheng Chenggong's serious illness, which took his life at the age of thirty-eight. After Zheng Chenggong's death, Xiamen's troops considered Zheng Jing the next leader in line since he was the first son, while Taiwan's troops believed Zheng Jing lost his integrity because of the scandal. They supported Zheng Xi, his younger brother, as the next leader. Then, the two leaders were fighting for the control of Zheng's army.

In October 1662, Zheng Jing launched an attack on Taiwan. After several tough battles, he defeated Zheng Xi's troops and took over the island. Zheng Jing not only established a huge military base on Taiwan but also a strong link between Taiwan and the adjacent area of the mainland. Like his father, he launched several large-scale expeditions against the Manchu to realize the dream of restoring the Ming dynasty in China.[3]

Although Zheng had no administrative experience, he depended on his minister Chen Yonghua, who had proved a very successful administrator of Taiwan from 1662 to 1680. After they took over the control of the island, Zheng's rulers terminated the Dutch colonial system and replaced it with a Ming-style administration by establishing the central government and local governments, including one metropolitan government at Anping and two counties at Tianyu in the north and Wannian in the south. The central government had six departments all under the leadership of the Han Chinese for the first time in Taiwanese history.

Among the most important policies of Minister Chen Yonghua was his developing military farms in Taiwan. To support a large army and its expeditions on the mainland for eight years, the Zheng government began to assign its battalions to establish many farms for securing food supply. About 50,000–60,000 troops were assigned to clear land and bring it into production trespassed on the hunting grounds of indigenous peoples. The soldiers engaged in cultivation, irrigation, farming tool improvement, and other agricultural productivities.[4] The staple food was rice. During the Dutch colonization, most Chinese rice farms were in the southern Taiwan. Now Zheng's army moved into the northern frontiers and cleared new land for farming. Soon the island became self-sufficient in food supply and was producing a surplus. They also engaged in other productive activities such as salt making, sugarcane processing, brick making, and handcrafts.

Many Chinese peasants also joined the land cultivation movement for new farming land during the 1660s–1670s. First, many Chinese immigrants came to Taiwan at night from the coastal regions of Fujian and Guangdong Provinces, which had been overpopulated and lacked farmland and other resources. Second, many families of Zheng's army (140,000–170,000 strong) left Xiamen and followed Zheng Jing to Taiwan. They too became small farm owners on the island. Third, the Qing court soon issued the sea ban to stop overseas trade and offshore fishing. Many Chinese fishermen joined the agricultural development in Taiwan. In 1672, there were more than 120,000 Chinese peasants in Taiwan, outnumbered the aboriginal people (about 60,000 at that time).

Since 90 percent of the Chinese came from Fujian Province, they carried on local tradition, customs, religions, and family values. Buddhism and Daoism (Taoism) were not among the popular religions. Minister Chen Yonghua emphasized Chinese classic literature and traditional education by building the first Confucian temple in the city of Tainan. He also began Chinese civil service examination in Taiwan to recruit the educated to serve in the government. He encouraged the establishment of schools in villages and cities. According to his new regulations, all children at age of eight must enroll in a school, which offered classic Confucian-Mencian curriculums.

Zheng Jing came from China, and he never gave up his dream of returning to the mainland. In 1673, the former Ming general Wu Sangui (Wu San-kui), then Yunnan governor of the Qing, asked Zheng Jing to join him and other Chinese generals to launch an anti-Qing rebellion in the south. Zheng agreed and took his army with him for the mainland in 1674, leaving Chen Yonghua behind at Taiwan.

Zheng's northern expeditions between 1674 and 1680 were not successful. First, the Ming generals did not trust each other. After Zheng Jing's landing, General Geng Jingzhong, commander of the anti-Qing force in Fujian, did not allow Zheng's force to move to inland areas. Offended and angry, Zheng attacked Geng and started a fight within the anti-Qing alliance in 1675 before their war against the Qing army. After Zheng took over several major cities in Fujian and Guangdong, General Wu Sangui had to mediate a peace between his two anti-Qing generals. Qing saw the internal conflict among the former Ming generals and tried to deal with one force each time. The Qing's strategy worked well, even though it took much longer to defeat the rebellion armies. In southeastern China, Qing attacked Geng's troops first. As expected, Zheng Jing did not help at all when Geng was circulated and attacked by the Qing main force. After they destroyed Geng's force, the Qing army started their attack on Zheng's troops in Fujian and Guangdong. Although Zheng fought fiercely, his army did not get any assistance from other anti-Qing forces. After six years of fighting against the Qing army on the mainland, Zheng lost all his territories in China and returned to Taiwan in 1680.

After his return, Zheng Jing faced a new power struggle in Taiwan. During the six years of his expeditions in China, his mother and his son had developed a political network with newly appointed officials in Taiwan. Since they did not like the returning senior officials and generals, they blamed the setback of the expeditions to these returning officers to prevent them from taking away their political and military positions. After several of Zheng's best officials and generals died, including Chen Yonghua, Zheng Jing became very sick and died in 1681. His death caused another round of power struggle, which further undermined the economy and defense of Taiwan.

QING'S CONQUEST, ADMINISTRATION, AND POLICY

The death of Zheng Jing and power struggle in Taiwan provided an opportunity for the Qing government to take over the island. In October 1681, Emperor Kangxi appointed Shi Lang (Shih Lang) as the commander in chief of the Qing attacking force against Taiwan. After two years of preparation, General Shi Lang decided to attack Penghu as the first step of his landing on Taiwan.

Shi Lang had been one of the best former generals of Zheng Chenggong since 1646. However, both had a strong personality and involved in personal conflict. The first incident took place when Zheng decided to attack the Qing army to save the Ming emperor. Shi Lang opposed Zheng's decision since their army was not strong enough to defeat the Qing army. Zheng did not listen and attacked the Qing army, which defeated the offensive force and launched a counterattack against Zheng's army. Shi Lang broke the Qing's circulation and rescued Zheng. Nevertheless, during the award ceremony, Zheng did not even mention Shi Lang's great effort. Then, one of Shi Lang's general violated the regulation and Shi Lang decided to discipline him. The general knew the personal issues between Shi and Zheng so he run to Zheng's headquarters and asked for protection. After Zheng promised his safety, Shi Lang still traced him into Zheng's headquarters and executed the general. Humiliated and upset, Zheng ordered to detain Shi

Lang. Although Shi was hiding, Zheng's officers searched his house and killed his father and brothers. Shi Lang left Zheng and surrendered to Qing, looking for his revenge. Since General Shi was one of few generals who knew naval warfare, the Qing court appointed him as the commander of the southern fleet of the Qing navy.

On June 29, 1683, General Shi Lang landed at Penghu with 20,000 troops and 300 war junks. In early July, he defeated the garrison under the command of General Liu Guoquan (Liu Kuo-hsuan), who thought the typhoon should have stopped the Qing's invading fleet in the Taiwan Strait as it had happened many years ago during the time of Zheng Chenggong. Although Liu and his troops fought bravely, they lost the defense after suffering heavy casualties, 12,000 out of 20,000 defensive troops. The military failure at Penghu seriously lowered the morale of Zheng's army in Taiwan since General Liu had the best force of the army. On September 23, 1683, Zheng Keshuang, grandson of Zheng Jin, surrendered to the Qing court and ended Zheng's regime in Taiwan.[5]

After the Qing took over Taiwan, there was a policy debate in the Qing court about the future of the island. Some of the Qing officials thought Taiwan not worth for any governmental efforts nor military garrison. However, Shi Lang and the others convinced Emperor Kangxi that an effective administration on Taiwan was strategically important and necessary. According to Shi, if the Qing gave up on its control, other powers would come and conquer it again. Then, the Qing had to spend more money and sacrifice more troops to fight again for the island. Kangxi agreed with Shi Lang and appointed him as the governor of Taiwan. Although the Qing limited any major development on the island, it was the first time when Taiwan was included in the official map of Chinese government in May 1684.[6]

Unprepared and unexperienced, the Qing court did not have an effective policy toward Taiwan, even though it included the island into its territory. Its early policy, inactive, indirect, preventive, and incomplete, was to prevent Taiwan from becoming an anti-Qing base again, rather than to reconstruct and develop the island. For most of the 202 years, from 1684 to 1886, Taiwan was placed under the provincial government of Fujian. After 1886, Taiwan was elevated to becoming the nineteenth province of China.

First, Beijing banned any contact between the mainland and Taiwan and did not allow any Chinese to cross the straits without official pass; even those who had permission were not allowed to bring their families with them. The immigration ban policy was aimed at a control of the population of Taiwan since it was "the land of rebellion and unrest."[7] Moreover, no Hakka was allowed to come to Taiwan with or without any permission. Second, iron making was not allowed in Taiwan without government license to prevent individuals from making iron weapons against the Qing. Third, all the officials and garrisons must be the mainlanders. Taiwanese could not serve in the military nor in the government. The Qing officials, officers, and soldiers rotated in a three-year term while they were not allowed to bring their wives and families with them to prevent any possible immigration. The policy undermined morale and effectiveness of the Qing government and garrison on Taiwan. Fourth, the Qing government closed the mountainous areas to separate the aborigines from the Chinese people by issuing the "Mountain Sealing Order" in 1721. All of these policies had negative impact on the economy, society, and ethnic minorities in Taiwan during the seventeenth and eighteenth centuries.

As the Chinese governor of Taiwan, Shi Lang began to establish his political control and military defense of the island. First, he organized an administration by establishing one prefectural and three county governments: the Taiwan Prefecture and Taiwan, Fengshan, and Zhuluo Counties. Shi appointed his generals to serve as county officials. Second, he maintained the loyalty of his army by carrying out the Qing's regulation that banned the Taiwanese people for military service. In the 1680s, Governor Shi had nearly 10,000 troops and 80 war junks. Third, he divided and controlled the population by issuing different policies to different Taiwanese people. For example, one of the Qing's regulations on Taiwan was to ban any immigration from China to Taiwan. Then, Governor Shi applied the ban on Hakka and Guangdong people, but not on Fujian immigrants. The regional and factional division started in the late nineteenth century still has its profound social and political impact on today's Taiwan.

Although the Qing continued no contact and immigration ban, the policy did not work well since there was a "considerable nighttime smuggling trade between Xiamen and the island."[8] During the years between 1683 and 1894, Taiwan experienced population increase, economic growth, and urban development. First, the population increase resulted from the waves of new immigrants from China in the 1700s. During the long reign of Emperor Qianlong, China experienced a population growth from 163 million in 1741 to 200 million in 1762. One of Qianlong's most impressive accomplishments was the incorporation of frontier territories into China. Many Chinese peasants left overpopulated provinces like Fujian and Guangdong and immigrated to Taiwan. Since Chinese immigrants continued to arrive, soon Taiwan became the land of immigration and the Chinese became later the majority of the Taiwanese people.

Chinese population increased tremendously in Taiwan during the 1700s–1800s. In 1684, when the Qing took over, about 400,000 Chinese lived in Taiwan. By 1691, the Chinese population increased to 545,000. By 1811, it reached 1.94 million and increased to 2.5 million by 1894.[9] Among the immigrants were about 45 percent from the Quanzhou region of Fujian Province, 35 percent from Zhangzhou region of Fujian, and 16 percent as Hakka from Guangdong Province. Most of the new immigrants were landless peasants or poor urban residents, who could not make it on the mainland. They believed Taiwan would offer new opportunity for their survival, and they were willing to work hard and start a new life on the island. Many of the Quanzhou immigrants arrived in urban areas and engaged in handcrafts and trade. The Zhangzhou immigrants lived on the plains and farmed in rice paddies and sugarcane fields. The Hakka people from Guangdong moved into the hill and mountainous areas and engaged in agriculture and other productive activities.

Second, Taiwan's economy experienced a rapid growth through a commercialization and market revolution. Before the Qing's takeover, Taiwan had a self-sustaining island economy, and most farmers worked on their farms to meet their family's need. The new immigrants brought to the island much-needed labor force, improved tools and irrigation, experienced skills, and better seeds of rice. By 1700, the opening-up of land for agriculture had added 68,800 acres for rice

The Chinese population increased in Taiwan from 400,000 in 1684 to 1.94 million in 1811 and to 2.5 million by 1894. Many Hakka immigrants came from Guangdong and Fujian. They moved into the mountainous areas, engaged in agriculture, and lived in their roundhouses (tulou), pictured above. (Ywjelle/Dreamstime.com)

production. Soon Taiwanese farmers could produce more than they needed. Then, the island became one of the major rice suppliers to the mainland. The Taiwanese merchants shipped rice to the markets in Quanzhou, Xiamen, and other seaports along the southeastern coasts. The exports also included deerskins; minerals; and other tropical farming items like sugar, pineapples, and spices.

The commercial farming saw the establishment of trade agencies, shipping groups, and organizations of specialized commerce, such as sugar industrial organization and textile industrial organization. To manage the population increase and economic growth, Taiwan established more local governments by adding one county and four metropolitan bureaus, including Chenghua County and Bureaus of Lugang, Tamsui, Penghu, and I-lian (Yilan) in 1787.

Third, as a result of trade and exports, urban development began in many of the early seaports like Tainan, Kaohsiung, and Lugang. The new urban cultures provided classic literature, Chinese arts, and civil service examination. In 1729, the government offered the civil service examination in Taiwan to recruit educated men to serve in the government and to win over the Taiwanese. During the Qing's administration, more than 250 Taiwanese passed the examinations and became degree holders. Urban culture further diversified when the Europeans returned to Taiwan after the 1868. Four cities were open for European trade and missionaries, Keelung, Kaohsiung, Tamsui, and Anping. The new international trade centered in the northern cities like Taipei since major trading items like tea and camphor were produced in the north. As a result, Taiwan's economic and political center moved from the south to north in the late nineteenth century.

NEWCOMERS AND NEW CONFLICTS

Early Chinese images of Taiwan were a mixed story. On the one hand, the island was described as a good opportunity for land, farm, and less government control. The Chinese images depicted an earthy environment and friendly islanders. On the other hand, Taiwan was pictured backward, hostile, and as having savages, and was full of danger and sickness. More and more Chinese were willing to take the risk as illegal immigrants to cross the Taiwan Strait.

When a large number of new immigrants arrived in Taiwan, they tried to fit into the diversified society, which at the same time adjusted to include newcomers. The new immigrants, however, had their difficulties at home and looked for new economic opportunities in the new frontier. Taiwan became a social release of the problems a poor peasant faced on the mainland, such as poverty, civil war, and Manchu racial discriminations. Nevertheless, after his arrival, everyone looked out for himself. It lacked communal bands of any kind. Accurately, the society appeared slowly with many regional and factional groups, secret organizations, religious sects, and even anti-Qing societies. Governor Shi Lang tried to restore standards of Manchu behavior and enforced some regulations, but he failed to deal with two major conflicts.

The major conflict was over land between the aborigines and Chinese new immigrants. At that time, the land in Taiwan was divided into two categories, virgin land and cultivated land. When new immigrants arrived, they could apply for virgin land from the Qing government. Most of virgin land located in the northern and eastern hilly regions of Taiwan. After the application was approved and the fees were paid, the immigrants and their families could move into that piece of land. Most cultivated land belonged to the aboriginal people, whom the immigrants had to deal with for any land rental or purchase. Most cultivated land located in the western plains and south of the island. Since the new immigrants did not know anything about the local affairs, they had to go through Chinese land agencies, or in many cases, the Chinese landlords, who had land ownership and managed land sales and rentals. These agencies and landlords also played an important role in irrigation and water-system development and management. Most farmers grew rice, which depended on water, while no single farmer could bring water from the nearby river to his rice paddy. They needed large investments to build water networks to cover hundreds and hundreds acres of land. Therefore, the land agencies and large landowners developed the water irrigation network by increasing the land rentals and sale prices.

There was much unrest in Taiwan under the Qing administration. Between 1683 and 1895, there were more than seventy mass riots in Taiwan. Among them were the Zhu Yigui's anti-Qing Rebellion of 1721 and the Lin Shuanwen Uprising of 1786.

Zhu Yigui (Chu Yit-gui) was an immigrant from Fujian and became a successful owner of a duck farm in Taiwan's Luohanmen (present-day Kaohsiung). He became popular since he was generous in helping local people and persistent against immoral conducts. In 1720, many Fujian merchants, Hakka farmers, and Chinese fishermen on Taiwan complained about the increasing taxation on the Taiwanese by the Qing government. They supported Zhu Yigui as their leader to call for open rebellion against the Qing government. Since Zhu had the royal surname of the Ming dynasty, they used it to mobilize the discontented Chinese to join the rebellion as anti-Qing movement. Hakka leader Lin Junying also joined the rebellion by bringing his people from the south.

In March 1720, Zhu and Lin attacked the Qing garrison at Tainan and defeated the Qing troops in April. Governor Shi Lang and many Qing officials fled Taiwan to the Pescadores. In less than two weeks, the insurgents took over the entire Taiwan.[10] After their military victory, however, Zhu and Lin could not overcome the limits of their regional and factional differences and split over a dispute about who should serve as the governor of Taiwan. All the Hakka troops left the rebel force for the north by following Lin Junying. Zhu Yigui had to defend the south himself when the Qing court sent its Fujian fleet under the command of Shi Shibian (son of Governor Shi Lang) and southern regional army with 22,000 troops. A month later, the Qing army defeated the rebellion army and captured Zhu. Then, Zhu was sent to Beijing and executed there.[11]

About sixty-five years later, in 1786, another large-scale incident took place in Taiwan against the Qing governor and lasted for two years. One of the reasons for this long-lasting anti-Qing movement was that it involved the most popular secret organization in Taiwan, "Tiandihui" (Heaven and Earth Society). It was founded in Zhangzhou of Fujian as a Chinese secret society against Manchu Qing regime. After it came to Taiwan with the Fujian immigrants, many Chinese joined the organization for their protection, communication, and socialization on the island. Lin Shaowen (Lin Shaon-wen) became the leader of Tiandihui in the 1780s. In 1786, several members of the Tiandihui were arrested by the Qing officials for their failed tax payments. Other members broke into the jail, killed the guards, and rescued these farmers. When the Qing governor sent his troops to the village, the members asked Lin to protect them. Lin called for Tiandihui's members to join an open rebellion against the Qing. He led his armed members and defeated the Qing troops. Then, Lin's army attacked the city of Changhua (Chenghua) and took over the entire county. During the battles, more than 2,000 civilians, including women and children, were killed.

In early 1787, the Qing government sent 50,000 troops from the mainland to put down the insurrection. Soon both sides engaged a long stalemate of nine months. Lin tried to get some involvement by the Hakka people; the latter did not only refuse any support, but also sent their troops to join the Qing against Lin's rebellion since the Hakka had been a long-time rivalry of the Tiandihui in Taiwan. On the other hand, the Qing army failed to take over Lin's base area around his hometown. It ended after Emperor Qianlong sent reinforcement to Taiwan in 1788.

EUROPEANS RETURN

Thus, Qing self-sufficient economy and China-centered regional trade were uninterested in new European trade. In 1793, when the British trade mission under Lord Macartney as the envoy of King George III sought to interest the Qianlong emperor in the establishment of trade privileges to British merchants and diplomatic representation in his court, the court absorbed British gifts as tribute and sent Macartney away without seriously considering his proposals. Thereafter, Europeans continued to pay in silver for Chinese goods. Between 1760 and 1780 alone, the net drain of silver from Europe to China had increased from three to sixteen million taels. Most of the silver originally came from Spain's American colonies. Unfavorable trade balance provoked the British to organize the production of opium in their Indian colonies and to introduce the addictive drug into China in order to create a new market for a commodity they could control.

Therefore, Qianlong was uninterested in expanding trade with Europe in the 1790s for several reasons. China had developed its own maritime trade with Southeast Asian countries such as Burma (now Myanmar), Malaya (now Malaysia), Thailand, Vietnam, and the Philippines, through its trading communities overseas. In other words, the Qing Empire already had long-standing existing outlets for international trade that presented less risk to its sovereignty. A maritime China along the coast centered its trade at Xiamen, and the Chinese traders "were ready to expand into international commerce as opportunity allowed."[12]

In the early nineteenth century, both the Jiaqing and Daoguang (Taokuang, r. 1821–1850) emperors continued Qianlong's closed-door policy and limited China's contact with the West to trade without extensive diplomatic relationships. Foreign trade had to go through the "Cohong" (government agency) at Guangzhou (Canton), the only city open to trade with Europeans. The British sold to the Chinese woolens and spices, while buying from China such items as tea, silk, medicine, and porcelain. Beginning in the second decade of the nineteenth century, cotton textiles became the major item of British export to China. However, owing to the Manchu rulers' closed-door policy, British trade with China was never large, and in fact, British trade with China was not particularly profitable. British merchants, who enjoyed a worldwide economic expansion and were the majority of the Westerners at Guangzhou, suffered a deficit in China trade. To reverse the negative balance of trade, the British began to ship large quantities of opium from India to China.

Emperor Daoguang decided to adopt a tougher policy to suppress the opium trade and maintain the traditional tribute system of foreign relations.[13] In 1839, Commissioner Lin Zexu launched an aggressive campaign against opium smoking and smuggling. After a series of skirmishes occurred between the Chinese and British, Commissioner Lin banned all British trade in China on December 6. Lin Zexu became a major Chinese hero in their first effort to resist the Western aggression.[14] To protect its merchants and expand its trading rights to the Chinese market, the British government declared war on China on January 31, 1840. Thus, the First Opium War began.[15] On July 28, eight British warships sailed further north and on August 9 arrived at Dagu near Tianjin, less than eighty miles from Beijing.[16] Under the threat of big guns, the Qing government began to waver. The Qing government then sent an imperial commissioner to a British warship to sign the Sino-British Treaty on August 29, 1842.[17] The First Opium War was over.

During the war, in July 1841, British warship *Nerbudda* attacked Keelung. In September, two British warships bombed Keelung again. The Qing garrison returned fire and forced the British retreats. In January 1842, British warship *Ann* reached the central coast of Taiwan. After it run into ground, the Chinese defense troops destroyed the British ship, and captured fifty-seven British sailors. In October, Britain sent another warship to Keelung to try to rescue the British prisoners. Although some British soldiers landed, they failed their rescue mission. After the Treaty of Nanjing, the Qing court punished its commanding officer in Taiwan.

After the First Opium War, China fought Britain and France in the Second Opium War of 1856–1857. That conflict would end the Chinese tributary system. There came the Arrow Incident on October 8, 1856, when a British flag was burned and crewmembers were arrested on the *Arrow*, a British-registered Chinese vessel at Guangzhou. After the Chinese governor refused to apologize, British gunboats moved in to bombard the city on October 23.[18] The so-called Arrow War began. Soon the French government decided on a joint expedition with Britain by dispatching a task force under the command of Baron Gross. In December 1857, the allied forces of Britain and France attacked and captured Guangzhou and then moved northward along the coast. In May 1858, they occupied Tianjin and then announced that they would soon attack Beijing.[19] During the Second Opium War, the capital Beijing was captured, and the Imperial Summer Palaces were sacked by a relatively small Anglo-French coalition force numbering 25,000. Without much choice, the Qing government sent representatives and asked for negotiating peace. The Arrow War was over. In June 1858, the Qing government signed the Treaties of Tianjin with Britain, France, the United States, and Russia.

The Treaty of Tianjin opened up more seaports for European trade in China, including Taipei and Anping in Taiwan. Soon Keelung and Kaohsiung were open as transportation depots for the two open seaports. After the opening of Taiwan, tea, sugar, and camphor replaced rice as the major exporting items from Taiwan. The rapid increase in international trade resulted in an important shift in Taiwan's agriculture from rice farming to tea, sugarcane, camphor, timber, and preserved fish. These new trading items also brought about new processing workshops, transportation, and shipping industries.[20]

Among new European merchants were British, French, Germans, Italians, and Austrians.[21] In 1862, Tamsui opened up and set up custom service. Other three cities followed during 1863–1865. The European countries also opened their consulate offices after the British opened its consulate office at Tamsui. Soon the British dominated Taiwan trade through the British East India Company. Opium became an important part of imports, which caused serious economic and social problems on the island. The textile products were the second-largest imports. In 1868, British and Taiwan Prefectural Government signed an agreement of camphor to allow the British to dominate camphor trade and price.[22]

After the opening of Taiwan, many European merchants, missionaries, and officials arrived in these four cities, including Taipei, Kaohsiung, Keelung, and Tamsui. Among the others were Catholic and Presbyterian missionaries who had more influence on Taiwanese people in the late nineteenth century. They opened Christian academies and schools, including girl schools; established modern hospitals; and conducted practical helps for the needy As a medical doctor and teacher, James L. Maxwell spent most of his life on Taiwan. Maxwell was from a Scottish family and graduated from Edinburg University in England. Then, he enrolled in the medical school of Paris University to study medicine. After his graduation, he was sent by the Catholic Church to Taiwan in 1865. He traveled to the mountainous, hard-to-reach villages of the aboriginal people to conduct practical helps for the needy. In 1868, he returned to Tainan and built the first hospital, the Old Building Hospital, in the city that later became present-day New Building Hospital. Rev. George L. Mackay arrived at Taiwan in 1871. He was a priest of the church as well as a dentist in Canada. He began to help the Taiwanese with their oral cavities and opened the first dentist clinic at present-day Taipei in 1879. Rev. Mackay established Oxford College in 1882 as the first higher education institute in Taiwan that later became today's Seminary of Taiwan. In 1884, he opened the Tamsui Girls Academy, which became the Tamsui Middle School later.

The opening of Taiwan not only brought in Christianity, Western technology and culture, international trade but also fundamentally changed the traditional trade pattern from a cross-strait trade between China and Taiwan to a global trade with many countries. Among the popular trading items were rice, sugar, tea, and camphor. Taiwan soon became the largest camphor supplier in the world since it had rich sources of eucalyptus in its mountains and deep forests. Taiwan also became one of few trading regions during the Qing dynasty that enjoyed a trade surplus over European trade.

JAPAN'S ATTACK, THE SELF-STRENGTHENING MOVEMENT, AND NEW PROVINCE

The opening of China after the two opium wars did not solve the problems between the Qing regime and the European powers since the Qing refused to form new relations with Western governments, institutions, and companies by maintaining traditional Chinese economic, political, and social systems. China fought three more foreign wars from 1884 to 1900 against the European powers, the United States, and Japan over trade and foreign intervention in neighboring countries. The Qing government lost all these wars, including the Sino-French War during 1884–1885, Sino-Japanese War during 1894–1895, and Box Rebellion in 1900. All of these wars and continuing European expansion and influence had a negative impact on Taiwan, especially the war with Japan, which made Taiwan the first Japanese colony in East Asia.

The success story of Meiji Japan from 1868 to 1912 only highlighted China's contemporaneous failure. Japan undertook speedy and comprehensive reforms, leading to its successful industrialization. In a short span of thirty-five years, Japan transformed itself from a feudal society into a major growing power in East Asia. Then, Japan began to challenge the existing international system in East Asia, a China-centered civilization and economy. Taiwan and the Pescadores were the first targets on Japan's list for its economic, military, and territorial expansion.

In 1871, Japan designed a "Pescadores Project" to plan to annex the island group into its territory. Later that year, sixty-nine Japanese fishermen from Ryukyu Island had a shipwreck and landed at Mudanshe (present-day Botan village, Pengdong County). Fifty-four of them were killed by the aborigines at Mudanshe. Twelve survivors returned to the Pescadores. Although Tokyo thought an opportunity to land on Taiwan, Japanese government was not sure about the Qing's reaction to such a military attack. In 1873, Japanese diplomat asked a Qing official in Beijing if the Taiwanese aborigines were under the Qing administration. The Chinese official tried to avoid any reliability of the Japanese killed in Taiwan and replied that the aborigines were not under the administration of the Qing government. It became an excuse for Japan to plan its attack on Taiwan in 1874.

On March 22, 1874, about 3,700 Japanese troops landed at Sheliao, present-day Pengdong County. They attacked Mudanshe fifteen days later and killed more than thirty aboriginal people. Thereafter, however, the invading troops faced a strong defense of the aboriginal vil-lagers around the area. Ironically, the Qing government had no idea about the Japanese invasion of Taiwan, until a British diplomat informed the Chinese officials in Beijing.[23]

The Qing court was shocked and sent Shen Baozhen, minister of transportation, as emperor's envoy to Taiwan for negotiations. In May, Shen arrived at Taiwan with 10,000 Qing army armed with rifles and guns. During the talks, the Japanese diplomats continued their aggressive policy to force the Qing government to accept Penghu as the territory of Japan, and to pay Japan 500,000 ounce of silver as victim compensations, war expenses, and other costs. It became a prelude to Japan's colonization of Taiwan twenty years later.

Nevertheless, the Mudanshe Incident became a wakeup call for the Qing government, which had just realized strategical and economic importance of Taiwan in international affairs. Thereafter, Beijing shifted its strategy from inactive to active policy. After the Mudanshe Incident, Shen Baozhen stayed in Taiwan for political and economic reforms by launching the "Self-Strengthening Movement" on the island. After the failed defenses in the two opium wars, the Qing had organized a nationwide effort to adopt Western technology and learn European military techniques to build a new Chinese armed force and strong defense. All these efforts between the 1870s and 1900s are referred to by Chinese historians as the Self-Strengthening Movement. The reformers, mostly Qing high-ranking officials, intended to save the Qing from being weakened by Western imperial aggression and to embrace appropriate strategies to strengthen the nation.

In the name of "strengthening the defense" of Taiwan, Minister Shen Baozhen established new defensive works along the coastal areas. The Qing lifted its bans on immigration from China and on families coming to Taiwan in 1874. Then, Shen opened the mountainous region of the aborigines by constructing three major roads into these hard-to-reach, remote areas. He ordered General Luo Dachun to command thirteen battalions to open the mountain in the north and build the northern road about sixty to seventy miles. General Wu Guangliang led three infantry battalions and Chinese labor force to move into the mountain to construct the central road about eighty to ninety miles. In the south, naval officers led soldiers and sailors to build the southern road about 130–140 miles. In the meantime, Shen lifted the bans on Chinese moving into the mountainous areas and on interracial marriage between the aboriginal and Chinese people in 1875.

To provide effective administration, Minister Shen expanded local governments to two prefectures and increased county governments from three to eleven. New Taipei Prefecture governed four local administrations, including Tamsui, I-lian, and Hsin-chu Counties and the Bureau of Keelung City. The existing prefecture of Taiwan added Hengchun, Pinan, and Pulishe to its five local governments, Taiwan, Fengshan, Changhua, and Chia-i Counties and Bureau of the Penghu. Shen accepted the fact that the Chinese residents of Taiwan considered Zheng Chenggong as a national hero against the Dutch despite his leadership in the anti-Qing movement to mobilize the Taiwanese and promote morale in anti-foreign powers. Shen also paid a lot of attention to improve the living condition, transportation, and education of the aboriginal people by building new roads, schools, and other facilities in the remote mountainous areas.

Minister Shen Baozhen also tightened the relationship between the Fujian provincial government and Taiwanese government. He asked the governor of Fujian to spend six months per year living in Taiwan (three months in the spring and three in the fall). Shen expanded Taiwan's government from one metropolitan administration to two in Taiwan and Taipei, and added four county governments. His efforts in local governmental development prepared Taiwan to be a province of China later. Shen faced some resistance against his reform efforts in Taiwan. For example, the Fujian governor could not spend an half of the year in Taiwan since he had to run a large province on the mainland. Although Shen modified his suggestion and agreed with three short visits annually, the Fujian governor still found it difficult to meet the requirements. Therefore, Shen believed and other officials agreed that the Qing needed to establish a provincial government on Taiwan for effective defense and better administration. Again, a new war with the European powers pushed the Qing to upgrade its administration on Taiwan to the provincial level.

After Shen was promoted to the South China governor general in 1875, Ding Richang, governor of Fujian Province, was appointed as the governor of Taiwan from 1875 to 1877. In his short tenure, Governor Ding continued Shen's policy and moved forward reform and modernization of Taiwan. He was the first governor who allowed the aboriginal people to take the Qing civil service examination and appointed those who passed the examinations with official positions in the government. Ding opened Taiwan's homestead promotion offices in Hong Kong, Xiamen, Fuzhou, and Guangdong to recruit more Chinese peasants to immigrate to Taiwan by offering land and government loans. He built the first telegram line in Taiwan about thirty-five miles between the prefectural government and Anping. In the meantime, he supported mining industry by sending officials to Keelung and investing in the coalmine there. The Sino-French War, or the Arrow War, further pushed the Qing's efforts on Taiwan's infrastructure, defense, and modernization.

The war between France and China, or the Sino-French War, during August 1884–April 1885 grew out of the Tonkin Wars during 1882–1885.[24] In 1884, at the start of the war, Paris ordered Admiral Amédée Anatole Courbet to threaten the Chinese naval base at Fuzhou and to occupy the coal-mining port of Keelung in Taiwan.[25] Admiral Courbet then attacked the Qing's Southern Fleet at the Fuzhou naval base. Within an hour all the Chinese ships were either sunk or on fire and drifting. Courbet estimated Chinese casualties at 2,000–3,000 men and put his own "cruel losses" at ten dead and forty-eight wounded.[26] After blowing up the docks and shelling the arsenal, the French steamed for the open sea. In three days, they methodically destroyed the Chinese barrier forts. In October, Courbet took his squadron to Taiwan to avenge the earlier repulse there. At Keelung, the French sank a Chinese frigate and sent ashore only 1,800 men. The Qing sent General Liu Mingchuan (Liu Ming-chuan) from China to defend Taiwan. Although Liu defended fiercely and seriously wounded Courbet, the French landing force eventually occupied the port and a neighboring harbor. With the Chinese unable to break the French naval interdiction of the seaborne rice trade between Taiwan and the Chinese mainland, however, they decided to seek peace. On June 11, 1886, Admiral Courbet died of his wound at the Pescadores.[27] A few days later, the Qing and the French signed the Treaty of Tianjin. After the Sino-French War, the Qing court fully recognized the strategic importance of Taiwan.

On October 12, 1886, Beijing proclaimed the founding of the Province of Taiwan. Taiwan became the nineteenth province of China. The Qing court appointed General Liu Mingchuan as the first provincial governor of Taiwan from 1886 to 1892.[28]

Governor Liu continued the Self-Strengthening Movement by establishing new administrative branches, appointing more officials, and carrying out reform and modernization. Among the reform policies, land tax reform was proved most important. As discussed early, most farming land in Taiwan had two layers of ownership. First, a wealthy landlord purchased a large land (thousands of acres) from the government and registered as its owner, who would pay land tax. Then, this large landowner divided the land into small pieces (a hundred acres) and rented them to smaller landowners. They divided the land again and rented them to the farms, who worked on the land. For many years, who should pay land tax and how much to pay had been the major problems in Taiwan.

Governor Liu focused his effort in establishing a bureau of land cultivation to deal with complicated landownership cases and re-categorize the land taxes in Taiwan.[29] He decided on 40 percent tax on the total property income of the large landowners. It certainly upset the wealthy but released the tax burdens on the small landowners, who were the majority of the farmers and supported Liu's land tax reform. Liu became a popular governor during his tenure of 1886–1891 by registering four million *mus* (615,000 acres) of land and bringing in 490,000 taels of silver more as annual land tax revenues.

Liu started constructing a manufacturing factory in 1885 in Taipei to make rifles, guns, and ammunition. In 1886, he built ten ship-loading sites at the harbors of Keelung, Tamsui, Penghu, Anping, and other seaports. He also opened factories to make water mines to protect these newly built shipyards. He purchased warships from the Europeans and rearmed his troops with European-style rifles. In 1886, Liu founded the general office of telegram in Taipei and began to construct the telegram lines between Fuzhou, Fujian Province, and Taiwan, the Pescadores and Taiwan, Tamsui and Taipei, and Tainan and Keelung, more than 1,300 miles. Taiwan became the first province in China to use telephone. In 1887, Governor Liu began to build the railway between Taipei and Keelung, which was completed in 1891. It became the first railway operated in China. In 1888, Governor Liu founded the general post office in Taipei with many branch offices across the island. The general post office purchased two postal ships for mailing services between Taiwan and the mainland. It also issued stamps, the first in Chinese postal service history. The most important reasons for Liu's success in early modernization of Taiwan were less Manchu resistance, less Qing's bureaucracy and corruption in Taiwan, and less inertia of the old system. Traditional China could not achieve modernization as Japan did because Chinese society was both so massive in size and so firm in organization. However, Taiwan rapidly shifted to Western models since the structure of the old society was not that durable.

NOTES

1. John K. Fairbank, Edwin O. Reischauer, and Albert M. Craig, *East Asian: Transition and Transformation*, revised edition (Boston, MA: Houghton Mifflin, 1989), 241–42.

2. Zhang Yongzhen, "Formative Period of a Chinese Dominant Society," Chapter 3 in *Taiwan shi* [History of Taiwan], 2nd edition, ed. Gao Min-shi (Taipei: Wunan tushu [Wunan Books], 2015), 93–94.

3. John F. Copper, *Taiwan: Nation-State or Province?* 4th edition (Boulder, CO: Westview, 2003), 35.

4. Hong Li-wan, "Era of Sea Powers in the Sixteenth and Seventeenth Centuries," Chapter 2 in *Taiwan shi* [History of Taiwan], 2nd edition, ed. Gao Min-shi (Taipei: Wunan tushu [Wunan Books], 2015), 86.

5. Compilation Committee, *Kangxi tongyi Taiwan dang'an shiliao xuanji* [Selected archival history materials on Kangxi's unification of Taiwan] (Fuzhou: Fujian renmin chubanshe [Fujian People's Press], 1983), on negotiations and agreements, no. 32, 5: 171–73.

6. Zhang, "Formative Period of a Chinese Dominant Society," 95–96.

7. Copper, *Taiwan*, 35.

8. Ibid., 103.

9. Jonathan Manthorpe, *Forbidden Nation: A History of Taiwan* (New York: Palgrave Macmillan, 2005), 113–14.

10. Shelley Rigger, *Why Taiwan Matters: Small Island, Global Powerhouse*, updated edition (Lanham, MD: Rowman & Littlefield, 2014), 17.

11. Manthorpe, *Forbidden Nation*, 121.

12. John K. Fairbank and Merle Goldman, *China: A New History* (Cambridge, MA: Harvard University Press, 1998), 195.

13. Xiaobing Li, *Modern China: Understanding Modern Nation* (Santa Barbara, CA: ABC-CLIO, 2015), 68–70.

14. Jonathan D. Spence, *The Search for Modern China*, 3rd edition (New York: Norton, 2013),150–152.

15. Immanuel C. Y. Hsu, *The Rise of Modern China*, 6th edition (Oxford, UK: Oxford University Press, 2000), 184.

16. Institute of Chinese History, China Academy of Social Sciences (CASS), *Jianming zhongguo lishi duben* [Concise text of Chinese history] (Beijing: Zhongguo shehui kexue chubanshe [China Social Sciences Publishing House], 2012), 440–41.

17. Jack Gray, *Rebellions and Revolutions: China from the 1800s to 2000* (Oxford, UK: Oxford University Press, 2002), 49–50.

18. Spence, *The Search for Modern China*, 176.

19. Frederic Wakeman, Jr., *The Fall of Imperial China* (New York: Free Press, 1975), 156–57.

20. Zhang Yongzhen, "Taiwan's Opening and Becoming a Province," Chapter 4 in *Taiwan shi* [History of Taiwan], 2nd edition, ed. Gao Min-shi (Taipei: Wunan tushu [Wunan Books], 2015), 147.

21. Rigger, *Why Taiwan Matters*, 17.

22. Su Ge, *Meiguo duihua zhengce yu Taiwan wenti* [U.S. China policy and the issue of Taiwan] (Beijing: Shijie zhishi chubanshe [World Knowledge Publishing], 1998), 13.

23. Wang Yufeng, *Taiwan shi* [History of Taiwan], 3rd edition (Taichung, Taiwan: Haodu chuban [How-Do Publishing], 2017), 102–3.

24. Guo Ming, *Zhongyue guanxi yanbian sishi nian* [Deterioration of the Sino-Vietnam relations in the past forty years] (Nanning: Guangxi renmin chubanshe [Guangxi People's Press], 1992), 4–5.

25. In October 1884, Courbet dispatched to Keelung the ironclad *La Galissonière*, the cruiser *Villars*, and a gunboat. The French bombarded the port and sent troops ashore, but this force was soon re-embarked. See Hsu, *The Rise of Modern China*, 328–29.

26. Keith R. Schoppa, *Revolution and Its Past; Identities and Change in Modern Chinese History*, 2nd edition (Upper Saddle River, NJ: Prentice Hall, 2006), 101.

27. Lian Heng, *Taiwan tongzhi* [A comprehensive history of Taiwan] (Beijing: Shangwu yinshuguan [Commercial Publishing], 1983), 282–89.

28. Chen Bisheng, *Taiwan defang shi* [A local history of Taiwan] (Beijing: Zhongguo shehui kexue chubanshe [China Social Science Press], 1982), 154–63.

29. Zhang, "Taiwan's Opening and Becoming a Province," 141–42.

6

Japanese Colonization, 1895–1945

In 1894, Qing lost the Sino-Japanese War and signed the Treaty of Shimonoseki in 1895, which ceded Taiwan to Japan. Taiwan became one of the Japanese colonies in the Pacific until the end of World War II. In three centuries, Taiwan had been successively ruled by Holland (1624–1648), Zheng of the Ming dynasty (1648–1684), and the Manchu of the Qing dynasty (1684–1895). Each had a different agenda. This, plus its own mobile character as a nation roving to reclaim land, made it impossible for Taiwanese to develop with a strong nationalistic consciousness until 1895.

From the beginning, Japan's colonial administration in Taiwan was sustained by its military and police forces. Its colonial policy changed from time to time and experienced four major developments in Taiwan. The first phase from 1895 to 1902 was a period of bloody military conquest and tight police control. All the Taiwanese governors were Japanese army generals or naval admirals. Imperial Japan solidified its rule by suppressing resistance, gaining control of the land system, and enforcing rigid administrative changes. Soon the Japanese governor-generals established a police state in Taiwan. The second phase from 1902 to 1919 became a constructive and progressive period when Japan attempted to extort not only political domination but also economic benefits. From 1902, Japanese chief civil administrators carried out reform and progressive policies to improve Taiwan's economy, infrastructure, and living standard. Their efforts changed Taiwan's status from an economic burden to a profitable colony of Japan. The third phase was from 1919 to 1937 when Japanese colonial government further enforced cultural and educational assimilation of Taiwanese people. During this period, all the governor-generals were Japanese upper house representatives, who were elected civilian officials, rather than the military men. The fourth phase began in 1937 when the war broke out between Japan and China. Japan carried out a new inclusive policy of Japanization to involve Taiwan in the war. After the Pacific War started between Japan and the United States in 1941, Taiwanese were required to show their loyalty to the emperor and make their sacrifice to winning Japan's war. Many of Taiwanese men served in the Japanese army, navy, marines, and engineering units. Many more served as combat laborers. Some young women served as military nurses and "comfort women" until 1945 when the war ended. Through the Japanese colonial period, the resistance movement continued against Japanese occupation, exploitation, and assimilation.

JAPAN'S WAR AND TAIWAN'S RESISTANCE

The Sino-Japanese War between 1894 and 1895 was a conflict between China and Japan primarily over control of Korea. During the Meiji Restoration, Japan was transformed from a divided state to an industrialized country and became the most powerful state in Asia by the end of the nineteenth century. As a newly rising power, Japan began to adopt an aggressive foreign policy, promoting overseas territorial expansion to protect its own interests and security as well as to expand its overseas trade. Korea naturally became the first target of Japanese expansionism.[1]

In Korea, public opinions were divided. Conservative Koreans still tried to maintain the traditional obedient relationship with imperial China, while the new, young reformists advocated the creation of a closer relationship with Japan and Western powers in the face of the decay of the colossal empire. In 1884, a group of pro-Japanese reformers overthrew the pro-Chinese conservative government of Korea. In spite of this successful coup, the pro-Chinese Korean armies, with the support of the Chinese troops, were successful in defeating the pro-Japanese reformers and in regaining control of the Korean government in a bloody counter-coup. These coup d'états led to not only the deaths of many pro-Japanese reformers but also the burning of the Japanese embassy and the deaths of several Japanese security guards and citizens.[2]

The Korean situation increasingly deteriorated, and the conflict between China and Japan intensified. In 1894, to answer the call of the Korean emperor, the Chinese government dispatched 3,000 troops to Korea to put down an antigovernment rebellion. The Japanese believed that the Chinese expeditionary force to Korea would violate the Convention of Tianjin and decided to send 8,000 troops to Korea. The Japanese troops afterward captured the emperor, occupied the imperial house in the capital of Seoul, and established a new pro-Japanese government on June 8, 1894.[3]

The Japanese army defeated the Chinese in a series of battles around Seoul and Pyongyang.[4] After Pyongyang fell to the hands of the Japanese army, the Chinese retreated from northern Korea and then took up defensive positions in fortresses along their side of the Yalu River, a river between the Korean Peninsula and China. The powerful Japanese army began to invade Manchuria after defeating the Qing army in October.

The modern Japanese navy defeated China's Beiyang Fleet at the mouth of the Yalu River at the Battle of Yalu on September 17, 1894. The Chinese navy, after losing eight out of ten warships, was forced to retreat behind the fortifications of the Weihaiwei naval base, and Japan's domination of the sea was secured.[5] The Japanese lost no time in launching a sudden land attack across the Liaodong Peninsula and smashed the rest of the Beiyang Fleet at the naval base with intense shelling from the heavy cannons on land. After Weihaiwei, Shandong (Shantung) Province fell to the Japanese on February 2, 1895, the Japanese quickly occupied Manchuria.[6]

After defeating the Chinese army and navy, on March 23, 1895, the Japanese military invaded the Penghu Islands off the west coast of Taiwan. In a short military campaign without any bloodshed, the Japanese overcame the islands defended by the Qing force and took over the major town of Makung. This successful campaign prohibited the Chinese forces in Taiwan from being strengthened and gave the Japanese government an opportunity to force the Qing government to surrender Taiwan to Japan in the negotiation thereafter. Poor preparation, inadequate training, and a great disparity between weapons and munitions were the major reason for China's defeat in the war.[7]

In addition, the war was fought largely with Li Hongzhang (Li Hung-chang)'s forces without any support from other Chinese generals.

Faced with these repeated defeats, the Qing government under great pressure was compelled to sign the Treaty of Shimonoseki on April 17, 1895. Under this treaty, the Qing government recognized the entire independence of Korea and surrendered the Liaodong Peninsula, Taiwan, and the Penghu Islands to Japan. The treaty provided that China pay Japan 200 million taels as reparation and that China have to conclude a commercial treaty with Japan to allow Japanese ships to operate on the Yangzi River, to establish factories in treaty ports, and to open four more ports to foreign trade. Japan forced the Chinese government to sign the treaty, but three European powers, especially Germany, Russia, and France, did not want to allow the Japanese to establish a colony on the Liaodong Peninsula in mainland China. As a result, Japan, under great pressure from the European powers, was compelled to stop colonization of the Liaodong Peninsula in exchange for another 30 million taels as indemnity on April 23, 1895.[8]

During the Sino-Japanese negotiations, Taiwanese were panic about Qing's position to sacrifice Taiwan in exchange for Japanese military withdrawal from China. After the treaty was signed in April, Governor Tang Jingsong (Tang Ching-sung) decided to save Taiwan from Japanese colonization by founding the "Taiwan Republic," an independence from the Qing government, on May 25, 1895. Tang proclaimed himself as the president of the Taiwan Republic.[9] The purpose of Tang's action was to stop Japan's taking-over rather than leaving the Qing dynasty.

On May 29, Japanese forces landed at Audi (or Aoli, present-day New Taipei), including 70,000 soldiers, 10,000 sailors and marines, and more than 40 vessels. The landing troops under the command of Major General Kawashima Kageaki soon occupied Keelung in the north. With fewer than 35,000 defending troops, President Tang fled Taiwan for Fuzhou on June 4. All the Qing generals, except Liu Yongfu (Liu Yung-fu), commander of the "Black Flag Army," also left Taiwan after Tang. The Hakka people organized volunteer force to resist Japanese landing forces. They mobilized Hakka peasants and engaged the Japanese with guerrilla warfare. Soon they joined Black Flag general Liu in the central areas and built a strong defense around Zhanghua (Changhua). After they lost the city, the joint forces continued their defense at Tainan in the south. In October, Tokyo sent more reinforcement and attacked Tainan from three directions. After Liu Yongfu escaped from the Japanese siege, the Taiwan Republic collapsed on October 21, 1985, and the organized resistance was over in November. During the resistance, more than 14,000 Taiwanese were killed and Japanese army lost 278 men.[10]

COLONIAL GOVERNMENT

From 1895 to 1902, the first phase of Japanese colonization was, military in nature, a period of bloody conquest and tight police control. Tokyo solidified its rule by suppressing Taiwanese anti-Japanese movements and enforcing rigid administrative changes. The first three Japanese governor-generals (1895–1898) established a police state under a direct monarchy colonization like the British system. Tokyo clearly stated its policy goal and means in several documents issued during 1895–1896, including the "Establishment of the Ministry of Colonial Affairs," "Regulations of the Governor-General in Taiwan," and "No. 63 Acts." Major General Kabayama as the first governor-general (1895–1896) of Taiwan announced the colonial regulations were in place and became effective on April 11, 1896.[11]

According to the "Regulations of the Governor's Council in Taiwan," the Meiji government established the Ministry of Colonial Affairs in Tokyo to supervise Japan's colonization of Taiwan. The ministry would nominate a Japanese governor-general for Emperor Meiji's approval to serve as the head of Taiwan's administration. Any governor-general nomination must have a ranking of army general/lieutenant general or naval admiral. Thereby, the governor-general of Taiwan would also serve as the command in chief of all Japanese army and naval forces on the island. Moreover, the governor-general would organize his administration by appointing his chief civil administrator as the executive head of the cabinet.[12] The "No. 63 Acts" further authorized the Japanese governor-general with legislative power in Taiwan after the Ministry of Colonial Affairs approved his laws. Nevertheless, his laws and orders were effective for three years. Thus, the Japanese governor-general had legislative, executive, judicial, and military powers in Taiwan. In 1906, "No. 63 Acts" were replaced by the "No. 31 Acts," which were not much different from the former. It was not until 1922 when Tokyo issued "No. 3 Acts" to limit the legislative power of the governor-general. The colonial government continued local administrative system established by the Qing dynasty and maintained the metropolitan bureaus and county governments.

From the very beginning, the Japanese military police became the most dreaded enforcers of the colonial directives. Their brutal oppression gave rise to deep-seated resentment and nationalistic resistance among Taiwanese against the Japanese rule. In 1898, Lieutenant General Kodama Gentaro was appointed by Tokyo as the fourth governor-general (1898–1906) to Taiwan. Governor Gentaro shifted the prime method for maintaining order from the military force to a new and enlarged police force. Under his rule, the police force totaled 17,000 Japanese officers with 5,000 operating in the aboriginal areas. From 1898 to 1902, more than 19,000 Taiwanese were arrested and/or executed for their anti-Japanese activities.[13]

There were three large-scale movements met by brutal Japanese suppressions. The first anti-Japanese movement was an armed rebellion under the command of Lin Shaomao in the south from 1891 to 1902. In 1898, Lin Shaomao organized an armed resistance against Japan's colonization of Taiwan. In the southern mountainous areas, his troops launched guerrilla fight and harassed the occupation force by cutting off Japanese communication lines, burning their warehouses, and executing pro-Japanese landowners and business owners. Newly arrived Japanese governor had to negotiate with Lin and recognize his own independent domain in exchange of his promise not attacking Japanese garrison in the south. Three years later, however, when the Japanese governor stopped most anti-Japanese resistance, he turned around and attacked Lin's domain in 1902. After Lin was killed, the armed anti-Japanese resistance ended.[14]

The second anti-Japanese revolt was the "Jiaobanian (or Xilaiyan) Incident of 1915" under the leadership of Yu Qingfang, Luo Jun, and Jiang Dingsan, who all participated in the armed rebellion of 1895. In February 1915, Luo Jun met Yu Qingfang, and they began to plan a revolt against the Japanese colonial government. In May, however, Japanese police discovered their plot, and Luo was arrested in June. Yu fled to the mountains and joined Jiang Dingsan, who had led a small-armed guerrilla force in the mountains. In July, they attacked several police stations and released arrested Taiwanese. On August 3, they launched an attack on the Jiaobanian, a town in Tainan County. After three days of fierce fighting, the guerrilla troops withdrew back into the mountains. The Japanese troops traced the Taiwanese into the mountain, and Yu was arrested on August 22. After the revolt, thousands and thousands of Taiwanese were arrested, and 866 rebels were sentenced to death.[15] In the following years, Japan tightened its control.

The third anti-Japanese movement was the well-known "Wushe (Masha) Incident of 1930" between the Taiwanese aborigines and Japanese colonists. Along with political colonization, Japan appropriated a variety of economic interests with no less passion on Taiwan's camphor and timbers. Most of the world's known stands of camphor trees were in those mountains. To get to these valuable trading items, Japanese colonial government started an active exploitation of forestry resources and effective control of the aborigines by stationing more than 5,000 Japanese police officers over the aboriginal areas, where the Qing regime had never asserted its authority there. When the Japanese police confiscated their hunting rifles and even hunting knives, the aboriginal people faced unavoidable conflicts with the colonial rules in the mountainous areas.

The Japanese governor tried to improve the relations with the aboriginal tribes by offering subsidies to giving up their hunting grounds, building schools for their children, inviting tribal chiefs to visit Japan, and encouraging the marriages between Japanese police officers and daughters of the tribal chiefs. It did not work since the Japanese officers left their aboriginal wives behind after they completed their service term of three years and returned to Japan. By the end, it became a huge humiliation to the aboriginal chiefs and their tribes.

On October 7, 1930, a Japanese police officer passed by the house of Mona Rudao, chief of Wushe village, Atayal ethnic group. Since the chief was presiding a wedding banquet for a couple in the village, he invited the police officer to join the party. Chief Rudao visited Japan in 1911. However, the Japanese officer did not like the food, and he beat Rudao's hand when the chief tried to bring him to the head-table. Chief Rudao felt shame and fought back. He became so upset that he asked the chiefs of other five villages to attack the Japanese on October 27, when the annual cultural and sport event would take place.[16] In the early morning of the 27th, aboriginal people attacked seven police stations and Japanese offices in the surrounding towns and villages. They captured 180 rifles and more than 23,000 rounds of ammunition. Around the noon, they launched a general attack on the Wushe School, which hosted the annual community event, and killed 197 Japanese, including women and children.

The governor-general sent 4,000 troops and police to stop the armed rebellion. It took three weeks for the Japanese troops to stop the majority of the aboriginal rebels. Chief Mona Rudao committed suicide, and his body was never found since he did not want his head to be cut off as a trophy for the Japanese. Many rebels, their wives, and children also committed suicide by hanging themselves in their hubs. During the conflict, the aborigines lost 644 people.[17] In 1931, Ota Masahiro arrived as the new governor-general. He identified the aboriginal groups in different categories between "allied tribes" as friendly groups and "protected tribes" as hostile groups for necessary monitoring, guarding, and even intervening.

EXPLOITATION AND ECONOMIC GROWTH

The second colonial phase from 1902 to 1919 became a progressive period when the Japanese colonial rulers attempted not only to control Taiwan but also to make it economically beneficial to Japan. Their efforts changed Taiwan's status from a financial burden to a profitable colony in a Japan-centered economy in East Asia.

Among the most important colonial administrators was Goto Shimpei, chief civil administrator between 1898 and 1906, under the fourth governor. His new deal policy included bringing foreign loans, respecting Taiwanese tradition, and improving local economy. Goto organized land survey, collected data about local heritage and tradition, and then made new, workable policy. His new policy proved successful and laid a solid foundation for Japan's colonial rule in Taiwan. After his years, Taiwan changed from depending on Japanese assistance to benefitting Japan. He pushed the improvement of sugarcane production, and his program worked very well by 1905. The land for sugarcane growing increased four times by 1938, and the total sugar produced multiplied by twelve times in the same year. His successful program met the increasing needs of Japan, which was a major importer of sugar.[18] In the 1930s, Taiwan also produced more rice than its people consumed and exported about one million tons a year to Japan.

During his tenure, Goto Shimpei encouraged foreign loans and investments on Taiwan's infrastructure construction. In 1902, Taiwan began the construction of the cross-island railroad from north to south, and it completed the railroad in 1908. Before the construction of the cross-island railroad, Taiwan had only thirty miles of railway in 1895. By 1905, it had 300 miles.[19] The new railway saved tremendous time for transportation between the southern and northern coasts. It had taken about eleven days for shipping goods from Tainan in the south to Taipei in the north before the completion of the railroad. Now it took only a half day to travel between the two cities. In the meantime, Taiwan started the construction of two new, modern harbors in Keelung and Kaohsiung and a hydroelectric power plant. Japanese capital was not only allowed to enter Taiwan but also encouraged to overwhelm the backward Taiwanese economy. Some of Goto's policies were controversial like allowing opium smoking, but only allowing governmental agencies to sell opium and enforcing heavy taxes on opium trade and consumption about 15–30 percent. The official opium selling continued until June 1945, two months before the end of World War II.

Goto brought in Japanese investment in establishing new companies for traditional industries like sugarcane processing. In 1901, the first modern company of sugar industry was founded with its processing factory at Qiaotou. The factory used machine and new power instead of traditional manual labor. As a result, the overwhelming majority of large firms in Taiwan were thereby owned and operated by the Japanese. Many of Japan's major banks, utility companies, and industrial giants established their operations in Taiwan, securely protected by the colonial administration. For this new Japan, the 1900s–1920s were a golden age. Rapid technological progress continued, the military continued to expand, and the infrastructure and the institutions of government continued to modernize. In 1930, the Wushantou Reservoir was completed as the largest reservoir in Asia.

By 1905, Taiwan was no longer depending on subsidies from Japan but was making a profit for Tokyo. During the 1910s–1920s, Japanese colonial rulers continued to build more manufacturing factories, modern mines, railways, and postal service for the first time, and most of the coal, iron, and food crops (including over half of the rice) were shipped to Japan. Western technology shocked closed Taiwanese society, but the influence from the West, including Christianity, science, and democracy, had little chance of being implemented under the long-lasting Japanese colonial rule.

In the late 1920s, however, Japan suffered a serious depression. The boom produced by World War I ended by 1921, resulting in substantial labor unrest in the industrial sector. Protectionism and tariffs introduced by the United States to protect its own industry placed high barriers on Japanese trade. High unemployment, over population, and acute shortages of raw materials all plagued the Japanese economy. The disparity between the rich (especially those who had profited from the war) and the poor caused popular resentment. The price of rice had also increased dramatically during the war, leading to the Rice Riots of 1918, in which tens of thousands people angry at the inflated price of rice attacked government offices and police stations across the country. Added to this were the Great Kanto Earthquake of 1923 and the subsequent fires that destroyed Yokohama and half of Tokyo, killing somewhere around 100,000 people and leaving three million homeless. Finally, in 1927 there was a crisis in the banking sector in which 25 percent of Japanese banks failed.

In order to solve these economic and political problems, voices for a campaign to further exploit colonies like Korea and Taiwan and win new territories such as Manchuria in China grew in popularity in Japan. Tokyo had a new policy on an "industrial Japan with agricultural Taiwan." Supporters included political rightists and the leadership of the Japanese army in particular. As a counterweight to the modernization of Japan, the military, the repository of conservative influence, had now expanded to include conscripts from relatively poor rural areas. They were receptive to the nationalistic narrative being fostered at the time, in part through the basic education they were provided with in the military.

CULTURAL ASSIMILATION

The third phase was from 1919 to 1937 when Japanese colonial government further enforced cultural and educational assimilation of Taiwanese people. During this period, all the governors came from the Japanese upper house, in which they were elected representatives rather than the military men. The political change took place in 1919 when Tokyo appointed Baron Den Kojiro as the first civilian governor-general of Taiwan. Representative Den and the civilian governors after him emphasized on winning Taiwanese' heart and mind by assimilating their colonial subjects into Japanese civilization through cultural changes, education, and propaganda.

Efforts aimed at cultural assimilation included such draconian measures as the outlawing of the Chinese language. Before 1919, Japanese government had a discriminated educational policy between Japanese and Taiwanese students. While Japanese students received elementary, secondary, and higher education, Taiwanese could only enroll in elementary schools to study Japanese language. During Japanese occupation, the rulers suppressed private schools in a moderate way while setting up public schools and primary schools to gradually implement its "policy of assimilation" through high-pressured "conciliation".[20] To imperial Japan, the public education system in Taiwan became solely another colonial tool devised to teach Japanese values and mores, another step toward molding the children into the emperor's subjects. In 1919, the Japanese governor reviewed the educational policy and terminated the discrimination policy. Thereafter, although the Taiwanese could enroll in secondary, vocational, and higher educational institutes, they had to pass the entry examination in Japanese. The Japanese language rather than ethnicity was the new requirement for school applications. In 1928, the Imperial University (later Taiwan National University) was founded with the same admission policy.

During the 1920s, many Taiwanese students and intellectuals joined the anti-Japanese cultural movement by resisting the Japanese cultural assimilation while encouraging the Chinese traditional culture. It became the mainstream of the anti-Japanese movement on Taiwan. Among its leaders were Lin Xiantang (Lin Hsien-t'ang), who opened his private schools in 1915 to teach Chinese language and culture. He had fund-raising among the Taiwanese business owners and landowners to open his private secondary schools. In 1920, Lin Xiantang and many Taiwanese students in Japan sent their petition to Japanese Diet for a Taiwanese legislative branch in Tokyo. After their petition was rejected, they founded the Taiwan Cultural Association on October 17, 1921. The association published its newsletters, newspapers, and a magazine, *Taiwan Youth Magazine*. It organized local associations, book clubs, and youth society, and sponsored summer schools, cultural seminars, and foreign film translations. These new cultural movements played an important role in shaping a new Taiwanese nationalism.

In February 1922, the association made the second petition to the Japanese Diet in Tokyo. Although rejected again, it shocked the Japanese governor in Taiwan, and he forced Lin to leave the association and cultural movement. Nevertheless, the third petition was made to the Diet again in February 1923 without Lin Xiantang. Then, these Taiwanese intellectuals established a permanent organization in Tokyo to help with the issue of Taiwan. The governor-general decided to take action by arresting most of the members of the cultural association in Taiwan in December 1923 and banned the association and its magazine on Taiwan. Nevertheless, the anti-Japanese cultural movement had a strong impact on the colonial society and brought up new cultural movement, peasant movement, socialist movement, and even Communist movement during 1925–1928.

After Meiji died in 1912, Emperor Taisho (r. 1912–1926) began some imperial reform on the constitutional monarchy to reflect increasingly diversified political and economic interest groups. Following the sweeping changes of the Meiji era, in the 1920s, different interest groups sought to find their place, and relative power, within the new Japan of the Taisho era. Though the new emperor was physically weak and died at a relatively young age, it was an important moment known as the "Imperial Democracy" in Japanese history. It was a time when more political parties emerged in Japan, including the Socialist Democratic Party and Communist Party. Labor unions gave workers a voice, and there were numerous strikes through the 1920s as they struggled with management. Emperor Taisho granted universal suffrage for males over the age of twenty-five. Social roles underwent further change. Women began to make up a large share of the labor force in factories and offices.

All of these had a positive impact on the Japanese colonies like Taiwan. In 1935, for example, the Taiwanese received some democratic privileges when they were allowed to vote for local representatives in provincial, county, and town's assemblies. In the first election, about 187,000 eligible males voted. Sixty-three Taiwanese were elected by the popular votes for the first time to serve in the local assemblies, only about 35 percent of 172 assembly members, since the half appointed by the Japanese provincial governors.[21] Thereafter, the number increased with more Taiwanese elected in city, county, and provincial assemblies. Nevertheless, the home-rule movement never reached the state level when democracy was steadily fading in the face of growing right wing and military powers.

As different groups competed for power in Tokyo, the new emperor, Hirohito, who acceded to the throne in 1926, became a much stronger symbol. Emperor worship reached its apex. Japanese people were told that the emperor was divine and the life goal of everyone should be utter devotion to the nation. The nationalism of the time had a religious, or perhaps crusading, flavor to it, and it had a strong negative impact on the colonies of Japan.

In 1937, Japanese governor-general officially banned all the newspapers in Chinese; terminated all the Chinese language classes in grade schools; and prohibited printing of any books, magazines, or documents in Chinese. In the meantime, the colonial government announced the Japanese as the "national language" of Taiwan. Later on, the colonial government opened 2,800 Japanese language schools to require all the Taiwanese to take Japanese as their speaking and writing language. All the service examinations, license tests, bibles, and Buddhist scripts must be in Japanese. By 1943, about 80 percent of Taiwanese could speak, read, and write in Japanese. By the early 1940s, Taiwanese were obligated to take Japanese names, both surnames and first names. Japanese claimed that they and the Taiwanese had the same origins and that the takeover by Japan was thus a natural development. When the Taiwanese became "imperial citizens" of the emperor, they should show their loyalty and make their self-sacrifices to the cause of imperial Japan.[22]

By 1945, when the Japanese colonization was over, there were too few Taiwanese with the education or administrative experience to form a viable government. Japan's colonial rule of Taiwan lasted for fifty years. Throughout the harsh colonial rule, Taiwanese jealously guarded their heritage and resisted Japanization with their lives. They effectively frustrated Japan's concerted attempts for cultural assimilation. By enduring long and cruel mistreatment, Taiwanese rejected Japan's overtures to make them second-class citizens. They remained resolutely nationalistic until the end of the ordeal. The legacy of Japan's colonial occupation was no less tragic in Taiwan; it provided a direct cause for the nation's division even before it recovered its lost sovereignty.

TAIWAN IN THE WARS

The fourth phase began in 1937 when Japan carried out a new inclusive policy of Japanization to involve Taiwan in the war with China by offering citizenship and recruiting Taiwanese youth into the Japanese imperial army. More than 270,000 Taiwanese men served in the Japanese army, navy, marines, and engineering units. Many more served as combat laborers. Some young women served as military nurses and comfort women. By 1945, when the war ended, about 30,000 Taiwanese died in Japanese military overseas.[23]

By 1937 armed clashes between the Japanese and Chinese troops at Lugouqiao, or the Marco Polo Bridge outside Beijing, had escalated into an all-out war between the Republic of China (ROC) and Japan. Japan's imperialist attempt to turn North China into a second Manchukuo led to the full-scale military confrontation between these two East Asian countries. Unlike the first Sino-Japanese War during 1894–1895, the second Sino-Japanese War, or the Anti-Japanese War in Chinese, was a long struggle of attrition that ended only by Japan's unconditional surrender to the Allies in 1945. Japan's territorial ambition on the Asian mainland soon drained its human and material resources at home. Taiwan and Korea as the colonies of Japan soon were mobilized for Japanese war efforts in Asia. In 1938, Taiwan began to enforce quota system to limit daily needs of Taiwanese and to send more food, manufactured goods, and other war supply to the Japanese front.

After Japan attacked Pearl Harbor, Hawaii, on December 7, 1941, the Allied powers expanded to include the United States and Republic of China. Between the war against Germany in Europe and the war against Japan in East Asia, World War II in the Asia-Pacific region is known as the Pacific War, the War in the Pacific Theater, or simply the War against Japan. Anti-Japanese independence movements in East Asia also joined the Allied war effort. Through the war, nationalism strengthened its hold on the East Asian people. It is interesting to note that Tokyo called it the "Greater East Asia War" at a cabinet meeting on December 10, 1941, after it attacked U.S. military bases at Pearl Harbor. The militarist-controlled government promoted its propaganda of "Asia for the Asians," freeing Asian peoples from European colonization and replacing the West to build a new Asian empire. Believing that Europe and America sought to slow down or even stop Japanese survival and success in building a strong military and modern country, Japanese militants decided to fight back by challenging the existing international order. The militarists' domination in the government doomed any diplomatic effort and peace negotiation.

Before the Pearl Harbor attack, Japan had already colonized Taiwan and conquered Manchuria, eastern and central China, French Indochina, and British Hong Kong. After Pearl Harbor, Japan continued its attacks on Southeast Asia and occupied American Philippines; British Malaya, Singapore, and Burma; and independent Thailand. In June 1942, Japanese armed forces conquered the Dutch East Indies and began to invade Australia and New Zealand. By that summer, Japan possessed a vast oceanic and continental empire stretching 4,000 miles from the Western Aleutian Islands south almost to Australia, and 6,000 miles from Burma in the west to the Gilberts in the east. Many people at home showed a strong support and appreciation of the superior military power of the Japanese invading forces.

In April 1942, the Japanese imperial army began to recruit Taiwanese for service since its total engagement in the Pacific against the U.S. armed forces demanded more troops. More than 1,000 Taiwanese young men signed up as the first group of volunteer soldiers. In August 1943, the Japanese navy began to recruit Taiwanese and 3,000 volunteers joined the naval force as the first group. In 1945, Japan began the universal conscription system, which required all the Taiwanese males between fifteen and sixty years of age and all females between seventeen and forty years of age must register for military services.

During the war, more than 270,000 Taiwanese men served in the Japanese military and fought over the Pacific islands. Many more served as combat laborers, technicians, and engineers who built Japanese airstrips, defense works, and roads. About 1,800 aboriginal people also served in the Japanese Special Force for the jungle warfare. The Japanese military institutionalized sexual slavery by forcing thousands of Taiwanese girls to become so-called comfort women serving Japanese soldiers in the Pacific War. Drafted to the "comfort stations" across Taiwan through deception and coercion, the majority of whom were virgins were subject to horrendous sexual abuse in the hands of

Japanese officers and soldiers. The brutalization of the comfort women went hand in hand with the Japanese military's desire to subdue the Taiwanese national spirit. They believed that their violating Taiwanese women was to be tantamount to conquering their homeland.

After January 1944, the Allied air forces began their heavy bombing of Taiwan as part of their offensive campaign against Japan. In October, for example, the U.S. air force with nearly 1,000 warplanes bombed Kaohsiung, Tainan, Pengdong, and Taitung to pin the Japanese forces on Taiwan during the Allied landing on the Philippines. Taiwan became as much as destructive as Japan in 1945. As Milton W. Meyer has argued, "Until Japan's defeat, no power in world history had achieved in Asia precisely the same extended imperial stature and the same widespread imperial boundaries. But Japan's temporary wartime supremacy was gained only at a great human cost to all parties concerned, built as it was on force and servitude. In 1941, Japan's position in Asia and the Pacific was paramount; in 1945, it became minimal."[24] Japan suffered an ultimate defeat and had to relinquish its long, hard-fought ambition to become a ruler of the Pacific region.

NOTES

1. Xiaobing Li, Yi Sun, and Wynn Gadkar-Wilcox, *East Asia and the West: An Entangled History* (San Diego: Cognella, 2019), 94.

2. Michael J. Seth, *A Concise History of Modern Korea: From the Late Nineteenth Century to the Present* (Lanham, MD: Rowman & Littlefield, 2010), 16–17.

3. Munemitsu Mutsu and Mark Berger Gordon, *Kenkenroku: A Diplomatic Record of the Sino-Japanese War: 1894–1895* (Princeton, NJ: Princeton University Press, 1982), 65, 77, 79–80.

4. James L. McClain, *Japan: A Modern History* (New York: Norton, 2002), 297.

5. S. C. M. Paine, *The Sino-Japanese War of 1894–1895: Perceptions, Power and Primacy* (Cambridge, UK: Cambridge University Press, 2005), 156.

6. Hans J. Van de Ven, "War in the Making of Modern China," *Modern Asian Studies* 30, no. 4 (October 1996), 737–56.

7. Wang Yufeng, *Taiwan shi* [History of Taiwan], 3rd edition (Taizhong, Taiwan: Haodu chuban [How-Do Publishing], 2017), 109–10.

8. Tao Wang, "Treaty of Shimonoseki," in *China at War*, ed. Xiaobing Li (Santa Barbara, CA: ABC-CLIO, 2012), 391–92.

9. Li Liyong, "Political Establishment of Japanese Colonial Rule," Chapter 5 in *Taiwan shi* [History of Taiwan], 2nd edition, ed. Gao Min-shi (Taipei: Wunan tushu [Wunan Books], 2015), 169.

10. Su Ge, *Meiguo duihua zhengce yu Taiwan wenti* [U.S. China policy and the issue of Taiwan] (Beijing: Shijie zhishi chubanshe [World Knowledge Publishing], 1998), 15–16.

11. Shi Lianzhu, *Taiwan shilue* [A concise history of Taiwan] (Fuzhou: Fujian renmin chubanshe [Fujian People's Press], 1980), 184.

12. Jonathan Manthorpe, *Forbidden Nation: A History of Taiwan* (New York: Palgrave Macmillan, 2005), 186–87.

13. Su, *Meiguo duihua zhengce yu Taiwan wenti* [U.S. China policy and the issue of Taiwan], 16.

14. Wang, *Taiwan shi* [History of Taiwan], 110.

15. Li, "Political Establishment of Japanese Colonial Rule," 174.

16. Shelley Rigger, *Why Taiwan Matters: Small Island, Global Powerhouse*, updated edition (Lanham, MD: Rowman & Littlefield, 2014), 20.

17. Li, "Political Establishment of Japanese Colonial Rule," 179.

18. Manthorpe, *Forbidden Nation*, 189.

19. John F. Copper, *Taiwan: Nation-State or Province?* 4th edition (Boulder, CO: Westview, 2003), 39.

20. C. Y. Chu and C. H. Yeh, "Taiwan's Private Education," *Chinese Education and Society* 28, no. 4 (July/August 1995), 76–97.

21. Manthorpe, *Forbidden Nation*, 178.

22. Chen Bisheng, *Taiwan defang shi* [A local history of Taiwan] (Beijing: Zhongguo shehui kexue chubanshe [China Social Science Press], 1982), 227–80.

23. Li, "Political Establishment of Japanese Colonial Rule," 205.

24. Milton W. Meyer, *Japan: A Concise History*, 4th edition (Lanham, MD: Rowman & Littlefield, 2013), 216.

7

From Colonial Rule to Authoritarian Government, 1945–1950

Taiwan had been colonized by Japan for fifty years from 1895 to 1945. During the Pacific War, the struggle against Japanese colonialism in Taiwan gained popular support, especially after 1943 when the Japanese governor planned to draft young Taiwanese for the Pacific War against the American forces. The draft stopped on August 15, 1945, when Emperor Hirohito surrendered to the Allied powers. Japan's sudden surrender created a power vacuum in the Japanese colonies and occupied territories in East Asian countries like Taiwan.

At the Cairo Conference in 1943, the Allied leaders including Franklin D. Roosevelt, Winston Churchill, and Josef Stalin agreed with Chiang Kai-shek (Jiang Jieshi, 1887–1975), president of the Republic of China (ROC) and chairman of the Kuomintang (KMT, Nationalist Party) that Japan's occupied Chinese territories, including Taiwan, "should be restored to the Republic of China."[1] At the Potsdam Conference in July 1945, the Allied powers reconfirmed their agreement on the returning Chinese territories. In the meantime, the anticolonial forces in Taiwan continued to request national support to complete their anti-Japanese movements, which had been escalated in the Pacific War.

Unfortunately, the ROC-appointed officials failed to deal with the inflation, corruption, power abuse, and mismanagement during the takeover of colonial Taiwan from Japan during 1945–1946. From February 28 to March 13, 1947, an armed uprising swept the island against Governor Chen Yi (Ch'en Yi), who had to call in the KMT troops to suppress the uprising by killing 28,000 Taiwanese. It later became known as the "2–28 Incident."[2]

From 1946 to 1949, Chiang Kai-shek was preoccupied by his war effort against the Chinese Communist Party (CCP) in the mainland and paid no attention to Taiwan's problems until 1948 when he lost decisive battles in Northeast and East China. In December, he appointed Chen Cheng (Ch'en Ch'eng), one of his best and most trusted generals, as the governor of Taiwan to prepare a general withdrawal to the island. On October 1, 1949, Mao Zedong (Mao Tse-tung, 1893–1976), chairman of the CCP, announced the founding of the People's Republic of China (PRC) after his People's Liberation Army (PLA) took over the mainland except Tibet (Xizang), Taiwan, and some offshore islands. In December 1949, Chiang moved the seat of his ROC government from China to Taiwan. Because of the civil war situation, martial law was implemented to regulate Taiwanese society immediately. Taiwan was basically an authoritarian dictatorship regime thereafter for thirty-eight years. In 1950, Chiang prepared for the final showdown with Mao by concentrating 200,000 KMT troops on Taiwan, which seemed to be the last battleground of the Chinese Civil War. Without a direct intervention of the United States, a Communist landing campaign was expected in the summer of 1950, less than five years after Taiwan was freed from the Japanese colonial government.

U.S. MEDIATION AND CHIANG'S CHINA

In 1944, U.S. president Franklin D. Roosevelt (FDR) approached issues of postwar China from an inclusive and global standpoint. Xiaoyuan Liu points out that FDR's policy planning was "primarily oriented toward dealing with other powers in Asia, but not with Asian peoples."[3] Even though the United States and the ROC fought as allies during the war, the leaders of the two countries found it extremely difficult to establish a partnership for a postwar order due to conflicting backgrounds and beliefs and incompatible visions for the future of East Asia.

President Harry S. Truman, who entered the White House after Roosevelt died in the spring of 1945, inherited "broad outlines" of U.S. East Asian policy adapted by FDR.[4] Lacking foreign policy experience and a personal familiarity with any Asian leaders, the new president relied heavily on advice from officials in Roosevelt's cabinet and State Department. Many historians agreed that Truman let others, such as Secretary of State Dean G. Acheson, NSC Policy Planning Staff Director George Kennan, and more importantly John Foster Dulles, take charge of the East Asian problems during 1945–1949. While the Truman administration undertook some policy planning for a postwar East Asia after the Allies' victory over Japan, Washington was unable to specify and finalize the plans with the ROC government.

In August 1945, the U.S. government just wanted to maintain the status quo of a wartime coalition between the Chiang government and Mao's Communists. In the fall, Truman sent Patrick Hurley, the U.S. ambassador to China, to Yan'an, the CCP capital, to pick up Mao and escort him to Chongqing for negotiations with Chiang.[5] In October 1945, Chiang and Mao signed an agreement, which provided for a joint coalition government under Chiang's leadership.[6] However,

Chiang Kai-shek's army suffered heavy casualties against Japan in World War II. After he lost the civil war to the Chinese Communist Army in 1949, Chiang moved the seat of his ROC government from China to Taiwan. (Library of Congress)

since both sides had different political agendas, the negotiations failed, and the two parties resumed their military conflicts in North China.

Following Hurley's resignation, Truman appointed General George Marshall, secretary of state and former head of the Joint Chiefs of Staff (JCS), as his envoy to China in December 1945. Secretary Marshall tried to use U.S. aid, which the ROC desperately needed, as a negotiating tool to force Chiang to accept terms that would also be acceptable to Mao. In fact, neither Chiang nor Mao would compromise, and they refused to cooperate with each other. The Chinese Civil War began on June 26, 1946, when Chiang launched an all-out offensive against CCP-held areas, culminating in a major attack in central China and other attacks throughout the country.[7] Seeing the momentum of civil war growing, George Marshall announced in January 1947 that his mission had failed.[8]

Compared with U.S. foreign policy planning, China had a focused and much narrower agenda, which proved pragmatic in its tenacious pursuit to gain national independence. China did not have the American sense of superiority, but rather a fear of the return to inferiority as a second-class nation like before the war. Both Nationalist and Communist parties approached postwar issues from an exclusive, China-centered, absolute nationalist calculation for an "independent and strong China."[9] They did not expect U.S. or Soviet hegemony nor the restoration of prewar European colonial powers in China. A retired KMT army general told the author that President Chiang Kai-Shek was convinced that the Roosevelt administration did not have a strategic plan for postwar China nor did the Truman administration consider China as a new power that would replace Japan in the position of dominance in East Asia after the war.[10]

At that moment, Chiang Kai-shek believed that he had no choice but rebuilt postwar China according to the KMT plan without the Communists. As the founder of the Nanjing government of the ROC in 1927, Chiang was the most important political and military leader of the KMT in the twentieth century. He was born in October 1887 to a salt merchant family in the coastal province of Zhejiang, just as the Qing dynasty (1644–1911) was crumbling. In 1908, young Chiang went to Japan to study at a military college. In 1911, after an uprising in the Chinese city of Wuchang involving New Army of the Qing dynasty, Chiang left Japan to become a regimental commander of the army that was revolting in Shanghai.[11]

During the 1911 Revolution, Chiang allied himself early on with Nationalist leader Sun Yat-sen (Sun Zhongshan, 1866–1925), first president of the new Republic of China, created after the Qing emperor's abdication in 1912. Sun soon realized that his new KMT party required a military if it was going to survive, let alone take control of the country. The Western powers spurned Sun's request for aid, and he turned to the Soviet Union, which readily offered to help create a new military force for the KMT. Sun sent Chiang to Moscow in 1924 to train with the Soviet Red Army, and he returned to play a critical role in the formation of a new KMT military. The first major project was the creation of a military academy. The Whampoa (Huangpu) Military Academy (the West Point of China) was founded on June 16, 1924, and Chiang was appointed its first commandant. After Sun died on March 12, 1925, of cancer, Chiang began his rise in the KMT, independent of Sun's patronage.[12]

General Chiang Kai-shek scored a round of victories with his new army in what is known as the Northern Expedition during 1926–1927. In just a few months, Chiang defeated two northern warlord armies and enticed other warlords to join him, and soon half of China was in KMT hands. Chiang entered Shanghai in March 1927, and the next month Chiang reestablished the ROC under KMT control in nearby Nanjing, with himself as president. Throughout this period, the CCP had enjoyed a privileged place within the KMT. However, with Chiang's victory in the Northern Expedition, the CCP became a political and ideological threat to his authority. On April 12, 1927, Chiang unleashed the "White Terror." In KMT-controlled areas, Communists were purged and killed, and the CCP was outlawed. The first CCP-KMT coalition ended.

As the CCP and KMT Civil War continued through the 1930s, Japan increased its territorial expansion onto mainland China. After the July 7, 1937, Marco Polo Bridge (*Lugouqiao*) Incident, in which Japanese forces attacked ROC troops, both Nationalist and Communist forces united again to fight a war with Japan that lasted until its defeat in 1945 by the United States at the conclusion of World War II. President Chiang suffered heavy losses during those years as the Japanese increased their territory in China. The ROC was forced to move its government several times, and it lost most of coastal China to the invading armies. Chiang instituted a policy of international diplomacy that had as its cornerstone an alliance with the United States, following Pearl Harbor, against Japan. As the Pacific War chipped away at Japanese hegemony in Asia, both the KMT and CCP forces began to see successes against a faltering Japanese war machine.

Although Generalissimo Chiang Kai-shek and his government survived the Pacific War after eight years (1937–1945) of bloody resistance against Japan's occupation of China, he lost China to the CCP during the Chinese Civil War from 1946 to 1949. His takeover of Japanese-occupied territories like Taiwan failed during 1946–1948. Soon after the war, corruption, power abuse, and mismanagement became rampant in the ROC government, which could not slow down the inflation, unemployment, and organized crimes across the country, especially in the major cities. Starving and disappointed by Chiang's failed policy, more and more people, including the Taiwanese, joined the antigovernment movements for their own survival.

CHEN'S TAKEOVER AND THE "2–28 INCIDENT"

On October 15, 1945, about 12,000 KMT troops arrived at Keelung, a seaport city of Taiwan, by American transit ships. On October 25, Governor Chen Yi arrived at Taipei and received the Japanese surrender. At that moment, the levels of public trust in the ROC government were high.[13] Taiwanese people had strong confidence in the ROC that had achieved the final victory of the war over Japan after eight years of bloody fighting on the mainland and fifty years of Japanese colonial rule on Taiwan. The long-colonized people developed a new vigor of nationalism that revealed a profound change taking place in the former colony and occupied territories. This new nationalism was no longer a traditional, Eastern cultural, or Han Chinese ethnic nationalism, but a modern, Western-style state nationalism that emphasized independence, self-government, state interests, and territorial sovereignty.

As in the mainland, Chen and the KMT officials rushed to "takeover" (*jieshou*) the Japanese assets and properties, including land, industries, transportation, communication, businesses, and banks in late 1945 and 1946. That winter, before any form of effective administration had been established in the cities, finance and commerce in the urban areas came under threat from newcomers who tried to use their government connections to enrich themselves. Nancy B. Tucker points out, "Under Chen's unscrupulous administration, the Nationalists systematically looted the island, stripping its people of as much as $1 billion in property."[14] Although Governor Chen himself avoided being entrapped by the riches of the island, his government's inability to deal with corruption tore into its legitimacy.[15] By 1946, the KMT garrison increased to 48,000 troops in Taiwan.

Taiwanese people began to lose their confidence and trust in the KMT government when it seemed to them that public resources and even private properties had been transferred to serve certain individual interests. KMT corruption spawned personal connections and made the government and bureaucracy personal instruments or vehicles of politicians. Therefore, the KMT government began to lose its credibility. However, even more important, these revenues went to individual officials, who then prevented the state from developing a free-market economy. This "official corruption" stopped the state from generating vital income; reducing its ability to decrease the portion of its revenue; and increasing its dependence on extortion, foreign aid, and higher taxes.[16]

It is conceivable that the draconian colonial rule of the Japanese caused the Taiwanese people to turn against the Chinese state. In fact, it appears more likely that it was the failure of state building during the KMT's control in Taiwan that cost the Chinese state its "legitimacy"—if indeed the "loss of legitimacy" is the best way to interpret the widespread resistance movement against the KMT government in February-March 1947. The KMT had a chance to promote major changes short of reform.

On the evening of February 27, six undercover agents from the Taipei branch office of the Taiwan Provincial Monopoly Commission accused a widow, Lin Chiang-mai, of illegally selling cigarettes on the street and tried to take away her cigarettes and money. The crowd became angry when the agents beat Lin, who begged for her money. One of the agents opened fire into the angry crowd and killed one of the observers. Next morning, February 28, in the capital city, many workers joined in a strike, students walked out of their classrooms, and shops were closed to protest the killing and demand the prosecution of the agents. In the afternoon, several thousand protesters marched to the governor's administrative office building, but they found themselves facing fully armed guards. The soldiers opened fire, killed three, and wounded several more.[17]

Then, the angry crowd gathered at the New Park (its name changed to the "2–28 Peace Memorial Park" in 1996) and called for an open rebellion against the KMT government. The antigovernment violence and armed conflicts against the KMT garrison began that evening in Taipei and soon expanded to most cities and towns such as Taoyuan and Hsinchu (Xinzhu) on March 1, to Taichung on the 2nd, and to Kaohsiung on the 3rd.[18] Many rebels became organized and armed themselves. Some local politicians, intellectual elites, celebrities, and scholars joined the uprising and played leadership roles with different political orientations. For instance, famous painter and professor Chen Cheng-po, a city council member of Taipei asking for democratic reform, joined the rebellion and became one of the leaders. The uprising leader Xie Xuehong was a Communist Party member and organized the "27 Brigade" of militias in Taichung and Pingtung to mobilize the residents for military actions.[19] His troops had three machine guns and more than 300 rifles. The KMT government became the common enemy for their coalition and cooperation.

Around 3:00 PM on February 28, Governor Chen declared martial law and ordered the military to fire on the armed residents. He also denounced all the self-organized groups as the Communist organizations, which were illegal. On March 5, he asked the ROC central government for military reinforcement since his troops had been reduced to 11,000 from 48,000 due to the civil war situation on the mainland. On March 8, the Twenty-First Infantry Division from Shanghai arrived at Keelung and Kaohsiung, totaling 13,000 troops. The military suppression campaign began from March 9 to 13 by attacking, shooting, looting, and making massive numbers of arrests. Many businessmen, reporters, lawyers, and newspaper editors were arrested and executed shorty. Several leaders were executed in the public. Even over one thousand middle-school students were arrested, and nearly a hundred of them were executed! Some of killings were random, while others were targeted. After the KMT troops wiped out the armed insurgents, the arrests, torture, and execution continued. On March 18, Bai Congxi, defense minister of the ROC, arrived and closed Chen's governor's administrative office. By the end of March, an estimated 28,000 Taiwanese were killed, while 120 officials, soldiers, and mainlanders were killed during the riots. It became known as the historic "2–28 Incident."

In April, Governor Chen Yi was dismissed and replaced by Wei Tao-ming (Wei Daoming), who established the Provincial Government of Taiwan. The new Taiwanese government included an administrative committee; about half of the committee members were Taiwanese. But the purge and investigation continued until May 16, when new Governor Wei Tao-ming took over the office and ended Chen's martial law.

The uprising not only opposed the GMD government but also drew a line between the Taiwanese and the mainlander, or "outsiders" (*wai sheng jen*), calling them such as "the pigs." The mainland seemed a world of policemen, brutal soldiers, corrupt officials, and dictators. More and more Taiwanese developed a negative view of the Chinese from the mainland and against their domination of the island during these early postwar years. Their agenda was different from any other postwar issues in China.

THE CHINESE CIVIL WAR (1946–1949)

Both the KMT government and CCP Party Center had different political agenda about post–World War II China. In the summer of

1946, the Chinese Communist and Nationalist armed forces began a full-scale war against each other for supremacy in the country. Chinese military historians divide the civil war into three phases. The first phase of the civil war began on June 26, when Chiang Kai-shek launched an all-out offensive campaign against Mao Zedong's "liberated regions" with a major attack in central China and other offensive campaigns from south to north.[20] From September to November, the KMT troops moved northward along four major railroads and tried to advance into the CCP-liberated regions. Chiang Kai-shek believed that if he could squeeze the CCP forces out of their bases within three to six months, he could win the war. The Communist forces made full preparations for fighting a new war against the KMT. The CCP forces totaled 1.68 million troops by the beginning of the war, even though the Red Army was, in fact, an army equipped with "millet plus rifles." They controlled the countryside with a population of about 100 million, while the KMT held the cities with larger populations. Mao adopted a new strategy in late 1946, "giving them tit for tat and fighting for every inch of land,"[21] and "offense in the north; defense in the south."[22] The goal was to maintain and concentrate a superior force to destroy the KMT effective strength.

The second phase of the war started in March 1947 and ended by August 1948. Since his all-out offensive campaign was failing, Chiang Kai-shek changed his war strategy from broad assaults to attacks on key targets. He concentrated his forces on two points: the CCP-controlled areas in Shandong and Shaanxi, where the CCP Central Committee and its high command had been since 1935. Chiang failed again.

In 1947, the ROC Constitution was created. Since the civil war had already been under way, the first session of the National Assembly in March 1948 argued that the new constitution authorized too little power for the president to deal with the serious war situation. The parliamentary majority agreed not to change the constitution but to add some "temporary provisions" to it. Thus was born the "Temporary Provisions Effective during the Period of National Mobilization for Suppression of the Communist Rebellion."[23] A very important fact of the "Period of National Mobilization for Suppression of Communist Rebellion" is *Jie Yan Fa* (literally translated as "vigilance measure law," or simply "martial law"). On December 10, 1948, Chiang Kai-shek announced martial law throughout China (except Xinjiang, Xikang, Qinghai, Taiwan, and Tibet). On May 19 next year, he included Taiwan as one of the areas under martial law. After its defeat in the civil war in late 1940s, the GMD government was forced out of mainland China and moved its government to Taiwan. The "Temporary Provisions" then would see even more extension and expansion in the next forty-plus years and leave deep marks in the history of Taiwan.

The third phase of the war lasted from August 1948 to October 1949. In the fall of 1948, the CCP armed forces reorganized as the People's Liberation Army (PLA) and began launching offensives from rural areas against KMT defenses in urban areas. This phase included three of the most important PLA campaigns in the war: the Liao-Shen Campaign (in northeastern China), Ping-Jin Campaign (in the Beijing-Tianjin region), and Huai-Hai Campaign (in eastern China). The three campaigns lasted altogether 142 days, during which 1.54 million KMT troops were killed, wounded, captured, or had revolted against Chiang Kai-shek's regime.[24] In terms of scale, or the number of enemies destroyed, the three campaigns were unprecedented in Chinese military history. Because of these offensive campaigns, all of Northeast, most of north, and the rest and central China areas north of the Yangzi River were liberated. Nearly all of Chiang's best troops were wiped out. In early 1949, the PLA had fifty-eight infantry armies, numbering four million men.[25]

To save the party, Chiang Kai-shek retired from his presidency on January 21, 1949, but continued to serve as the chairman of the KMT. In fact, it was his personal network rather than a well-organized party that helped maintain his power in the KMT. Therefore, Chiang continued to tolerate the corruption, malfeasance, and fraud that existed in his political party. Although Chiang was aware of negative impact of corruption, he knew that the termination of personal network and loyalty, party's power and control of the government, and party-owned and party-run businesses (*Dangchan*) would destroy the KMT political base and eventually destroy the party itself. KMT political culture tended to emphasize group harmony and hierarchical relationships. Access to the state resources was achieved through political network; having loyal party members in positions of authority, in turn, allowed for the incumbent to control and benefit from the illegal exchange of public decisions for money and political support. This was clearly the case inside the KMT, where corruption, personal favoritism, loyalty, and patronage were closely entangled. Party members were socialized to sacrifice their personal life to serve the interest of the political group and party.

After Chiang Kai-shek's temporary step-down, Vice President Li Tsung-jen (Li Zongren, 1890–1969) came to the forefront as interim president (January 1949–March 1950). The peace talks between the KMT and CCP began on April 1 and ended on April 20 when both sides failed to reach an agreement.[26] The PLA then ordered one million troops to cross the Yangzi River on April 21. Two days later, Nanjing, the capital of the ROC, fell. The PLA pressed on in its drive into the northwest, southwest, and central China. On August 5, the U.S. State Department issued its "White Paper on China," officially known as *United States Relations with China*, a move to defend U.S. China policy. Dean Acheson, then secretary of state, explained that the situation of China's civil war was out of America's control. The 1,054-page document emphasized that the major reason for the KMT military failure was its armed forces, which "did not have to be defeated; they disintegrated."[27]

After its publication, the *China White Paper* was sharply criticized by all sides, especially the Chinese Communist leaders, who seemingly had found evidence to back up their accusation that the United States had supported Chiang's war efforts and had sent money and weapons for Chiang to kill millions of Chinese people. Mao Zedong used anti-American rhetoric to mobilize millions of Chinese peasants to join the Communist war efforts against Chiang's regime. By September, the PLA occupied most of the country except for Tibet, Taiwan, and various offshore islands. The KMT lost several million troops as well as its control of mainland China to the Communists in the civil war. On October 1, 1949, Mao declared the birth of the PRC in Beijing.

FROM THE MAINLAND TO THE ISLAND: CHIANG'S AUTHORITARIAN GOVERNMENT

After his forces were ousted from mainland China, on December 8, 1949, President Chiang Kai-shek moved the seat of his ROC government to Taiwan. In late 1949 and early 1950, Chiang Kai-shek prepared for the final showdown with Mao in the last battle of the civil war while concentrating his troops on four major offshore islands: Taiwan, Hainan, Zhoushan (Chou-shan), and Jinmen (Quemoy).[28] Taiwan lies 120 miles away from the mainland and had a population of some four million in 1949. Chiang concentrated 200,000 troops on Taiwan. Hainan Island had a population of one million, and he deployed 100,000 men in its defense. Jinmen, with a population of 40,000 at that time, is not in the open ocean but lies in Xiamen (Amoy) Harbor and is surrounded by the mainland on three sides, less than two miles away from Xiamen. With 60,000 troops, Jinmen was also prepared to defend against attack.[29]

After retreating to Taiwan, Chiang's government officially announced martial law in Taiwan on March 14, 1950, and started to enforce laws that would make it illegal for assembly, organization, demonstration, petition, and strikes. For example, no other political party or

The History of Taiwan

organizations were allowed to form except the KMT. Speech, publication, and correspondence were under close watch by the government, and no personal liberty was allowed at all (civilians now might face court-martial). Censorship on the news media also began throughout the country. Thereby Taiwan became one of the "war zones." Martial law denied a lot of freedom, which citizens should enjoy under the protection of the constitution, such as freedom of travel (restriction on leaving Taiwan or traveling overseas), for thirty-eight years until 1987.

To explain such restrictions, the ruling KMT government always argued that it was an absolute necessity to strengthen the military power and government support in order to prevent any effort by the Taiwan independence movement so that Chiang Kai-shek could continue to call for his goal of "returning to the mainland."[30] From the first day of his arrival at Taiwan, Chiang had announced publicly that the first priority of this government was to "counterattack the mainland" (*fangong dalu*) and "return to China."

In fact, during the early years, the KMT government had to strengthen Taiwan's defense in the face of a pending PLA invasion from the mainland. It was very essential for the government to implement martial law to maintain Taiwan's survival, which was the biggest issue, and without it there would be no place to talk about "returning to the mainland." The KMT government also justified its policy by arguing that martial law provided the badly needed stability in Taiwan and such stability would help Taiwan in its economic development without too much trouble for people's everyday life. The argument of the KMT is that the political authoritarianism with one-party rule plus martial law "actually helped Taiwan in its modernization, making it one of the most developed areas in Asia."[31] Generally speaking, most scholars accept this argument, though they also pointed out the high price paid for it.[32]

For the PLA on the mainland, the offshore operations became an important and difficult issue in late 1949, because of its lack of amphibious experience and a naval force. The PLA had learned a hard lesson from its amphibious attack on the Jinmen Island, a small island group lying less than two miles off the mainland. After taking over Xiamen on October 17, the Tenth Army Group of the PLA Third Field Army ordered its Twenty-Eighth Army to prepare a landing campaign against the Jinmen Island. On October 24, the Twenty-Eighth Army attacked the Jinmen Island. As the first wave of 10,000 troops landed, they found themselves tightly encircled by the KMT garrison and suffered heavy casualties. KMT air and naval forces destroyed two hundred small fishing junks, collected around Xiamen by the PLA for landing, before they could land reinforcement.[33] With no boats, the Tenth Army Group, 150,000 strong, could not reinforce the Jinmen landings. The Twenty-Eighth Army lost 9,086 landing troops, including more than 3,000 prisoners, while the KMT only lost about 1,000 defenders.[34] A retired KMT army general recalled that the Battle of Guningtou not only boosted the troops' morale but also convinced his father that the KMT government could survive on these islands by building up a strong defense.[35]

One of the best army groups in the PLA Third Field Army lost three regiments on the Jinmen beaches. Shocked, Mao drafted a circular with a warning to all PLA commanders, "especially those high-level commanders at army level and above," that they "must learn a good lesson from the Jinmen failure."[36] Mao suggested that all concerned armies take time to train for cross-strait operations in order to have their troops better prepared for future landings. Mao asked his coastal army commanders to "guard against arrogance, avoid underestimating the enemy, and be well prepared."[37] In early November, Mao instructed Su Yu to postpone the attacks on the islands in the East China Sea.[38] Su was deputy commander of the Third Field Army, with one million troops in Southeast China, and in charge of PLA offshore offensive campaigns. In the meantime, Su also warned the high command that it would be "extremely difficult to operate a large-scale cross-ocean amphibious landing operation without air and sea control."[39] On November 18, on his way to Moscow, Mao drafted a lengthy telegram to Marshal Lin Biao (Lin Piao). This message was the first systematic consideration of PLA amphibious operations by the top Chinese leaders.[40]

To better prepare an amphibious campaign, in December, the high command established the PLA navy (PLAN) with Xiao Jinguang (Hsiao Kin-kuang) as the commander.[41] Xiao became vice minister of defense in 1954 and was promoted to grand general in 1955. It is important to note that at this time the Chinese were numerically and technologically inferior to the KMT navy (KMTN).[42] The KMTN had a total tonnage of 100,000 at that time, while the PLAN had 51 small warships, landing crafts, and support vessels, totaling 43,000 tons.[43] Since the PLA did not have a modern navy, they would require Soviet aid.

Mao traveled to Russia to gain Soviet financial and material support to the PLA cross-strait attack on Taiwan and other offshore islands. Mao spent two months in Moscow to convince Stalin and negotiate a Sino-Soviet agreement. In February 1950, Mao and Zhou Enlai signed a huge naval order with Stalin at Moscow, after they completed the "Sino-Soviet Friendship and Mutual Assistant Treaty." Zhou was political, diplomatic, and military leader of the PRC, serving as its premier during 1949–1976 and foreign minister during 1949–1958. His most notable achievements were in the diplomatic realm. According to the agreement, the Soviet Union would arm a new Chinese naval force with ships and equipment worth $150 million, half of the total loan package Stalin granted during Mao's two-month stay.[44]

Returning from Moscow in February 1950, Mao called a meeting of the PLA high command. During the discussions, Mao instructed Nie Rongzhen (Nieh Rong-chen), acting chief of the General Staff, along with Su, to plan attacks on Jinmen and Taiwan, with an emphasis on training airborne forces and preparing an additional four divisions for amphibious maneuvers.[45] On March 11, Su met Xiao to discuss the first detailed plan, in which the Third Field Army and the navy would deploy 500,000 troops to attack Taiwan. The field army would send its Seventh and Ninth Army Groups, totaling 300,000 troops, as the first landing wave on Taiwan. The Tenth Army Group, plus the other three armies, totaling 200,000 troops, would be the second landing wave.[46] The Thirteenth Army Group of the Fourth Field Army remained as a reserve for the attack. The Nineteenth Army Group would deploy its three armies along the coast as a mobile force. Total forces for the invasion of Taiwan would include nearly 800,000 men. In April, the Central Military Commission approved the Su-Xiao plan, and soon after, the Ninth Army Group began landing training along the southeastern coast near Shanghai.[47]

In the meantime, Mao approved the Fourth Field Army's attack on Hainan Island. In April 1950, about 100,000 men of the Fifteenth Army Group, Fourth Field Army, crossed the twenty-mile-wide Qiongzhou (Ch'iong-chou) Strait in the South China Sea and successfully landed on Hainan. The landing forces quickly overran the KMT garrison and captured the entire island. A month later, the Seventh and Ninth Army Groups of the Third Field Army occupied the Zhoushan Islands in the East China Sea. In the late spring of 1950, the people on both sides of the Taiwan Strait expected an imminent PLA attack on Taiwan.[48]

David Finkelstein points out that, even though President Truman did not recognize new Communist China after it was founded in October 1949, neither did he give full support to Chiang Kai-shek on Taiwan after Chiang moved the seat of the ROC government to the island later that year with two million Nationalists from the mainland. Truman and his secretary of state Dean Acheson vigorously warded off pressures from domestic critics of their policy. They did not use the U.S. Navy to protect Taiwan from an attack from the mainland. At an NSC meeting in December 1949, Truman rejected the Joint Chiefs of Staff (JCS) recommendation of helping the KMT government defend Taiwan and dispatching a military mission to the island.[49] On December 23, 1949, the State Department sent a secret memorandum on Taiwan to its diplomatic and consular officials in the Far East, informing them of the U.S. hands-off policy toward Taiwan. The memo pointed out that the fall of Taiwan to the Chinese Communists was widely expected. The island had no special military significance. It was politically, geographically, and strategically a part of China, and "Formosa is exclusively the responsibility of the Chinese government."[50]

In his statement of January 5, 1950, Truman repeated this American proposition toward Taiwan again. In keeping with the terms of the Cairo Declaration, Potsdam Proclamation, and terms of Japanese surrender, Truman stated clearly that "Formosa was surrendered to Generalissimo Chiang Kai-shek, and for the past four years, the United States and the other Allied Powers have accepted the exercise of Chinese authority over the island." The United States, Truman added, "has no predatory design on Formosa . . . nor does it have any intention of utilizing its armed forces to interfere in the present situation." That means the United States would not intervene in a Communist attempt to seize Taiwan. "Similarly the United States will not provide military aid or advice to Chinese forces on Formosa. It does not have any intention of gaining its special right or privilege or establishment of military base at Formosa."[51] Confronted by the increasing influence of the Soviet Union, Truman's strategic dilemma in China in early 1950 included limited resources for a global containment. His primary concern was to determine what the United States could possibly do to prevent the Chinese Communists from further challenging U.S. security interests in the long run.

Given these assessments, Truman's advisors had reached a consensus by early 1950 that China alone, under Communist control, would not enhance the Soviet capability of undertaking military aggression based on Asia's strategic potential unless the Communists controlled Japan as well. Therefore, according to Shuguang Zhang, a complete fall of China to the CCP should not necessarily result in an immediate threat to U.S. security interests in the Asia-Pacific area, at least in the foreseeable future.[52] Thus, the idea of a "defensive perimeter" in the Western Pacific became the predominantly accepted solution. In Acheson's address before the National Press Club on January 12, he outlined this "defensive perimeter" as it had been designed in NSC document No. 48/1 two weeks earlier. The American defense perimeter in the Western Pacific ran along the Aleutians through Japan and the Ryukyus to the Philippines. The Taiwan area was left out of this defense line.[53] Apparently, strategic and security considerations were the decisive factors structuring Truman's policy toward Taiwan in early 1950. A general line to guide this hands-off policy "is to conduct a strategic offensive in the 'West' and a strategic defensive in the 'East.' "[54] Zhang argues that regarding Europe, not Asia, as its strategic focus, the Truman administration did not want its effort, attention, and resources diverted in China.[55]

However, the Truman administration's aid to Chiang Kai-shek has largely been ignored, or treated only briefly, because the KMT, as well as Truman, "lost China" to the CCP by the end of the Chinese Civil War. *The China White Paper* calculated a total of $3 billion as U.S. aid provided by the Truman administration for the Chiang government during the civil war between 1946 and 1949. This joint effort is all too commonly dismissed as solely a sterile phase of the wartime U.S.-ROC alliance or as a precursor of the upcoming CCP takeover, both of which have been given more detailed attention.[56] It was not until June 1950—when North Korea invaded South Korea—that Truman shifted his Taiwan policy making from "hands-off" to "hands-on" and engaged East Asian countries like Taiwan in the Cold War.

NOTES

1. U.S. Department of State, *Foreign Relations of the United States, 1943, Cairo and Tehran* (Washington, DC: U.S. Government Printing Office, 1976), 404. Hereafter cited as *FRUS*.

2. Su Ge, *Meiguo duihua zhengce yu Taiwan wenti* [U.S. China policy and the issue of Taiwan] (Beijing: Shijie zhishi chubanshe [World Knowledge Press], 1998), 78–79.

3. Xiaoyuan Liu, *A Partnership for Disorder: China, the United States, and Their Policies for the Postwar Disposition of the Japanese Empire, 1941–1945* (Cambridge, UK: Cambridge University Press, 1996), 301.

4. Robert G. Sutter, *U.S.-Chinese Relations: Perilous Past, Pragmatic Present* (New York: Rowman & Littlefield Publishers, 2010), 48–49.

5. In 1944, to avoid a collapse of the CCP-GMD coalition, U.S. ambassador Hurley visited Yan'an, Mao's wartime capital, and proposed a joint postwar government in China. See Patrick Hurley, "Aide Memoirs," September 25, 1944; and his letter to President Roosevelt accompanying the memoirs, September 25, 1944, *Ambassador Patrick Hurley Papers*, University of Oklahoma Library, Norman, Oklahoma.

6. Compilation Committee of ROC History, *A Pictorial History of the Republic of China* (Taipei, Taiwan: Modern China Press, 1981), 2: 259.

7. Lanxin Xiang, *Recasting the Imperial Far East: Britain and America in China, 1945–1950* (Armonk, NY: M. E. Sharpe, 1995), 142.

8. Xiaobing Li, *A History of the Modern Chinese Army* (Lexington: University of Kentucky Press, 2007), 71–77.

9. Xiang, *Recasting the Imperial Far East*, 30–31.

10. A retired general of the KMT army met with the author and other scholars at Rongzong [Glory's General] Hospital in Taipei, Taiwan, on May 26, 1994.

11. Justin E. Burch, "Jiang Jieshi (Chiang Kai-shek)," in *China at War: An Encyclopedia of Chinese Military History*, ed. Xiaobing Li (Santa Barbara, CA: ABC-CLIO, 2012), 184–87.

12. Yi Sun and Xiaobing Li, "Mao Zedong and the CCP: Adaptation, Centralization, and Succession," in *Evolution of Power: China's Struggle, Survival, and Success*, eds. Xiaobing Li and Xiansheng Tian (Lanham, MD: Lexington Books, 2014), 31.

13. Peter Zarrow, *China in War and Revolution, 1895–1949* (New York: Routledge, 2005), 330–31.

14. Nancy Bernkopf Tucker, *Taiwan, Hong Kong, and the United States, 1945–1992: Uncertain Friendships* (New York: Twayne Publishers, 1994), 27.

15. Suzanne Pepper, *Civil War in China: The Political Struggle, 1945–1949* (Berkeley: University of California Press, 1978), 155–60.

16. Arvind K. Jain, ed., *Economics of Corruption* (Boston: Kluwer Academic, 1998).

17. Chen Shichang, *Zhanhuo 70 nian Taiwan shi* [Post-war Taiwan in 70 years] (Taipei: Shibao wenhua, 2015), 45.

18. Gao Mingshi, *Taiwan shi* [History of Taiwan], 2nd edition (Taipei: Wunan tushu, 2015), 265.

19. Wang Yufeng, *Taiwan shi* [History of Taiwan], 3rd edition (Taizhong, Taiwan: Haodu chuban [How-Do Publishing], 2017), 152.

20. For the detailed events in the Chinese civil war, see Xiaobing Li, *The Cold War in East Asia* (London: Routledge, 2018), 53–54, 57–59.

21. Mao Zedong, "The Situation and Our Policy after the Victory in the War of Resistance against Japan," in *Selected Works of Mao Tse-tung* (Beijing: Foreign Languages Press, 1977), 4: 14.

22. Mao, "Greet the New High Tide of the Chinese Revolution," in *Selected Works of Mao Tse-tung* (Beijing: Foreign Languages Press, 1977), 4: 119–24.

23. Harvey J. Feldman, ed., *Constitutional Reform and the Future of the Republic of China* (New York: M. E. Sharpe, 1991), 3–4. Also see Government Information Bureau, ROC Executive Yuan, *A Glance at ROC* (Taipei: ROC Government Printing Office, 2000), 20–23.

24. Odd Arne Westad, *Decisive Encounters: The Chinese Civil War, 1946–1950* (Stanford, CA: Stanford University Press, 2003), 205–11.

25. Qian Haihao, *Jundui zuzhi bianzhixue jiaocheng* [Graduate Curriculum: Military Organization and Formation] (Beijing: Junshi kexue chubanshe [Military Science Press], 2001), 40.

26. Mao, "Order to the Army for the Country-Wide Advance," in *Selected Works of Mao*, 4: 387–97.

27. Richard M. Fried, *Nightmare in Red* (New York: Oxford University Press, 1990), 89.

28. Defense Ministry, Republic of China (ROC), *Guojun houqin shi* [Logistics history of the GMD Armed Forces] (Taipei, Taiwan: Guofangbu

shizheng bianyiju [Bureau of History and Political Records of the Defense Ministry], 1992), 6: 199–200.

29. Ibid., 6: 200–201.

30. Government Information Bureau, ROC Executive Yuan, *A Glance at ROC*, 20.

31. Taiwan's GNP per capita increase more than a dozen times during the period from 1952 to 1977. See Ge Yong-guang, *Taiwan Stories: Politics* (Taipei: Government Information Bureau, ROC Executive Yuan, 1999), 2–8.

32. Xiansheng Tian, "A Lesson to Learn: The Origins and Development of the Constitutional Reform in Taiwan," in *Taiwan in the Twenty-first Century*, eds. Xiaobing Li and Zuohong Pan (New York: University Press of America, 2003), 195.

33. Chief General Hau Pei-tsun (KMT army, ret.), interview by the author in Taibei, Taiwan, in May 1994. Hau served as the KMT army commander on the offshore islands during the PLA attack on Jinmen in 1949. Then, he served as the defense minister of the ROC in the 1980s.

34. Compilation Committee of ROC History, *A History of the Republic of China*, 2: 297. The KMT army officially claimed PLA casualties about 20,000 men, including 7,200 prisoners. According to the author's interviews both in Taiwan and in China, 10,000 PLA casualties seem most acceptable.

35. A retired KMT army general met with the author and other scholars at Rongzong Hospital, Taipei, Taiwan, on May 26, 1994.

36. CMC document, "Circular on the Setback of Jinmen Battle, October 29, 1949." It was sealed and issued by the CMC. In 1987, the Archives and Research Division of the CCP Central Committee found that Mao drafted the original document. The division reprinted it from Mao's manuscript and included it in Mao, *Jianguo yilai Mao Zedong wengao* [Mao Zedong's manuscripts since the founding of the state] (Beijing: Zhongyang wenxian chubanshe [CCP Central Archival and Manuscript Press], 1993), 1: 100–101. Hereafter cited as *Mao's Manuscripts since 1949*.

37. CMC document, drafted by Mao, "Circular on the Lesson of Jinmen Battle, October 29, 1949," ibid., 1: 101.

38. Two of these CMC telegrams were drafted by Mao to Su Yu. The first one is the "Telegram for the Operation Plan of the Dinghai Campaign, November 4, 1949," and the second is the "Telegram: The Disposition of the Dinghai Campaign, November 14, 1949." The latter reads, "In view of the military failure on Jinmen, you must check out closely and seriously all problems, such as boat transportation, troop reinforcement, and attack opportunity on the Dinghai Landing. If it is not well prepared, we could rather postpone the attack than feel sorry about it later." Ibid., 1: 118, 120, 137.

39. General Ye Fei, *Ye Fei huiyilu* [Memoirs of Ye Fei] (Beijing: Jiefangjun chubanshe [PLA Press], 1988), 608. Ye was the commander of the Tenth

Army Group during 1949–1955. *Xinghuo liaoyuan* Composition Department, *Zhongguo renmin jiefangjun jiangshuai minglu* [Marshals and generals of the PLA] (Beijing: Jiefangjun chubanshe [PLA Press], 1992), 1: 58–59.

40. Military History Research Division, China Academy of Military Sciences (CAMS), *Zhongguo renmin jiefangjun zhanshi* [War history of the PLA] (Beijing: Junshi kexue chubanshe [Military Science Press, 1987), 3: 359.

41. Yang Guoyu, *Dangdai Zhongguo haijun* [Contemporary Chinese Navy] (Beijing: Zhongguo shehui kexue chubanshe [China Social Sciences Press], 1987), 17.

42. The first group of eighty-nine PLA air force pilots graduated from the training schools in May 1950. The PLA air force organized its first division in Nanjing with fifty Soviet-made fighters and bombers. The KMT air force on Taiwan had about two hundred fighters and bombers at that time. Meanwhile, the PLA navy expanded to fifty-one medium warships, fifty-two landing boats, and thirty support vessels, totaling 43,000 tons. The KMT navy had a total tonnage of 100,000 at that time. Defense Ministry, ROC, *Guojun houqin shi* [Logistics History of the KMT Armed Forces] (Taipei: Guofangbu shizheng bianyiju [History and Political Publication Bureau of the Defense Department], 1992), 6: 262, 277.

43. Ibid., 6: 277.

44. Yang, *Dangdai Zhongguo haijun* [Contemporary Chinese Navy], 48, 52.

45. Mao's telegram to Liu Shaoqi, "Approval of Disposing Four Divisions for Landing Campaign, February 10, 1950," Mao's comments on the "Proposal of Attacking Dinghai First, Jinmen Second, March 28, 1950, Mao to Su Yu, "Instructions on Paratroops Training," in *Mao's Manuscripts since 1949*, 1: 256–57, 282.

46. Grand General Xiao Jinguang, *Xiao Jinguang huiyilu* [Memoirs of Xiao Jinguang] (Beijing: Jiefangjun chubanshe [PLA Press], 1988), 2: 8, 26.

47. He, "The Last Campaign to Unify China: The CCP's Unrealized Plan to Liberate Taiwan, 1949–1950" in *Chinese Warfighting; the PLA Experience since 1949*, eds. Mark A. Ryan, David M. Finkelstein, and Michael A. McDevitt (New York: M. E. Sharpe, 2003), 82–83.

48. A retired KMT army general met with the author and other scholars at the Rongzong Hospital in Taibei, Taiwan, on May 23, 1994. He also recalled that Chiang Kai-shek and the KMT intelligence had the information on the PLA landing preparation in the spring of 1950.

49. *Time Magazine*, January 2, 1950, 11–12.

50. U.S. Department of State, "Military Situation in the Far East: Policy Memorandum of Formosa, December 23, 1949," *Hearings before the Committees on Armed Services and on Foreign Relations*, Senate, 82nd Congress, First Session (Washington, DC: Government Printing Office, 1951), part iii, 1667–69.

51. Truman's statement in *Hearings before the Committees on Armed Services and on Foreign Relations*, Senate, 82nd Congress, First Session, *ibid.*, 1671.

52. Shuguang Zhang, "Revolution, Security, and Deterrence: The Origins of Sino-American Relations, 1948–1950," *Chinese Historians* 3, no. 1 (January 1990), 18.

53. U.S. Department of State, *State Department Bulletin* xxii, no. 551 (January 23, 1950), 116.

54. Doak Barnett, *China and the Major Powers in East Asia* (Washington, DC: Brookings Institute, 1977), 223–24.

55. Zhang, "Revolution, Security, and Deterrence," 22.

56. David Finkelstein, *Washington's Taiwan Dilemma, 1949–1950: From Abandonment to Salvation* (Fairfax, VA: George Mason University Press, 1993), 208.

8

Cold War Island: Conflict and Control, 1950–1972

In 1949, the Nationalist, or Kuomintang (KMT), government fled to Taiwan with 800,000 troops and nearly one million government officials, families, and war refugees. The KMT asserted that their government, the Republic of China (ROC), had jurisdiction over the whole of China after the Chinese Communist Party (CCP) won the civil war and established the People's Republic of China (PRC). From 1950 to the 1970s, both Taipei and Beijing maintained the one-China policy, which stated that Taiwan is part of the Chinese territories, and both of them pursued China's eventual reunification. However, Beijing and Taipei differed on the key issue of which government was sovereign. From the first day when he arrived at Taiwan, Chiang Kai-shek, ROC president, had announced publicly that his goal and the first priority of his government was to "return to the mainland" by counterattack (*fan-gong dalu*). However, since China's armed forces, or the People's Liberation Army (PLA), were prepared for a large-scale amphibious attack on Taiwan, Chiang's immediate task was appropriately how to defend the island in the 1950s. The Taiwan Strait became and has remained a front of the civil war between the Communists and Nationalists.

The United States, the third player in the Taiwan-issue game, has been deeply involved in this Chinese problem. Before and after 1949, the United States was a close ally of the KMT. When the PRC was established in 1949, Washington refused to recognize the new Beijing government but chose to continue its diplomatic relationship with Taipei. Washington also supported Taipei's position that the ROC was the legitimate government of the whole of China and made a commitment to the defense of Taiwan after the Korean War broke out on June 25, 1950.

The Korean War played a decisive role in the initial development of relationships between Taiwan, China, and the United States.[1] On June 27, two days after the Korean War broke out, President Truman announced that the U.S. Seventh Fleet would be deployed to the Taiwan Strait to prevent a Chinese Communist attack on KMT-held Taiwan. Truman's order became the turning point in the U.S. Taiwan policy and had a strong impact on the future of Taiwan. Under the presidential directive, the United States for the first time committed its armed forces to the defense and security of the ROC government. The Truman administration shifted its strategy on Taiwan from the hands-off policy to a military commitment. The new policy was a reflection of the president's view on East Asia that Taiwan could survive the Chinese Civil War by joining the "free world" in the global Cold War. A retired KMT army general told the author that it was in the Korean War when the U.S. government recognized the strategic importance of Taiwan in the Cold War.[2] Thereafter, the Taiwan Strait became a point of friction between the PRC and the United States.

In retrospect, Truman's new policy of 1950 disengaged the Chinese from their hot civil war while engaging them in the global Cold War. The Truman legacy was keeping the military struggle "cold" in the Taiwan Strait and creating the foundation and opportunity for political and international competition in which both Chinese parties could find alternatives or even a peaceful solution over their civil struggle. Truman did not intend to postpone the Chinese Civil War or provide Beijing with a different reason to attack Taipei. Tucker points out that "Truman had no plans to create two Chinas or to secure independence for Taiwan."[3] The Chinese leaders in Beijing took Truman's policy change seriously, and they had to stop their landing operation against Taiwan. The island's status quo had inherited much since that summer. It had secured the ROC in Taiwan from a major military showdown with the PRC on the mainland in the 1950s, it had preserved the political unity and social stability of Taiwan through the 1960s, and it had provided an opportunity for the island's economic growth in the 1970s.

THE KOREAN WAR AND TAIWAN'S DEFENSE

On June 25, 1950, North Korea launched a surprise attack on South Korea, commencing the Korean War. Two days later, having reached a consensus with Capitol Hill and the Pentagon, Truman ordered the Seventh Fleet to patrol the Taiwan Strait. He shifted U.S. position to a "hands-on" commitment toward the safety of Taiwan.[4] Finkelstein argues, "Taiwan was neutralized for purely military-strategic reasons. Washington could not allow the island to be occupied by enemy forces while U.S. ground troops were committed to a land war in Korea."[5]

China had been preparing its landing campaign against Taiwan since the founding of the PRC. The Seventh Fleet's presence in the Taiwan Strait totally changed the balance of military power in the Chinese Civil War. The Communist leaders faced a serious challenge—America's direct involvement in the Chinese civil struggle, which would transform the conflict into an international confrontation. With Washington's direct involvement in the Taiwan Strait, the PLA now confronted the most advanced military force in the world—the U.S. armed forces. The Seventh Fleet's presence in the Taiwan Strait marked a turning point in the cross-strait situation.[6] An amphibious campaign against U.S. forces in the Taiwan Strait in the summer of 1950 could have been a military disaster for the PLA. U.S. general Douglas MacArthur said that a Chinese Communist attack on Taiwan that summer would face "such a crushing defeat it would be one of the decisive battles of the world—a disaster so great it would rock Asia, and perhaps turn back Communism."[7] Truman's order secured the ROC by preventing a well-planned landing on Taiwan by the end of June 1950, and on June 30, the PLA high command postponed the landing operation.[8]

Beijing watched Washington closely as the American military presence and support to Taiwan's defense increased on a daily basis. After June 28, more than a dozen American warships and supply ships from the Seventh Fleet arrived at Keelung and Kaohsiung, two major seaport cities of Taiwan. In July, the American warships began their patrol in the Taiwan Strait. Meanwhile, American diplomats and military strengthened their ties with the ROC government. On July 31, MacArthur led a high-level U.S. military delegation, including sixteen generals, on a visit to Taiwan in order to strengthen the island's defenses and bolster GMD morale. Thereafter, Chiang Kai-shek also met Vice Admiral Arthur D. Struble, commander of the Seventh Fleet at Taipei. Chiang and his generals convinced their American partners that the PLA would land in Taiwan soon and direct U.S. military support was critical to the island's defense.

Thus, in July, Chinese leaders made a significant shift in strategy; instead of landing at Taiwan, they were now defending Manchuria.[9] Mao Zedong met other top leaders and discussed the military situation in Korea. After the meetings of the CCP high command, Premier Zhou Enlai (Chou En-lai, 1898–1976) briefed Russian ambassador Nikolai Rochshin in Beijing.[10] Beijing believed it was necessary for China to bolster forces in Northeast China along the Chinese-North Korean border. It was only after the Korean War broke out that China's military began to see significant strategic changes, from focusing on attacks on KMT-held islands to protecting the mainland. The concept of national defense against a possible Western invasion became the cornerstone of China's new strategic culture and their military modernization in the 1950s. Considering these new developments, Mao ordered the PLA to put off all offshore offensive operations.[11]

On August 4, 1950, the first combat group of American fighters and bombers from the U.S. Thirteenth Air Force arrived at the Taibei air base.[12] Before the end of August, the Truman administration sent $140 million in military aid to Taiwan.[13] On September 18, the State Department approved the first military assistance program to Taiwan, totaling $9.8 million that included weapons, ammunition, and equipment to guarantee the island's safety. In September, top KMT commanders discussed the defense of Taiwan with Major General Howard M. Turner, commander of the Thirteenth Air Force, and Rear Admiral Francis P. Old, commander of the U.S. Naval Force in the Philippines. Subsequently, the United States organized a Military Advisory Assistant Group (MAAG) for Taiwan.[14] Taiwan was now in a much better defensive state against a possible PLA attack. Even though MacArthur doubted that "the Red Chinese might commit themselves to such folly," he prayed "nightly—that they will."[15]

On February 9, 1951, Washington and Taiwan reached an agreement of "mutual defense and assistance." On February 16, the U.S. Defense Department received a financial package of $67.1 million as military aid to Taiwan and Thailand, $50 million of which was for Taiwan.[16] In May, the Truman administration provided $21 million in military aid to Taiwan's naval and air force improvement.[17] On May 1, the U.S. MAAG was established in Taiwan. To ensure the island's safety, the American advisors became actively involved in improving the combat effectiveness of KMT forces, including reorganizing Chiang's troops into thirty-one infantry divisions. In August, General William Chase, leading advisor of the American group in Taiwan, reported to Washington that he and his advisory group had planned to aid and train a total of 600,000 Chinese Nationalist troops.[18] By the end of September 1951, the total number of American military advisors reached 280.[19]

In the years 1949 to 1953, the Truman administration's military aid to the ROC had the effect of discouraging China from a large-scale landing. Chen and Li state, "But the active role that China played in East Asia also turned this main Cold War battlefield into a strange 'buffer' between Washington and Moscow. With China and East Asia standing in the middle, it was less likely that the United States and the Soviet Union would become involved in a direct military confrontation."[20] Chinese military involvements in Korea from 1950 to 1953 had promoted the CCP to international status, projecting a powerful image of China as the vanguard of the Communist countries against Western powers such as the United States.

CHIANG'S AUTHORITY AND CONTROL

With a secured national defense and political consolidation in place in the early 1950s, President Chiang Kai-shek and Nationalist leaders began to think of Taiwan as a permanent home rather than returning to the mainland. They felt they were needed in Taiwan, and they saw their presence as a chance to prove that their ideology was superior to Communism. From 1950, Chiang focused his efforts on three areas as his priority to consolidate his control of Taiwan. The first effort was the GMD party reform through organizational purge, institutional changes, and a new membership drive. The second was to allow village, township, and county elections to mobilize Taiwanese support to the central government. The third, and one of the most important ones, was land reform. All of the three policy efforts had worked and laid a solid foundation for the survival and success of Chiang's regime for thirty-nine years, when Chiang Kai-shek served as the ROC president for five terms from 1950 to 1975. According to the 1947 Constitution of the ROC, each presidential term was six years. Then, his son Chiang Ching-kuo served as the president from 1975 to 1989.

In 1950, Chiang Kai-shek, chairman of the KMT, launched a much-needed political reform to clean up the KMT by stopping factional politics and individual control by Chen Li-fu and Chen Guo-fu and their "Central Club" (CC) group. The Japanese invasion during 1937–1945 and the Chinese Civil War seriously weakened the KMT as a party. Because Generalissimo Chiang Kai-shek was preoccupied by the continuing total wars, diplomatic efforts, and shifting capital city (three times through these years), the Chen brothers controlled the Party Center and established their own personal network. It became the KMT wartime culture in twelve years to develop personal networks, establish fractional and sectional groups, and use public resources to cater to particularistic loyalty, even if the same activities would be perceived as corrupt in the West. In particular, the norm of reciprocity embedded in KMT political culture socialized people to treat corrupt exchange as neutral and acceptable. The attempts to form the KMT into an elite, popular party with a strictly hierarchical organization were dropped, and the party's policies suffered under the thousands of big and small compromises it had to strike for wartime needs with local power holders, including warlords, bandits, and Communist guerrilla forces.

In July 1950, KMT chairman Chiang Kai-shek dismissed Chen Guo-fu from his Party Center positions. In August 1951, Chiang approved a travel fund of $50,000 for Chen Li-fu and his family to immigrate to America and settle in New Jersey. Thereafter, the CC group collapsed and ended its control of KMT. Then, Chiang created the KMT National Reforming Committee to reorganize the local committees and recruit Taiwanese into the party. Many appointed committee members were Chiang's own followers, including his son, Chiang Ching-kuo, who was appointed as the chairman of the KMT Taiwan Committee. In 1952, the KMT held its Seventh National Congress at Taipei with two major agendas: revising the KMT Constitution and reelecting the members of the Central Committee. Its members were reduced from 460 of the Sixth Central Committee in China to 32 members of the Seventh at Taiwan. After the Congress, Chiang Kai-shek regained his total control of the KMT as the political foundation for his authoritarian government until his death in 1975.

In the meantime, KMT chairman Chiang Kai-shek also tightened the party's control of the military, which needed to follow the fundamental principle and system of absolute party leadership of the armed forces. In other words, the party's army should support Chiang by showing its loyalty to the Party Center. In 1950, Chiang purged different factions from the army and established his personal control of the military. He jailed hundreds of the generals and executed more than fifty of them before the end of the year. In 1955, Chiang detained General Sun Li-jen (Sun Liren), army chief and commander of the Taiwan defense, by charging him with failure to report Communist spies in his staff. General Sun was detained for thirty years before his death in 1990. In the year of 1955, more than 300 generals and officers were accused and purged with charges of conspiracy under Sun. Some of them died of torture or were executed.[21] In the early 1950s, Chiang Kai-shek created the General Department of Political Tasks in the Defense Ministry and appointed his son Chiang Ching-kuo as the first director. In July 1950, Chiang Ching-kuo opened the Political Officers Academy to train the party's officers for the services needed to maintain the party's control of the military. Chiang's regime continued to control the resources and personnel management for the military budget and professional careers.

Because of the unique civil war situation, martial law had been implemented to regulate Taiwanese society for thirty-eight years. Ruled under martial law, Taiwan was basically an authoritarian dictatorship regime. In 1949, the government began to implement a residential identification system and control the border: nobody could enter or leave Taiwan, or traveling overseas, without the government's permission.[22] In June 1950, the government promulgated the "Regulations to Eliminate the Enemy Spies" to ban freedom of speech, press, assembly, strike, public rally, and political organization. Its articles provided the "principal punishments," including criminal detention, fixed-term imprisonment, life imprisonment, and the death penalty for any "connection, communication, and cooperation with the Communists," or any antigovernment propaganda or other acts that were committed to the goal of overthrowing the political power.

The ruling KMT government possessed enormous power and used it ruthlessly to crash any dissent and activity regarded as threatening to its power. In addition, ROC president Chiang Kai-shek controlled the judicial system, law enforcement, intelligence, mass media, and civil organizations such as trade unions, women federation, and youth groups. Any speech that included controversial political materials was made publicly or disseminated to overseas audiences; those involved would be soon arrested and punished. Undercover secret agents were posted everywhere to report any antigovernment conversation or action through common people's daily life. Police could arrest and detain any person without warrants from a court. In most cases, police arrested individuals without notifying their family members. After a person was arrested, the individual did not know how long he or she would be held by police. During detention, torture, abuse, and insulting of prisoners remained prevalent through four decades. The death penalty was common for those who were against the government. Often, executions were carried out on the same day as the sentencing. According to official statistics, between 1949 and 1970, more than 140,000 people were arrested for 30,000 political crime charges. More than 4,000 of them were executed, and 9,000 were sentenced to life in prison.[23]

From 1949 to 1989, Taiwan was under an authoritarian government and people lived in the "White Terror" (*baise kongbu*). During the 1940s–1950s, the government made connection with Communists a capital crime, with charges like conspiracy, illegal rallies, and antigovernment plots. Soon, all the antigovernment complaints and political disagreements were considered pro-Communist activities and those who were involved in such activities faced serious charges. Among the other major purges were the Chiong Ho-tong (Zhong Haodong) and Cai Hsiao-qian cases. Chiong Ho-tong was the principal of the Keelung Middle School. Dissatisfied with the government policy, he began to print an underground newspaper *Guangming bao* (*Brightness Newspaper*) to explore the dark side of Taiwan. In August 1949, he was charged with a conspiracy against the government, and many of his students and teachers in the middle school were also arrested for their "anti-government activities." On October 14, 1950, Principal Chiong was executed. Other teachers and students faced lifetime prison terms or long jail time. In April 1950, Cai Hsiao-qian was arrested for organizing the CCP's committees in Taiwan. Hundreds and hundreds were charged since the government made it clear, "Better to kill one thousand non-Communists by mistake than allow a single true Communist to slip through the net."[24]

In the early 1960s, the government expanded its suppression to democratic and independent activities in Taiwan. Among the major charges were the Lei Chen (Lei Zhen) case in 1960, Shih Ming-teh (Shi Mingde) in 1961, the *Xingtai hui* (Reviving Taiwan Society) case in 1962, and Peng Ming-min in 1964. Lei Chen was an important KMT official with some liberal ideas as a committee member of the Executive Yuan and editor of a couple of journals in China. After he came to Taiwan with Chiang Kai-shek in 1949, Lei created *Ziyou Zhongguo* (*Free China*) journal to help the government by promoting anti-Communist and liberal ideas. But after 1955, tension arose between the government and the journal, which explored the problems of the dictatorship and complaints of Taiwanese people. In 1960, the conflict became personal between Chiang Kai-shek and Lei Chen, when the journal publicly opposed Chiang's attempt to revise the constitution in order to serve a third term (another six years) as the ROC president. On September 4, Lei was charged as an "enemy spy" and sentenced to ten years in prison. Many of the editors, reporters, and supporters of the journal were also arrested. Thereafter, Chiang revised the constitution and served five terms as the president until his death in 1975.

LOCAL ELECTION AND LAND REFORM

With Truman's guaranteeing the island's security and economic aid in the early 1950s, the KMT government undertook various kinds of reform and instituted new policies aimed at promoting popular support and economic development. As the "outsiders" or "other people" ("people from other provinces," *wai sheng jen*), Chiang's government in an effort to establish a connection with Taiwanese people allowed local elections of village, township, city, and district leaders and assemblies as well as provincial assembly elections to be routinely held. In 1950, the government passed the "Autonomy Outlines for Counties and Cities in Taiwan." However, the provincial governor and mayors of municipalities directly under the central government were still appointed by President Chiang Kai-shek himself.[25] As a result of the coexistence of authoritarianism and local autonomy, a "two-layer political system" emerged in Taiwan where Chiang established a dictatorship at the top with a total control of the party, army, and central government, while the Taiwanese people had limited democracy at the village, township, and city levels. The problem of the "two-layer system" was that there was not much interaction and transaction between the center and the locals, who stayed in their own exclusive circle.

Moreover, the KMT also permitted the discussion and debate of Western liberalism but banned Marxism and socialist thought. It insisted upon strict adherence to the 1947 Constitution with the intent of reactivating it to establish full democracy when conditions permitted. The ruling party also allowed regime critics to hold public meetings and critically evaluate the regime as long as the authorities judged that such behavior did not threaten the party-state rule. The Taiwan government even passed a law in 1969 permitting a small quota of national representatives to be elected every three years. According to Linda Chao and Ramon H. Myers, the balancing act between maintaining authority and power and nurturing a democracy paved the way to the later democratic movement.[26] Taiwan's people gradually learned to play by the rules of democracy. Even so, popular elections for public officials are only one of the many variables that define a political system, judged by criteria like power distribution, civil liberties, political contestation, and the autonomy of interest groups, along with public elections, Taiwan before 1986 was definitely an authoritarian political system.

The most important progressive policy in the 1950s was land reform. The first step of the land reform was to reduce the rent burden of tenant farmers under the old ownership structure of land, by decreasing the previous rent rate of 57 percent in average and 70 percent at the highest level to a uniform rent of 37.5 percent. According to the land policy issued on April 4, 1949, landlords were allowed to collect below the rate but not above and were required to fix the rent period to six years or more by a formal contract instead of an uncertain period by oral contracts. This measure raised and stabilized the income expectation of the tenants and gave incentives of production and investment. Statistically in the three years after the reform, the increased income was invested into reproduction to the extent of three-quarters by the tenant farmers.[27]

The second step of the land reform started in 1951 was the sale of publicly owned farming land, 22 percent of all the farming land in Taiwan, to the tenant farmers at a low price and quota. The quota was three acres maximum per farming family. The price level was 2.5 times of annual output of the land and could be paid in ten years by installments without interest, which meant that a tenant farmer could obtain the land by paying a rent of 25 percent for successive ten years.

The final reform step was to carry out the "Farmland Owned by Farmers" policy in 1953. The government first bought the excess farmland from landlords who were legally permitted to own and cultivate only up to three acres per family. The purchase was made in payments of 70 percent by bonds in kind with an interest rate of 4 percent annually and 30 percent in stock shares of the privatized state-owned enterprises. Then the government sold the farmland to the tenant farmers in the same way as the sale of public land. By the third step of the reform, with the effects of the previous two steps, nearly all the non-farming landlords disappeared and the self-farming and semi-self-farming farmers grew to about 87 percent of the rural population, which by data showed a great promotion of agricultural production, labor input, labor productivity, and re-cultivation level. Farmland in Taiwan after this time was strictly owned by cultivating farmers. John F. Copper points out that the land reform "was a resounding success; so much so that Taiwan's land reform program still provides a model for other countries to study and emulate."[28] Land reform and Taiwan's overall successful economic development plans, both of which were overseen by U.S. aid advisors, also made Taiwan a showcase of U.S. foreign aid and improved the Nationalist government's image in the international community.

After he entered the White House in January 1953, President Dwight D. Eisenhower continued Truman's policy to disengage the Chinese in the Taiwan Strait. After the Korean Armistice was signed in July 1953, China shifted its attention and efforts against "American imperialists" from Korea to Taiwan. When the Korean War was over, Beijing had hoped to see U.S. withdrawal from the Taiwan Strait. But the Korean Armistice did not end the Taiwan problem, nor did it lead

Chiang's land reform and U.S. aid in the 1950s preserved Taiwan's security, political unity, and social stability through the 1960s and provided an opportunity for the island's economic growth in the 1970s. The island's economy depended, in part, on the rice harvest, depicted above. (Paul Almasy/Corbis/VCG via Getty Images)

to the Seventh Fleet's withdrawal. Instead, America's increasing involvement dashed Beijing's hopes for a possible end to the Chinese Civil War. Chinese leaders suspected that the United States was carrying out a policy of "unleashing Chiang." Since the establishment of the PRC, the question of how to deal with the United States was not only a foreign policy issue for Beijing; rather, it was an issue concerning the very essence of the Chinese revolution.[29]

In 1954, Beijing perceived unmistakable indications that Taipei–Washington collaboration was accelerating. If China did not send a quick and effective message to the United States, Beijing believed, American cooperation would legitimize Taiwan within international politics, hindering Beijing's goal to gain full acceptance as a significant member of the international community. The Central Military Commission (CMC) of the CCP decided in July that the PLA would launch attacks in September on the Dachen (Tachen) Islands off the Zhejiang (Chekiang) coast and the Jinmen Island off the Fujian (Fukien) coast in the Taiwan Strait.[30] By the summer of 1954, KMT troops still held nineteen islands off China's coast. They are geographically divided into two groups. The first group is the Taiwan Strait island group, which has six offshore islands. This group includes Jinmen and Mazu, lying a few miles south of the

mainland, off Fujian Province. Second, the East China Sea group
has twelve offshore islands, including the Dachens. This group lies
to the east of China, off Zhejiang Province. In addition, there are
another dozen much smaller uninhabited islands, also very close to
the mainland, and within hit-and-run range of both the KMT army
and the PLA.

THE TAIWAN STRAIT CRISES

On September 3, 1954, the PLA artillery in the Fujian front began a
heavy bombardment of Jinmen and Mazu to reduce the re-enforcement
and supply shipments from Taiwan to these islands.[31] The Taiwan Strait
Crisis of 1954–1955, or the First Taiwan Strait Crisis, began between
China and Taiwan. On November 1, the PLA began its air and naval assault on the Dachens. For four days, PLA bombers and fighters raided
the Dachens, flying more than one hundred sorties and dropping over
one thousand bombs.[32] They now dominated both air and sea around
the Dachens, and a landing at Yijiangshan (Yikiangshan) seemed imminent.[33] Nonetheless, a retired KMT army general recalled that Chiang
Kai-shek visited the Dachens and strengthened the garrison's morale
by clearing some rumors that Taiwan's high command would evacuate the KMT troops from these islands. Then, the Dachens' garrison received reinforcement and more supplies.[34]

The PLA high command called a halt to await the outcome of negotiations on a mutual defense treaty between the U.S. and Taiwan,
that might or might not include the offshore islands. The Washington-
Taiwan Mutual Defense Treaty was signed by the Eisenhower administration on December 2.[35] On January 18, 1955, the PLA landed at
Yijiangshan, a KMT-held, a half square mile islet, seven miles north of
the major Dachen Islands, to test the mutual defense treaty and U.S.
defense commitment. KMT garrison at Yijiangshan numbered only
about one thousand troops armed with some sixty artillery pieces and
one hundred machine guns. The PLA's 10,000 men attacking forces had
an overwhelming numerical superiority. By the next day, the PLA had
annihilated all remaining KMT pockets of resistance. The KMT lost its
entire garrison of 1,086 men, including 567 dead and 519 prisoners. The
PLA suffered 1,592 total casualties.[36]

The Eisenhower administration, for its part, persuaded Chiang Kai-
shek to withdraw his troops from the Dachens with American assistance. Between February 8 and 12, the Seventh Fleet helped the KMT
evacuate some 25,000 military and 18,000 civilian personnel from the

Dachen Islands.[37] At the same meeting that decided the Dachen's evacuation on January 20, 1955, Eisenhower and Secretary Dulles agreed that abandoning all the offshore islands would be a "great blow to Nationalist morale and that the U.S. must therefore assist in defending Quemoy and Matsu as long as the PRC continued to threaten Taiwan."[38] To implement this policy, Eisenhower requested authorization from Congress for the United States to participate in the defense of Jinmen, Mazu, and other islands in the Taiwan Strait. On January 29, Congress passed the "Formosa Resolution," which authorized Eisenhower to employ U.S. armed forces to protect Taiwan from a possible PLA invasion. Beijing backed down on April 26 when the Chinese premier offered to negotiate with the United States at the Bandung Conference. Zhou Enlai said that the PRC wanted no war with America, that "the Chinese people are friendly to the American people," and that his government was willing "to negotiate with the United States for the reduction of the tensions in the Taiwan Strait."[39] The 1954–1955 Taiwan Strait Crisis was over. On August 1, 1955, the Chinese-American ambassadorial talks began at Geneva.

Keeping the two sides apart was not easy. The Second Taiwan Strait Crisis erupted over the offshore islands of Jinmen and Mazu on August 23, 1958, when the PLA heavily bombarded the islands. In the following two months, several hundred thousand artillery shells exploded on Jinmen. At one point, a PLA invasion of the island seemed imminent. Jinmen had a total of 88,000 troops and 50,000 residents, who totally depended on supplies from Taiwan, requiring at least 400 tons of supplies per day—transportation and logistics thus were the critical vulnerabilities of the Jinmen garrison.[40] If the PLA could cut off or restrict the flow of supplies, it would undermine the garrison's effectiveness. The Chinese intended to create a blockade of these supplies, leading to a possible withdrawal of the KMT garrison from those islands like the Dachen evacuation in 1955.

By August 25, the PLA's heavy shelling had totally cut off the Jinmen Islands from Taiwan. After ten days of shelling, the Jinmen garrison only received a very small percentage of its regular supplies through a limited and ineffective airlift and some nightly shipping. In response to the rapidly escalating PLA threat, the Eisenhower administration reinforced U.S. naval forces in East Asia and directed U.S. warships to help the KMT protect Jinmen supply lines. On September 7, seven American warships (two cruisers and five destroyers) escorted two KMT supply ships sailing to Jinmen. Meanwhile, U.S. planes began escorting KMT shipments to Jinmen and equipped GMD F-86 fighters with new air-to-air missiles, their first ever introduction to combat. These became a huge tactical obstacle for PLA pilots. The PLAAF discovered that the GMD had air-to-air missiles on September 24 only when PLA fighters were shot down by the missiles in an engagement with KMT fighters.[41] The blockade of Jinmen was becoming more and more difficult to sustain.

Chinese leaders seemed willing to accept the fact that the PRC would not fight the United States over the offshore islands if the Americans made a commitment to their defense. On October 5, the CMC issued an instruction, drafted by Mao, that rationalized the slowdown in shelling by claiming that while the PLA could have seized Jinmen, it would have been merely a short-term victory. China would leave Jinmen linked to Taiwan to avoid giving the United States a pretext for instigating a "two Chinas plot." The nation's unification and the liberation of Taiwan were much more important in the long run than the recovery of a few offshore islands. Mao called it the "noose strategy." It meant that Beijing would leave the islands such as Jinmen and Mazu in Chiang's hands as a burden on America. Beijing, however, could use the islands as the "noose" to serve its own goals in the international arena.[42]

Thus, by October 5, 1958, the tension in the Taiwan Strait began to ease, though a small-scale shelling of Jinmen continued in order to carry out Mao's "noose policy." From August 23 to October 6, 1958, the PLA shelled the Jinmen Islands and surrounding waters with 474,900 rounds. The PLA claimed to have sunk twenty-one KMT gunships and transport ships, damaged another seventeen; shot down eighteen KMT airplanes; and inflicted more than 1,000 KMT casualties.[43] Beyond the shelling, Mao's policy toward the Taiwan Strait had changed from a military confrontation to a political consideration, the nature of the Cold War, and ultimately the international politics over the civil war.[44]

ECONOMIC RECOVERY

When the Chiang government moved to Taiwan, its economy was characterized by high inflation, low productivity, and an influx of population from the mainland. About two million people moved across the straits and migrated from mainland. In 1948, the inflation rate reached 1,145 percent. In 1949, the inflation rate reached 181 percent.[45] Only a few industries remained after the heavy bombing of Allied forces during the Pacific War, including sugar refining and some textile manufacturing.

From 1949 to 1959, continuing U.S. aid stabilized Taiwan's economy and currency system. On May 17, 1951, the National Security Council passed the "NSC No. 48/5" document and decided to provide more economic and military aid to Taiwan in order to further strengthen Taiwan's economy and guarantee Taiwan's defense.[46] By the end of the year, U.S. aid to Taiwan reached $98 million, but only about 13 percent of the total was military aid while 87 percent consisted of economic and technological help. From 1951, much of the U.S. aid was used in infrastructure and the agricultural sector. In 1952, U.S. aid to Taiwan totaled $81.5 million, including only $13.3 million military assistance. In 1953, U.S. annual aid to Taiwan rose to $105 million, with more than 74 percent of that amount allocated to economic and technology aid. Besides the governmental aid, the United States also provided financial and material help to Taiwan during the early 1950s through the industrial counterpart fund, the Joint Commission on Rural Reconstruction (JCRR), and other assistance projects.[47] JCRR was an organization sponsored by the United States that aimed at modernizing Taiwan's agricultural system and land reform. Lee Teng-hui, then a professor of economics at the National Taiwan University and later the president of the ROC, worked at JCRR during 1957–1960. U.S. aid in the 1950s slowed down inflation, provided the reconstruction's needs with U.S. manufactured goods and agricultural technology, and purchased Taiwan's agricultural items. American advisors stationed in Taiwan and the Taiwanese sent abroad for education were all directed at rebuilding the economy.

In 1949, Chiang Kai-shek appointed Chen Cheng as the governor of Taiwan. During his tenure, Chen carried out his first economic policy with a focus on agricultural development, including land reform, monetary reform, and support for private enterprises. At the beginning of the 1950s, the Taiwanese government focused on agriculture by issuing favorable farming policy, freeing rural labor, and increasing agrarian exports. National employment in the agricultural sector reached 56 percent in 1950. The performance and productivity of rural economic activities, most of which was achieved by laborers or workers in the villages, had an important influence on the development and industrialization of the economy. The government labor policy provided the rural laborers with some important rights, including first, every rural laborer in the farming family had his or her ownership of land after the land reform. Second, every rural laborer had the right to choose his or her career or type of work in the labor market, which ranged from farming to animal husbandry, fishery, forestry, agricultural product processing, transportation, and trade. If a rural laborer chose to work in non-farming field for a long time, he or she would change the status from a farmer to a non-farm worker, businessman, or others. Third, each rural worker had the right to move or migrate from one place to another, for example, from a rural to an urban area or from an inland to a coastal area. The right of rural laborers to move was one of the crucially necessary conditions for industrialization in developing countries. Fourth, the rural laborer had the right to own, accumulate, and invest his or her money and treasures, or material property. Along with the land reform and the growth of farming and non-farming works, rural laborers had more and more income and wealth. The government did not levy high taxes on the rural income but encouraged farmers to own and save more and more by the legislation and policy, which gave favorable terms on interest and loans to farmers who made deposits in the agricultural societies, the farming banks, and so on.

After successful land reform, the start of its industrialization process, and some years of peace and stability, Taiwan introduced a new monetary system and initiated interest rates, foreign exchange, and trade control. In the late 1950s, a major priority of the government program was aimed at developing Taiwan's own electricity, fertilizer, and textile industries to replace the exports from America. The government took advantage of the enterprise tradition, the large amount of increasing funding and monetary capital from mainland China, the skilled and professional workers withdrawn from the mainland to Taiwan with Chiang Kai-shek, and the high level of market demand to push ahead with the Taiwanese economy by a clear and official definition of the rights of private capital. The government adopted policies to support private enterprises and industries, which included the establishments of the "Productivity Center" and "Industry of Hand-Made Goods Promotion Center" in order to provide professional training, guidance on production techniques, product designs, and so forth. The growth rate of the gross domestic product reached 12 percent in 1952. In 1953, the Taiwanese government implemented its First Four-Year Economic Plan. Governor Chen Cheng's economic policies focused on agricultural development and guaranteed food supply for Taiwan with surplus. In the mid-1950s, Taiwan exported rice, sugar, and tea to Japan worth more than $100 million a year. It became the most important revenue for the Taiwanese economic recovery. About 90 percent of Taiwanese exports were agricultural produce by 1959.

Realizing Taiwan's small domestic market, Taiwan's government adopted a second policy of "export promotion" in the late 1950s, which continued throughout the 1960s. Governor Chen Cheng established several "Export Manufacturing Zones" around the major cities like Kaohsiung, attracting foreign investments from America and Japan; offering manufacturing jobs to surplus laborers in rural areas; and also sharing new technology with Taiwanese light industries like textile, papermaking, and food processing. From 1961 to 1964, Taiwanese exports averaged a growth rate of 31 percent per year. Its economic growth rate rose steadily and in 1964 reached double-digit figures, 12.6 percent, for the first time since 1951.[48] Soon Taiwan secured an international reputation as an exporter to the world.

In 1964, U.S. aid to Taiwan stopped; almost simultaneously, Taiwan's economy took off. Starting from the Fourth Four-Year Economic Plan in 1965, Taiwan began its first economic plan without U.S. economic aid. In 1966, the share of heavy industry in total industrial output reached 52 percent, exceeding that of light industry for the first time. By 1968, the output of the manufacturing industry hit 24 percent, for the first time exceeding the share of agriculture (about 22 percent).[49] At the same time, Taiwan's economy had been increasingly dependent on United States and Japan. Its share of exports to the United States reached 26 percent, and its share to Japan was 18 percent in 1967. It also set off a continuous trade surplus with United States in 1968. Over the next two decades, Taiwan enjoyed the world's fastest-growing economy. A decade and a half of successful Nationalist rule after 1949 had made Taiwan more prosperous than it had ever been.

In the 1960s, successful industrial development attracted foreign investments, especially those from America and Japan, to Taiwan's newly established manufacturing, mining, papermaking, and food-processing industries. In 1966, the government created many "Manufacturing Industrial Zones" around the major cities to support the foreign-owned factories and businesses. The government also carried out policies of privatization of the state-owned enterprises, set up the uniform taxing ratios to private and public firms, and reduced the entry barriers to the industries that were previously controlled by governments to encourage fair competition. In this way, the government replaced the entry permits of some industries, such as rubber, matches, soap, light bulbs, and wheat flour industries, with uniform standards of quality and operation evaluations. The government also made an effort to establish a good business environment for private firms, such as building some public enterprises to produce the products or services that the private firms were not willing or able to provide, carrying out the construction of infrastructure, and reducing the very high rate of inflation to levels of around 10 percent. Through all

of the aforementioned measures by the government, the responsibili-
ties and rights of the private capital were clearly defined and the right
of profits was especially defined and protected.

In the urban sector of Taiwan, laborers also obtained almost full
definition of the rights of labor property. During the period of industrialization in Taiwan during the 1960s–1980s, unlike some other developing economies (like South Korea) with more and more laborers
absorbed into large enterprises, the laborers who worked in large
enterprises occupied a minority of all urban laborers. They were
usually protected by the regular operation and government regulations to large enterprises in Taiwan. Their rights of labor property
were embodied in the normal wages and salaries payment, working
conditions, and fair treatment in daily work, which were provided
by the large enterprises, most of them with public ownerships. On
the other hand, nearly 70 percent of the urban employment took
place in private mid- and small firms that were characteristics of a
traditional family economy as mentioned earlier. The government
took responsibility to protect the legal and reasonable rights of the
common employees or self-employed workers, but the rights of the
laborers were also protected to a certain extent by traditional business practices.

EDUCATION REFORM

Economic development fostered governmental and social reforms,
including political openness, cultural revitalization, and educational
reforms. Taiwan began to create a more efficient government. President Chiang Kai-shek and his KMT Party made moves to rid the
government and ruling party of corruption and incompetence.[50] The
Taiwanese people gradually learned to play by the rules of the authority. After the central government moved to Taiwan and the Communists' takeover of the mainland, Chinese traditional culture began to
be revitalized in Taiwan. Intellectuals, scholars, and educators advocated to "inherit Chinese culture critically and develop it creatively."[51]

With an active role by the central government, compulsory education
was extended from six to nine years (six-year elementary and three-
year junior high school) in 1968. For the economic development of labor-intensive industries, junior vocational schools were terminated and
senior vocational schools were fully supported by the government. In
the 1970s, to meet the urgent need for manpower, many two-year junior colleges or five-year technical ones were established. With the transformation of the economic structure from labor-intensive industries to

capital- and technology-intensive ones, public four-year technical institutes were set up to meet the higher-level need for manpower. Now, the school system in Taiwan is six years for primary school, followed by three years of junior high school. Afterward, three years of senior high school, vocational schools, or five-year technical schools are the choices available for students. Postsecondary education includes three years of junior college or, usually, four years of college/university with the exception of departments such as dental and medical science, which take six and seven years, respectively.[52]

Private schools also were developed and provided education to 28.65 percent and 69.46 percent, respectively, of senior high and college students in 1955 and 1968.[53] The government supported private school development and issued the "Program for the Development of Junior High School Education." Along this line, the provincial and metropolitan governments also supported vocational schools, technician learning centers, and re-educational programs sponsored by private sector.

The political climate of centralization in the past was reflected in the unified Curricular Standard in secondary and primary education. The Ministry of Education supervised the National Institute of Compilation and Translation, which compiled, edited, reviewed, and adopted all the textbooks, supplementary readings, and instructional materials for all the public schools of nine-year compulsory education. Many of the educational textbooks served KMT political agenda and promoted governmental policies and programs with emphases on loyalty to the party, anti-Communism, and national interests. All the students in middle schools, high schools, and colleges received political education and military training to prepare them for active service. All the male citizens in Taiwan according to the regulations had to serve at least two years in the military when they were eighteen years old. The KMT also established party branches in all the public schools and appointed party branch directors as the school administrators. Most public school teachers were the members of the KMT. They recruited new GMD members from high school seniors and college undergraduate and graduate students.

In conclusion, the Truman administration was confident—in the global Cold War in general and on the Taiwan Strait in particular—that the horror of another massive conflict could be contained and avoided, and that the United States and its allies could preserve the balance of power based on the status quo. After Truman's idealistic policy toward the Chinese Civil War failed in 1949, his new policy toward Taiwan became realistic after the summer of 1950. The Truman administration made a strong commitment to the security and safety of Chiang Kai-shek's government. President Truman put his faith in the development and future of the Taiwanese economy and society. He recognized the strategic and political importance of Taiwan in the U.S. containment policy in Asia. Carrying on Truman's Taiwan policy, President Eisenhower renewed and legalized the U.S. commitment by signing the Mutual Defense Treaty with Taibei in 1954. In the meantime, China began to move into the central stage of the global Cold War between the Soviet Union and the United States. Thereafter, the U.S. Taiwan policy continued without major changes until 1972, when President Richard Nixon adopted a rapprochement toward China. Both China and Taiwan have survived the Chinese Civil War and the global Cold War without a major showdown in the Taiwan Strait.

NOTES

1. Dennis Van Vranken Hickey, "U.S. Arms Sales to Taiwan: Institutionalized Ambiguity," *Asian Survey* 26, no. 12 (1986), 1324.

2. A retired KMT army general met with the author and other scholars at Rongzong [Glory's General] Hospital in Taipei, Taiwan, on May 26, 1994.

3. Nancy Bernkopt Tucker, *Strait Talk: United States-Taiwan Relations and the Crisis with China* (Cambridge, MA: Harvard University Press, 2009), 13.

4. Xiaobing Li, "Truman and Taiwan: A U.S. Policy Change from Face to Faith," in *Northeast Asia and the Legacy of Harry S. Truman: Japan, China, and the Two Koreas*, ed. James I. Matray (Kirksville, MO: Truman State University, 2012), 127–28.

5. David M. Finkelstein, *Washington's Taiwan Dilemma, 1949-1950: From Abandonment to Salvation* (Fairfax, VA: George Mason University Press, 1993), 332–33.

6. Chief General Hau Pei-stun, interviews by the author in Taipei, Taiwan, during May 23–24, 1994. Hao served as the commander of the KMT front artillery force on Jinmen Island in 1950.

7. General Douglas MacArthur's words are quoted in General Matthew B. Ridgway, *The Korean War* (Garden City, NY: Doubleday, 1967), 37.

8. A retired KMT army grand general met with the author and other scholars in Taipei, Taiwan, during May 23–24, 1994. He felt released when he was informed of the U.S. Seventh Fleet's patrol in the Taiwan Strait in June 1950. See also Xiao Jin'guang, *Xiao Jin'guang huiyilu* [Memoirs of Xiao Jin'guang] (Beijing: Jiefangjun chubanshe [PLA Press], 1988), 2: 26.

9. Major General Xu Yan (PLA), *Mao Zedong yu kangmei yuanchao zhanzheng* [Mao Zedong and the war to resist the U.S. and aid Korea], 2nd edition (Beijing: Jiefangjun chubanshe [PLA Press], 2006), 59.

10. After he received Roshchin's telegram to Moscow, Stalin confirmed the Chinese leaders' concerns of a possible UNF invasion of North Korea. In his telegram to Zhou Enlai on July 5, 1950, Stalin agreed: "We consider it correct to concentrate immediately nine Chinese divisions on the Chinese-Korean border for volunteer actions in North Korea in case the enemy crosses the 38th parallel. We will try to provide air cover for these units." "Filippov (Stalin) to Chinese Foreign Minister Zhou Enlai (via Soviet ambassador to the PRC N. V. Roshchin)," Ciphered telegram No. 3172, *Archives of the President of the Russian Federation* (hereafter *APRF*), Fond 45, Opis 1, Delo 331, List 79, in "New Russian Documents on the Korean War," Kathryn Weathersby trans. and ed., in Woodrow Wilson International Center for Scholars (Washington, DC), *Bulletin: Cold War International History Project* 6–7 (Winter 1995/1996): 43.

11. Grand General Hau Pei-stun, interviews by the author in Taipei, Taiwan, during May 23–24, 1994.

12. Vice Admiral Arthur D. Struble, "The Commander of the Seventh Fleet to the Commander of Naval Forces, Far East, February 27, 1951," U.S. Department of State, *FRUS, China, 1951*, 7: 1509.

13. U.S. Department of State, *FRUS*, 6: 414.

14. Major General William C. Chase (U.S. Army) arrived in Taiwan on May 1, 1951, to establish JUSMAAG-China. For more details, see Finkelstein, *Washington's Taiwan Dilemma*, 336.

15. MacArthur's words are quoted in Ridgway, *The Korean War*, 37–38.

16. Truman to the secretary of state, February 16, 1951; Truman to the secretary of defense, February 16, 1951; and "Memorandum for the President, February 16, 1951," in Mutual Defense File, *Papers of Harry S. Truman*, Box 26, Truman Library, Spring Field, Missouri.

17. Truman to the secretary of state, May 4, 1951; Truman to the secretary of defense, May 4, 1951; and "Memorandum for the President: Request for Allocation of Mutual Defense Assistance [MDA] Funds to Provide Additional Military Assistance to Formosa, May 3, 1951," in Mutual Defense File, Folder 4, Confidential File, ibid.

18. U.S. Department of State, *FRUS, 1951*, 6: 37–38.

19. Karl Lott Rankin, *China Assignment* (Seattle: University of Washington, 1964), 174.

20. Chen Jian and Xiaobing Li, "China and the End of the Global Cold War," in *The Cold War: From Détente to the Soviet Collapse*, ed. Malcolm Muir, Jr. (Lexington: Virginia Military Institute Press, 2006), 121.

21. Chen Shichang, *Zhanhuo 70 nian Taiwan shi* [Post-war Taiwan in 70 years] (Taipei: Shibao wenhua, 2015), 103.

22. Wang Yufeng, *Taiwan shi* [History of Taiwan], 3rd edition (Taizhong, Taiwan: Haodu chuban [How-Do Publishing], 2017), 156.

23. Gao Mingshi, *Taiwan shi* [History of Taiwan], 2nd edition (Taipei: Wunan tushu, 2015), 274.

24. Chen, *Zhanhuo 70 nian Taiwan shi* [Post-war Taiwan in 70 years], 100.

25. Qi Guang-yu, *The Development of Constitutionalism for the ROC: The Constitutional Evolution since 1949* (Taipei: Yangzhi Cultural Publishing, 1998), 4–28.

26. Linda Chao and Ramon H. Myers, *The First Chinese Democracy: Political Life in the Republic of China on Taiwan* (Baltimore, DE: John Hopkins University Press, 1998), 17, 122.

27. Wang, *Taiwan shi* [History of Taiwan], 157.

28. John F. Copper, *Taiwan: Nation-State or Province?* 4th edition (Boulder, CO: Westview, 2003), 47.

29. For example, Mao, "Where Is the Nanjing Government Going?" and "Address to the Preparatory Meeting of the New Political Consultative Conference," in *Mao Zedong xuanji* [Selected works of Mao Zedong] (Beijing: Renmin chubanshe [People's Press], 1991), 4: 1447, 1465–66.

30. Dong Fanghe, *Zhang Aiping zhuan* [Biography of Zhang Aiping] (Beijing: Renmin chubanshe [People's Press], 2000), 2: 664–65; Xiaobing Li, "PLA Attacks and Amphibious Operations during the Taiwan Strait Crises of 1954–1955 and 1958," in *Chinese Warfighting; the PLA Experience since 1949*, eds. Mark A. Ryan, David M. Finkelstein, and Michael A. McDevitt (New York: M. E. Sharpe, 2003), 148.

31. KMT and CIA officers on the scene were surprised by the timing of the artillery shelling. See CIA, "Report on the Chinese Offshore Islands Situation, September 9, 1954," CIA Official File, 50318-Formosa (1), box 9, International Series, *Dwight D. Eisenhower Papers*. Eisenhower Library, Abilene, Kansas.

32. Ma Guansan, deputy commander of the ZFC naval force, "Remember the Combat Years in the East China Sea," in *Sunjun huige zhan donghai* [Three services wield weapons in East China Sea combat], eds. Nie Fengzhi et al. (Beijing: Jiefangjun chubanshe [PLA Press], 1985), 29.

33. Dong Fanghe, *Zhang Aiping zhuan* [Biography of Zhang Aiping], 2: 674–75; Han Huaizhi, *Dangdai Zhongguo jundui de junshi gongzuo* [Military affairs of Contemporary China] (Beijing: Zhongguo shehui kexue chubanshe [China's Social Science Press], 1989), 1: 216–17.

34. A retired KMT army general met with the author and other scholars at Rongzong Hospital in Taipei, Taiwan, on May 26, 1994.

35. Thomas J. Christensen, *Useful Adversaries: Grand Strategy, Domestic Mobilization, and Sino-American Conflict, 1947–1958* (Princeton, NJ: Princeton University Press, 1996), 60, 194.

36. Di Jiu and Ke Feng, *Chaozhang chaoluo; guogong jiaozhu Taiwan haixia jishi* [Record of the CCP-GMD confrontation in the Taiwan Strait] (Beijing: Zhongguo gongshang chubanshe [China Industrial and Commercial Publishing, 1996], 210–12.

37. In February 1955, the Seventh Fleet deployed aircraft carriers, cruisers, and up to forty destroyers, to cover the evacuation of the Dachens. *New York Times*, January 25 and February 7, 1955.

38. "Memorandum of Discussion at the 232nd Meeting of the National Security Council, January 20, 1955," in *FRUS, 1955–1957*, 2: 70–71.

39. Xinhua News Agency, *China's Foreign Relations: A Chronology of Events, 1949–1988* (Beijing: Foreign Languages Press, 1989), 525.

40. Grand General Hau Pei-stun, interview by the author in Taibei, Taiwan, in May 1994. Hau served as the garrison commander in Jinmen from 1957 to 1960. Then, he became the chief staff of the GMD army and the defense minister of the ROC in the 1970s and 1980s. He retired from the military and served as the ROC premier from 1990 to 1993.

41. Wang Dinglie, *Dongdai Zhongguo kongjun* [Contemporary Chinese Air Force] (Beijing: Zhongguo shehui kexue chubanshe [China's Social Sciences Press], 1989), 345; History Compilation and Translation Bureau, ROC Defense Ministry, *8–23 Paozhan shengli 30 zhounian jinian wenji* [Recollection for the 30th anniversary of the victorious August 23 Artillery Battle] (Taipei: Guofangbu yinzhichang [Defense Ministry Printing Office], 1989), 33–34.

42. Mao, "Some Viewpoints about International Situation," speech at the Fifteenth Meeting of the Supreme State Council, September 8, 1958, in *Mao Zedong waijiao wenxuan* [Selected diplomatic papers of Mao Zedong] (Beijing: Zhongyang wenxian chubanshe [CCP Central Archival Manuscript Press], 1994), 348–52.

43. Shen Weiping, *8–23 Paoji Jinmen* [8–23 Bombardment of Jinmen] (Beijing: Huayi chubanshe [Huayi Publishers], 1999), 2: 842; History Compilation and Translation Bureau, ROC Defense Ministry, *8/23 Paozhan shengli* [Victorious 8–23 Artillery Battle], 30, 34.

44. Peng, "The Order of the PRC Defense Ministry," drafted by Mao, *Mao Zedong junshi wenxun: neibuben* [Selected military works of Mao Zedong] (Beijing: Jiefangjun zhanshi [PLA Soldiers' Press], 1981), 1: 368–69.

45. Zuohong Pan, "Democracy and Economic Growth: A Taiwan Case Study," in Xiaobing Li and Zuohong Pan, eds., *Taiwan in the Twenty-First Century* (New York: University of America Press, 2003), 144.

46. U.S. Department of State, *FRUS, 1951*, 6: 37–38.

47. For more details about the financial and economic aid, see Air Pouch 181, October 14, 1954, 794a, 5-MSP/1054, RG, *U.S. State Department Files*, Record Group 59, National Archives, College Park, Maryland.

48. Pan, "Democracy and Economic Growth: A Taiwan Case Study," 146.

49. Copper, *Taiwan: Nation-State or Province?* 48.

50. Linda Chao and Ramon H. Myers, *The First Chinese Democracy: Political Life in the Republic of China on Taiwan* (Baltimore, DE: The Johns Hopkins University Press, 1998), introduction.

51. W. S. Fu, *Critical Heritage and Creative Development* (Taipei: Dongda Publishing, 1991), 21, 152–53.

52. C. Yu and H. L. Pan, "Educational Reforms with Their Impacts on School Effectiveness and School Improvement in Taiwan," *School Effectiveness and School Improvement* 10, no. 1 (March 1999), 72–86.

53. C. Y. Chu and C. H. Yeh, "Taiwan's Private Education," *Chinese Education and Society* 28, no. 4 (July/August 1995), 66–97.

9

Aftershock: Reform and Transformation, 1972–1995

The 1970s were a time when Taiwan experienced big diplomatic and political turmoil. In February 1972, President Richard Nixon met Mao Zedong in Beijing as the first U.S. leader who had ever visited Communist China since it was founded in 1949. Nixon's visit caused a political earthquake in East Asia among the U.S. alliances.[1] Although Taipei was fully aware of Washington's policy change in East Asia during the late years of the Vietnam War, Chiang Kai-shek and his government had not yet figured out a workable alternative to avoid diplomatic disasters. By that time, Taiwan had been replaced by the People's Republic of China (PRC) in the United Nations in 1971. Then its diplomatic relations with Japan and the United States were terminated in 1972 and 1978, respectively. In 1979, Deng Xiaoping (Deng Hsiaoping, 1904–1997), China's new leader after Mao, visited the United States and met President Jimmy Carter as the first Chinese Communist leader who had ever visited Washington. The Taiwan Relations Act of 1979 passed by Congress pledged the United States to "resist any resort to force," but left open just what action the United States might

actually take.[2] The government of the Republic of China (ROC) had a
strong impression that the U.S. was leaving Taiwan as well as getting
out of East Asia. There was even a fear among Chiang Kai-shek's regime that the United States might use Taiwan as a bargaining chip for
a Sino-American rapprochement.

Nevertheless, tremendous changes in Taiwan's political regime
began in the late 1970s and continued until the early 1990s. Its political
reform and democratization were influenced by forces that included
U.S. policy change and international pressure. The process of political changes can be divided into two broad phases in 1988. The years
of 1978–1988 were a period of authoritarian government, decorated
with an element of limited democracy. Lifting martial law (emergency
decree) in 1988 initiated a new stage of transition to democracy, which
also went through several substages of its own thereafter. Constitutional reform was a very important part of Taiwan's democratization
during 1989–1996. The constitution that was passed in the late 1940s
never had a chance to establish its authority because of the Chinese
Civil War between the Nationalists and Communists as well as the
martial law enforced by the Kuomintang (KMT) government in the
following decades. However, with the waves of reforms since the
late 1980s, great efforts have been made to restore the long-ignored
constitutional authority, and it has become scholars' consensus that
Taiwan is making great strides toward a democratic society. The democratization process in Taiwan promoted its economic growth. With
limited natural resources and a short history of scientific and technological development, economic takeoff took place in the 1970s and
completed in Taiwan after thirty to forty years of independence from
the colonialists.

NIXON SHOCK AND THE TAIWAN RELATIONS ACT

In the early 1970s, President Nixon and his national security advisor
Henry Kissinger initiated a new U.S. foreign policy, détente, to replace
the containment policy of the previous decades, which had involved
the United States in the Vietnam War since 1965. Consequently, Washington's China policy also changed dramatically and sought to extend
rapprochement with Beijing. The immediate purpose for Washington's Sino-U.S. rapprochement was to stop China's aid and assistance
to North Vietnam to end the unpopular war in Vietnam and to unite
with China in the two countries' confrontation with Soviet Union.
For the United States, Taiwan was much less important in that bigger
game of international politics. All of this paved the way for Nixon's
historic visit to China in February 1972.

The Shanghai Communiqué, issued during Nixon's visit to the PRC, signaled a major shift in America's policy toward Taiwan. The United States officially abandoned its long-standing position that Taiwan's regime was the legitimate government of the Chinese people. In addition, the United States reserved the right to provide Taiwan with the arms necessary to defend itself against any aggression by the PRC. The United States attempted to deter China from attacking Taiwan with its insistence on a peaceful reunification. The United States never spelled out what actions it would take in the event that China began hostilities against Taiwan. The diplomatic wording in the communiqué allowed the United States to keep a military presence in the Taiwan region and to use military force to respond to any military action taken against Taiwan.[3]

After Mao died in 1976, Deng Xiaoping became the new Chinese Communist Party (CCP) leader and changed the direction of China by ending Mao's revolution and emphasizing the four modernizations of industry, agriculture, national defense, and science and technology.[4] In 1978, he launched an unprecedented seismic reform and an opening to the outside world to bring the "four modernizations" to China. Deng pursued a new relationship with the United States, paying the first ever PRC state visit to that country and meeting with President Carter. Both attended a special ceremony where the U.S. government officially recognized the PRC and established a diplomatic relationship with China on January 1, 1979.

At that moment, Washington ended its diplomatic relations with Taipei and recognized Beijing as the only legitimate government of China, though the United States continued to support Taiwan through the Taiwan Relations Act of 1979, which replaced the U.S.-Taiwan Mutual Security Treaty.[5] Washington's official China policy and its new position on the Taiwan issue included: first, the United States recognized that the PRC was the only legitimate government of China. The United States acknowledged the position held by both sides of the Taiwan Strait that there was one China and Taiwan was part of it. However, the United States tacitly did not acknowledge that the mainland had sovereignty over Taiwan.[6] Second, the United States continued to maintain unofficial cultural and economic relations with the people of Taiwan. Third, after the United States and China established official diplomatic relations, a special legislation—the Taiwan Relations Act of the U.S. of 1979—was adopted to conduct unofficial relations with Taiwan. The key point of this legislation was that it mandated the executive branch to provide Taiwan with its self-defense needs, and to consult Congress in case Taiwan's security was endangered. Beijing strongly opposed the Taiwan Relations Act in that it violated Chinese sovereignty over Taiwan. On August 17,

In 1979, Deng Xiaoping, China's new leader after Mao, met President Jimmy Carter as the first Chinese Communist leader who had ever visited Washington when
the two countries normalized their diplomatic relations. Meanwhile, Congress
passed the Taiwanese Relations Act, which pledged the United States to "resist
any resort to force." (National Archives)

1982, Beijing and Washington reached a new agreement on the Taiwan issue, in which Washington promised to gradually reduce its
arms sales to Taiwan in both quality and quantity as the tension in the
Taiwan Strait was diminished. On the other hand, the Reagan administration privately promised Taiwanese authorities that the United
States would not set a time to stop selling arms to Taiwan.[7] Fourth,
the United States would accept any peaceful solution between the
two sides of the Taiwan Strait.[8]

   Since 1979, Deng Xiaoping had gradually adopted a "peaceful reunification" and "one country, two systems" policy to settle the Taiwan issue. First, Beijing appealed to the Taiwan authorities to reunify
the nation peacefully. Beijing proposed that the two sides should have
santong (three links, i.e., commercial, postal, and travel) and *siliu* (four
exchanges, i.e., academic, cultural, economic, and athletic) as the first
step to "gradually eliminate antagonism between the two sides and
increase mutual understanding."[9] In the 1980s, Deng put forth his
"one country two systems" formula for the Hong Kong, Macao, and
Taiwan questions. According to the formula, Taiwan, as a special administrative region after reunification of China, would enjoy a high

degree of autonomy. Taiwan's current social and economic systems would remain unchanged. Taiwan would maintain its current administrative, legislative, and judiciary power and some powers in foreign affairs. In particular, Taiwan would maintain its own armed forces.[10] In 1989, Deng retired from his position of the Central Military Commission chairman of the CCP.

After Deng's retirement, Jiang Zemin became the top CCP leader of the new generation from 1989 to 2002. Jiang continued Deng's "one country two systems" policy. On July 1, 1997, Britain returned Hong Kong to China and the Jiang government established an autonomic government of the Special Administrative Region (SAR) of Hong Kong. In December 1999, Portugal returned Macao to China, and Beijing established the SAR government of Macao. In the 1990s, President Jiang Zemin made more concessions to Taiwan in support of reunification. He suggested that the two sides could talk on any topic, including national anthems, the national flag, and the name of the nation after reunification under the one-China principle, which is the bottom line of a peaceful reunification.[11]

CHIANG CHING-KUO AND THE *FORMOSA* INCIDENT

Although Taipei was caught off guard in 1971 when Washington suddenly announced Nixon's plan to visit Beijing in February 1972, President Chiang Kai-shek quickly made several responses, including making his son Chiang Ching-kuo chairman of the Executive Yuan as the state executive chief or the premier in 1972. Thereafter, Chiang Kai-shek began to pass political power to Chiang Ching-kuo since his health dramatically declined after an earlier car accident. Taiwan began a new period as the "Chiang Ching-kuo Era" (1978–1989).[12] As the founder of the ROC government on Taiwan in 1949, Chiang Kai-shek died on April 5, 1975, after he served five terms as the ROC president on Taiwan (1949–1975).

After Chiang's death, his vice president Yen Chia-kan (Yan Jiagan, 1905–1993) became interim president from 1975 to 1978 to complete Chiang's fifth term of the presidency (1972–1978) according to the 1947 Constitution of the ROC. In fact, Chiang Ching-kuo had political power of the KMT and controlled the administration since he had been premier as the chairman of the Executive Yuan since 1972. Young Chiang had a quite different political background from other KMT leaders.

Chiang Ching-kuo was born at Fenghua, Zhejiang Province on April 27, 1910, the first son of Chiang Kai-shek. In 1925, his father

Chiang Kai-shek sent Ching-kuo to the Soviet Union for his higher education at the Yat-sen University in Moscow, where he joined the Russian Communist Party (*Bolshevik*). In April 1927, Chiang Kai-shek terminated the KMT-CCP coalition by purging CCP members, raiding the Soviet Embassy compound in Beijing, and dismissing all 140 Soviet military and political advisors from their posts in the KMT army and ROC government.[13] In retaliation, Moscow expelled Chiang Ching-kuo from the university and sent him to Siberia to serve in the Russian army. A retired KMT army general told the author that the Russians held his brother as a hostage for more than ten years as punishment for his father's anti-Soviet and anti-Communist policy.[14] After Chiang Ching-kuo issued a public statement to denounce his father's betrayal of the revolution and criticize his anti-Soviet policy, he was allowed to leave Siberia in 1928 and worked at the Ural Heavy Machinery Plant, Urals, Yekaterinburg. During his working years, he married a factory worker Faina Vakherevich on March 15, 1935. Eventually, after Chiang Kai-shek established the KMT-CCP coalition for the second time against the Japanese invasion of China in January 1937, Josef Stalin allowed Chiang Ching-kuo to leave the Soviet Union in April with his Russian wife and a two-year-old son.[15]

After his return to China, Chiang Ching-kuo was appointed county commissioner in Jiangxi (Kiang-shi) Province in 1938. Then, he served as commander of the district security force, regional air defense command, and regiment command from 1939 to 1945 during the Anti-Japanese War. Among his major contributions to Chiang regime's survival of the war was his leadership role in the KMT youth corps (*Sanqing Tuan*), which had mobilized hundreds of thousands of young men to join the KMT army during the war.

Facing the economic difficulties after the war ended in 1945, Chiang Kai-shek began his economic reform in 1947, including an anti-corruption policy in 1948. Pressure also came from the U.S. government, which continued to support the Chiang regime after World War II. Chiang Ching-kuo and several leading generals urged Chiang Kai-shek with a crackdown on corruption and the misuse of public funds. The reform policy was finally announced on August 19, 1948, with a new currency, the Gold Yuan (*Jinyuanjuan*). Chiang Ching-kuo was sent to Shanghai, the financial and economic center of China as well as the main battleground against corruption and mismanagement in the KMT. Westad describes, "The young Jiang went to his new task with determination and substantial public support. More than most GMD leaders, Jingguo realized that the campaign which he was at the helm of might be his party's last chance to stabilize the political and economic situation before the military showdown with the CCP."[16] Chiang Ching-kuo struck hard on the corruption in Shanghai by putting more than 3,000 officials and businessmen in jail within two weeks. Some of those in prison were Shanghai's best-known Chinese businessmen, who were called the "big tigers."[17] Among others were Green Gang leader Du Yuesheng's own son, charged with black-market stock exchange trading. Chiang Ching-kuo also organized paramilitary forces to raid warehouses and suspects' homes, placed "Secret-report boxes" in the streets, and issued new laws and regulations. They had contributed significantly to the dissatisfaction of local people with the regime and the mobilization of opposition groups.

Although Chiang Ching-kuo's "Great Tiger Hunt" (*Dahu*) was successful in controlling prices against inflation, solving corruption cases against political protection and cover-ups, and slowing down public complaints against the government, his anti-corruption efforts did not stimulate the economy and could not last long in Shanghai. In September, after only four or five weeks of the anti-corruption movement, the shelves of shops became empty since the retailers could sell goods eight or even ten times higher in the surrounding provinces and other cities. The manufacturing factories were closed because the owners could not keep up with the cost of production when they had to purchase the raw materials at high prices from other regions. By October 1948, Chiang Ching-kuo's anti-corruption movement was over.[18]

Following his father to Taiwan in 1949, Chiang Ching-kuo served as the director of the KMT Taiwan Provincial Committee, the General Department of Political Tasks of the ROC Defense Ministry, and vice minister of defense. From 1965 to 1969, Chiang Ching-kuo served as the defense minister of Taiwan. Thereafter, he served as the vice premier of the Executive Yuan. In 1972, he became the premier or the chairman of the Executive Yuan.

After Chiang Kai-shek died in 1975, Interim President Yen Chia-kan (1975–1978) supported Chiang Ching-kuo's executive decision making and prepared young Chiang for the presidency. On May 20, 1978, Chiang Ching-kuo became the president of the ROC and served the sixth (1978–1984) and seventh (1984–1990) terms until he died on January 13, 1988.[19]

The KMT government under Chiang Ching-kuo's new leadership initiated a democratic breakthrough, replacing martial law with new laws and promised political reform. These remarkable events resulted in the legalization of political opposition and the lifting of martial law. Faced with new crises through the mid-1980s, Chiang Ching-kuo instructed the KMT to study political reform. Even before martial law was lifted, the opposing political forces illegally established a political party, the Democratic Progressive Party (DPP), in 1986 after the *Formosa Incident* (or Kaohsiung Incident) in 1979.

After Chiang Ching-kuo took over office in 1978, Taiwan began opening up to liberal ideas and public opinion that differed from the KMT propaganda of the past twenty-nine years. In August 1979, a new monthly journal *Formosa* was published in Kaohsiung discussing Taiwan's issues and consciousness, which had been banned during the Chiang Kai-shek era. Among its founders were Huang Shin-chieh (Huang Xinjie), Chang Chun-hung (Zhang Junhong), Chen Chu, Lin Yi-hsiung (Lin Yixing), and several other liberal intellectuals. *Formosa* (*Taiwan, or Meilidao*, the Beautiful Island) soon became a popular journal and had more than 100,000 subscriptions within a few months across Taiwan.[20] The journal editorial board planned a human rights memorial public rally at a city park on December 10, 1979, the "International Human Rights Day." After the Kaohsiung government rejected their application for the event, they decided to hold the public assembly as a protesting demonstration on that day. In the afternoon, armed police and soldiers clashed with tens of thousands of the protestors in the city streets. After the clash, all of the leaders, journal editors, and other activists were arrested, including Huang Shin-chieh, a member of the Legislative Yuan.[21] This became known as the "*Formosa* (or Kaohsiung) Incident."

The incident became a starting point for a new Taiwanese movement from 1979 to 1986 when the journal editors and protesting leaders faced charges in the court. Their defendants, their families, defense lawyers, and supporters became the first organized participants in this movement, including Chen Shui-bian, then a defense lawyer for Huang Shin-chieh and later the Taiwanese president.[22] In 1980, the eight most prominent leaders of the "*Formosa* Incident" (or the "Kaohsiung Eight") were sentenced to jail from twelve years to life imprisonment, including Annette Lu, later the vice president of Taiwan. On August 28, 1986, over 130 leading opposition dissents gathered in Taipei and founded the DPP, the first publicly established opposition party in Taiwan since 1949.[23] The KMT authorities did not take any repressive actions. The opposing party's political skill and Chiang Ching-kuo's wise and enlightened political leadership both contributed to resolution of the crises without bloodshed.[24]

THE END OF MARTIAL LAW

On July 15, 1987, the ruling Nationalist (KMT) Party decided to officially lift martial law (or emergency decree) and the ban on new political parties the following year, thus starting to move away from authoritarian rule toward democracy. Many factors caused this change of policy. One of the factors is the fact that the elections that had been going on for years even during the martial law era. In reality, local elections had never stopped in Taiwan since 1946 after the ROC government took the island back from Japan. Elections to choose representatives for their village, city, county, and provincial governments were an important part of Taiwan people's lives.[25] Since their retreat from mainland China, the KMT leaders also allowed many elections on different local levels even when martial law was in effect. This laid the foundation for future democratic reform. During the same time, Taiwan's economy began to take off, bringing about wealth for the whole society. Along with this economic prosperity came the political consciousness of Taiwan's people as citizens of the country—they started demanding more participation in political life. Different interest groups began to form, but there were conflicts between them and they had to take more active roles in defending their own interests. That explains why more and more people were involved in political activities.

International development, to a great extent, also helped to push Taiwan toward democracy. After the United States formalized its relationship with mainland China in 1979, the pro-Taiwan force in the American Congress passed the Taiwan Relations Act to counter balance the shock to Taiwan.[26] But even this friendly act showed signs of Americans' unhappiness about the lack of civil rights under Taiwan's ongoing martial law. Though there was no direct criticism, everybody could see that the United States hoped Taiwan would improve its image in front of the world. Foreign Minister Mark Chen (Chen Tang-shan) told the author that during the 1970s, many Taiwanese students in the United States began to organize overseas democratic societies and published political journals against the authoritarian government of Taiwan. He became one of the dissent student leaders when he studied at the University of Oklahoma for his MS and Purdue University for his PhD.[27] After his return, Chen was appointed foreign minister of the ROC during 2004–2006 and secretary-general of the President Office under Chen Shui-bian during 2007–2008. The democratic reforms that were going on in the neighboring countries, such as in South Korea and the Philippines, also put heavy pressure on the Taiwan leaders to move away from authoritarian rule. Mainland China's policy experienced some changes too. The earlier slogan "We must liberate Taiwan!" has given its place to "peaceful unification" (though military action has never been excluded) since late 1970s. The tense military confrontation across the Taiwan Strait began to "thaw," giving Taiwan's government more room to consider lifting martial law.

However, the most important force behind Taiwanese leaders' decision to lift martial law was the fast development of Taiwan's political opposition forces. During the martial law era, these opposition groups had gained more and more strength through local elections, not only getting more votes but also moving into more offices. Apparently, political diversification was taking shape. The famous "Zhongli Incident" on November 19, 1977, was a good example of the increasing strength of the opposition groups and their determination to challenge the government.[28] After this serious challenge to government authority, opposition forces began to see their ranks expanding quickly and their activities covering more areas. At the same time, government policy began to soften. Though martial law was still in effect, the government allowed the publication of many political journals and most of the street demonstrations. Although new political parties were still illegal, many political entities were functioning. Many of these so-called *Tangwai* (or *Dangwai*, non-KMT) people worked together and strongly challenged the KMT in the 1980 election.[29] The opposition politicians cooperated and criticized the ruling party in a manner that people in Taiwan had never experienced. In September 1986, they even officially declared the birth of a new party, DPP. This development definitely forced the ruling KMT government to think about lifting martial law and putting political liberalization into effect. Without the challenge from new political forces, the KMT might not have moved to change its policy in a hurry. Nobody should deny the role the DPP played in this change of policy.

At the same time, Chiang Ching-kuo also promoted native-Taiwanese KMT members to some key positions in the regime with the intention of diversifying Taiwan's leadership image and easing societal tension accumulated from the long-term and high-handed KMT rule.[30] Among the others were Lee Teng-hui, a Taiwan-born local official who was hand-picked by Chiang and promoted to the KMT Party Center as vice president and then Chiang's successor. Chiang Ching-kuo announced in December 1985 that the next president would not come from the Chiang family. However, Chiang's original intention of doing reforms was not to enliven the pro-independence movement or split the KMT, but mainly to boost the declining legitimacy of the KMT and make Taiwanese society more open and humane under "soft authoritarianism."[31] Therefore, when Chiang legalized the DPP's existence as an oppositional party, some expected that Chiang might wish to follow the models of Japan or Mexico to implement an electoral contest system, but with the KMT as an unchallengeable party to rule.

That does not mean, however, the KMT leaders' determination to change Taiwan's political scene played a junior role. Many scholars agree that the KMT leaders were the true motivating force behind the political reforms in Taiwan. For example, the KMT leaders were already talking about lifting martial law and the ban on political parties even before the DPP was born. After the DPP's establishment, the KMT government did not take any action to crack down the new political enemy. Instead, the government leaders tried to establish communication with the DPP, which was still not legal at the time. On October 15, 1986, the Central Committee of the KMT, under the leadership of Chiang Ching-kuo, passed two important resolutions. The new National Security Act and a modified Civil Organization Act ended martial law and the ban on new political parties, though they still required the newly registered political parties "to follow the Constitution, fight against communism, and not to pursue Taiwan independence." In late June 1987, the Legislative Yuan officially announced the end of martial law, and the Executive Yuan, at the same time, also announced the end of more than thirty executive orders that had something to do with martial law. By then, some scholars argued, Taiwan indeed moved into "a truly transitional 'twilight zone' that is neither authoritarianism nor democracy," an important step toward constitutional government.[32]

Nonetheless, this policy change has proved to be critical in pushing Taiwan into quick transition to a pluralistic society, but also opening the window for political mobilization of Taiwanization by allowing the DPP to run for office. There were two unintended consequences of Chiang Ching-kuo's political reforms. One is the emergence of a strong contending party, the DPP, with a pro-independence stance, and the other the fragmentation of the KMT party machinery. The DPP, in its early form, was a loosely organized political oppositional group called the "*Tangwai* (Non-KMT) Movement."[33] The lifting of the ban in 1986 made it possible for the movement to form the DPP to challenge the domination of the KMT. However, the DPP's indigenization movement had never been so popular until this movement came to converge with pro-indigenization factions inside the KMT headed by Lee Teng-Hui. Together, they effectively acted upon the ideal of Taiwanization. In this sense, Taiwan's democratization has been complicated by the Taiwanization movement seeking independence since its beginning.

With martial law officially lifted on July 15, 1987, Chiang Ching-kuo made his final monumental contribution to Taiwan's democracy before his death in January 1988. With the ending of the one-party system and martial law, Taiwan thereafter entered a phase in which

Lee Teng-hui, Chiang Ching-kuo's successor, initiated a series of lib-
eralizing reforms that contributed to Taiwan's final transition to a real
democracy.[34]

LEE AS THE FIRST TAIWANESE PRESIDENT

Lee Teng-hui was born into a police officer's family in a village of
Taipei County, Taiwan, on January 15, 1923. During the Japanese colonial period, he had to adopt a Japanese name Iwasato Masao. His
older brother served in the imperial Japanese army and was killed
in the Philippines. During his college years, Lee Teng-hui was also
enlisted in the Japanese army, and his artillery unit was deployed in
Japan until the war ended in August 1945. After his return to Taiwan
in 1946, Teng-hui enrolled in the National Taiwan University (NTU)
and majored in agricultural science.[35]

After his graduation in 1948, Lee taught at NTU as assistant instruc-
tor. In 1951, he was awarded a foundation scholarship and was able to
go to America to study agricultural economics at Iowa State University. After he received his master's degree in 1953, Lee returned to his
teaching at NTU as a lecturer. He also worked as an official in the Bureau of Agriculture and Forestry of the Taiwan Provincial Government.
In 1957, Lee Teng-hui was promoted to professor in the Department of
Economics at the National Taiwan University. In the meantime, he also
worked as an economist with the Joint Commission on Rural Reconstruction (JCRR). During the "White Terror" of Chiang Kai-shek, Lee
Teng-hui was under investigation for his connection and participation
in the CCP movement.[36] In 1960, Lee was arrested by the Investigation
Bureau. After being jailed for four months, he was released without
any charge. In 1961, Lee was baptized in Taiwan.

In 1965, Lee was awarded a full scholarship from the Rockefeller
Foundation and came back to America to study at Cornell University
for his doctoral degree. In 1968, he received his PhD in agricultural
economics from Cornell University, and his award-winning disserta-
tion, *Inter-Sectoral Capital Flows in the Economic Development of Taiwan,
1895–1960*, was published by the Cornell University Press in 1971.
After his return from America in 1969, Dr. Lee continued his jobs as
a professor at NTU and section chief at JCRR. In August 1971, Lee
Teng-hui was introduced to Chiang Ching-kuo, then vice chairman
of the Executive Yuan. Chiang recognized Lee's potential and asked
him to join the KMT. In October, Dr. Lee became a party member of
the KMT.[37]

In 1972, Chiang Ching-kuo, now chairman of the Executive Yuan, appointed Lee Teng-hui as a political commissioner, the youngest among all the ministry-level officials, responsible for agriculture. In November 1976, Lee became a member of the KMT Central Committee. In 1978, he was appointed as mayor of Taipei. In December 1979, Lee Teng-hui became one of the top leaders when he was appointed by Chiang as a member of the Standing Committee of the KMT Central Committee. Lee became the governor of Taiwan Province in 1981 and vice president, next to Chiang Ching-kuo, in 1984.[38]

On January 13, 1988, Lee Teng-hui became the interim president (1988–1990) of Taiwan on the same day that Chiang Ching-kuo died. After defeating political opposition from both the "Palace Faction," or the KMT old-guards from the mainland, and the Chiang family members and loyalists, Lee called for the Thirteenth National Congress of the KMT in July 1988, and he was elected the chairman of the KMT.[39] At the national congress, Lee appointed sixteen Taiwanese into the Central Committee, more than one half of the committee members. He began to reduce the authoritarian power of the KMT under Chiang's regime during 1949–1988. He did the same to the Executive Yuan, replacing the elderly KMT bureaucrats with younger Taiwanese technocrats with advanced degrees from America and Europe just like himself to serve as ministers and committee chairs in the administration. He shifted the political power from the mainlanders to the grassroots elected officials in Taiwan.[40] After he completed the seventh term (1986–1990) of the Chiang Ching-kuo's presidency, he continued to serve the eighth term (1991–1995) and the ninth term (1996–2000) as the president. Among his major political achievements during his twelve years of presidency was his constitutional reform, including a direct general election of the president and reducing each term of the presidency from six to four years.

THE CONSTITUTIONAL REFORM

With political support from Interim President Lee Teng-hui, during 1989–1991, the National Assembly, which increased its legislative power by amending the constitution to elect the president and vice president, was subjected to its first genuine popular election on Taiwan. In March 1990, the National Assembly called its Eighth Session. At the meeting, some deputies proposed increasing funds for the meeting, making the Assembly meeting an annual event, restoring its power to initiate and review constitutional amendments, and prolonging deputies' terms from six years to nine years. Such a move made many people unhappy. To them, it seemed the deputies were increasing their own power at will, though many of them were never popularly elected in Taiwan. In the meantime, students from Taipei's universities and colleges started a peaceful demonstration in front of the Chiang Kai-shek Memorial Hall, calling for the Assembly to disband, to end the "Temporary Provisions," and to schedule a "National Affairs Conference" for Taiwan's democratic reform. By March 21, 1990, about 6,000 students started a hunger strike to force the government to take quick action. This largest student movement in twentieth-century Taiwan put huge pressure on the government.[41] The next day, the ruling KMT government backed down. President Lee Teng-hui met with the student leaders and agreed on calling the National Affairs Conference to schedule democratic reform, among the students' cheers. The same day, Lee also announced the decision nationwide. Immediately after that, the ruling KMT consulted the DPP and other political organizations and interest groups. By the end of April, the preparation for the conference was well under way, and on June 26, the conference officially raised its curtain in Taipei, signaling a very important beginning of Taiwan's political reform.[42]

Representatives from the ruling KMT, the DPP, non-partisan groups, and academics attended the conference. The discussion at the meeting followed, generally speaking, two guiding lines: amplifying constitutional rule and unifying the country. It, however, also covered many subtopics such as reform in the National Assembly, local government functions, central government system, means of constitutional reform, and policies regarding cross-strait relations. Heated debates indeed brought about quite a few consensuses. The most important ones included the constitutional reform, the end of "the Period of National Mobilization for Suppression of the Communist Rebellion," and the repeal of the "Temporary Provisions," to be carried out by a representative part of the government. Following the conclusion of the conference, the ruling KMT quickly put together a planning team for constitutional reform (July 11), with Vice President Lee Yuan-tsu (Li Yuansu) as its leader, making sure the reform remained under the leadership of the ruling party. With great effort, the team put forward a whole set of reform topics, including issues on the National Assembly, the Control Yuan, the election of president and vice president, the relationship between the Legislative Yuan and the Executive Yuan, the ways the constitution was to be amended, and the end of the Temporary Provision. These plans would lay the basic foundation for future constitutional reforms.

The National Assembly started the first phase of constitutional reform in early April 1991. But soon after the meeting convened, the DPP representatives suddenly decided that the amendments presented by the KMT's Constitutional Reform Task Force could not represent the DPP's major ideas. They threatened to give up their earlier position of negotiation and called for a large-scale mass demonstration. The threat worked. The ruling KMT had to hold an overnight discussion session with the DPP representatives, who were able to force their ideas into the KMT amendments. The National Security Council, the Bureau of National Security, and Bureau of Executive Personnel would see a "sunset" procedure, putting the three agencies' future in the hand of the second National Assembly by the end of 1993. By April 22, ten amendments had passed the Assembly ending the Temporary Provisions, and on April 30, President Lee Teng-hui officially announced the abolishment of the Temporary Provisions and the adoption of the ten new amendments to the constitution.

Immediately after the first phase of reform, the KMT determined to take the leadership role in the process and set up its task force for the second phase of constitutional reform. By the end of 1991, the KMT won a landslide victory in the election for the National Assembly, gaining 318 seats out of 403. This gave the KMT the necessary overwhelming majority (3/4), making it possible for them to guide the next phase of reform. The opposition, especially the DPP, could only play a loud but junior role. On December 19, 1992, Taiwan's voters elected the entire Legislative Yuan for the first time in the history of Taiwan.

The second phase of reform increased the power of the National Assembly, which now had the authority to approve the presidential nominations to the Judicial Yuan, Examination Yuan, and the Control Yuan though the term of the Assembly deputies shrank from six years to four. The reform also changed the structure of presidential elections: Starting from 1996, the president and the vice president would be elected directly by voters, not the National Assembly any more. Although the presidential terms shrank from six to four years, the president now had more power. He or she could nominate more officials in the central government, including the vice president of the Judicial Yuan, Supreme Court justices, the vice president of the Examination Yuan and committee members, and the president of the Control Yuan and committee members. (Of course, he or she needs the approval from the National Assembly.) The reform also increased the difficulties to impeach the president and vice president; one-sixth of National Assembly's members could propose the impeachment, but simple majority would not work now. A two-thirds majority was necessary for any

impeachment procedure to move ahead. It also changed the organizations and the functions of the Examination Yuan, the Judicial Yuan,
and Control Yuan, along with changes regarding local governments.[43]

Obviously, many participants from different parties in the second
phase of constitutional reform ignored the important principle that
the constitution as the basic law of the land should not be subject to
frequent and drastic changes. They paid too much attention to their
own parties, or even their individual interests and refused to listen to
others. The issue of direct presidential election as the focus of debate
never got any consensus, and the DPP even withdrew from the meeting. So the National Assembly, generally speaking the KMT members
alone, could only set the general direction for direct election but never
touched the issue of how this could be done, thus leading to the 1995
third phase of constitutional reform.

The third revision of the ROC Constitution combined the eighteen
amendments proposed during the first two phases of reform and put
them into the new ten amendments. The contents of the ten amendments include: the creation of the positions of president and vice president in the National Assembly; adjustment of the National Assembly's
authority—the power to fill the vice president's vacancy if necessary;
the power to propose the impeachment of president and vice president; discuss and approve the proposed presidential impeachment
and vice president by the Control Yuan; the authority to amend the
constitution; the power to approve the constitutional revision proposals by the Legislative Yuan; the right of approval of a president's
nomination; the direct election of the president and vice president by
1996 (the ninth president). The impeachment of president and vice
president became more difficult. Not only more than one quarter of
the National Assembly members' petition and two-thirds majority ap-
provals are required, but the approval of more than half of the population is also a must.[44]

ECONOMIC AND SOCIAL CHANGES

From the 1970s to the 1990s, Taiwan experienced tremendous economic growth and urban development. Some of economists and
historians called them the "Taiwan Miracle."[45] During the Chiang Ching-kuo era, he accomplished the "Ten Major Construction Projects"
and "Twelve New Development Projects," including the creation of
the China Steel Corporation, Kaohsiung Super-Sized Ship Building
Yard, Petro-Chemical Park, Chong-shan (Yat-sen) Highway, Chong-
cheng (Chiang Kai-shek) International Airport, and nuclear power
plants. All of these major construction projects contributed to the

"Taiwan Miracle" and helped its economy during and after the Nixon Shock and Middle East Oil Crises in the 1970s. Chiang successfully transformed Taiwan's economic focus from export-oriented manufacturing to domestic needs-based productivity.

However, mainly pushed by its expanding exports, Taiwan's economy garnered four continuous years of double-digit growth rate through the 1970s. That growth was abruptly terminated by the first oil crisis in 1974. The huge oil import burden caused the economy's growth to drop to a creeping 1.2 percent. Looking at Taiwan's economic growth on average basis during the twenty years from the 1960s to the 1980s, it is a remarkable performance. From the mid-1960s, Taiwan entered industrialization period with a transformation from light manufacturing to heavy industries, including transportation, communication, construction, and energy industries. During the next two decades, Taiwan enjoyed an average annual growth rate nearly 10 percent. Through the 1970s, the leading industries included electronics, chemical fibers, equipment, and instrument.

In the 1980s, improvement of the relations between Taiwan and the mainland China promoted trade and investments across the Taiwan Strait. After Deng Xiaoping launched the economic reform in China in 1978, Beijing began to look for trade opportunities, new technology, and direct investment from Taiwan. In 1987, the Taiwanese government lifted martial law and allowed its citizens to travel to the Chinese mainland. In the meantime, China established special economic zones in the southern cities like Shenzhen and Zhuhai and offered favorable terms for direct investment and joint ventures of Taiwanese business, manufactures, and banks in China. Soon China became Taiwan's largest trading partner. Through the 1980s, the annual gross domestic product of Taiwan maintained around $100 billion, and its gross domestic product per capita reached $4,500 in 1988. In 1991, President Lee Teng-hui launched the "Six-Year Development Plan." His economic policy aimed to promote Taiwan into the top twenty nations in per capita income in the world. Taiwan's economic miracle contributed to further social and educational changes.

The total education budget of Taiwan increased from only 1.37 percent of the GNP in 1951 to 6.85 percent in 1997. There were 5.2 million students in schools of all types and levels, forming 23.89 percent of the total population in Taiwan. In other words, almost one-fifth of the population attended school. There were 6,628 schools, 183 schools per 1,000 square kilometers, and 195,742 teachers in 1987, and 7,562 schools, 209 schools per 1,000 square kilometers, and 251,768 teachers in 1997. In ten years, the number of schools increased by 14.1 percent, and the number of teachers increased by 28.6 percent.[46]

In 1983, the Taiwanese Ministry of Interiors established the Bureau of Professional Training, which issued the Act of Work Training in 1983 and the Act of Labor Standards. Both acts required the companies, institutes, and employers to provide on-the-job training, internships, workshops, and professional developments for their employees. The government also made more investments in the public education, vocational training, and higher education. In 1985, for example, the Taiwanese government invested 22.1 percent of its educational budget in its higher education, higher than China's 20.6 percent in the same year.

In 1997, Taiwan had 6,848 educational institutes with more than five million students. More schools were open for adult and continuing education, foreign languages studies, and college annual entry examination preparations. In 1997, the enrollment rate from middle school to high school was 92 percent, and from high school to college was 62 percent.[47] Through the twentieth century, more Taiwanese students came to America for high education and postgraduate studies with or without governmental sponsorship or educational scholarship. From 1953 to 1975, about 32,000 Taiwan students enrolled in American four-year colleges or graduate schools for their degree programs in these twenty-two years, about 1,500 students a year. After President Nixon visited Beijing in 1972 and the U.S. government normalized its relationship with China in 1979, the number of Taiwanese students who came to the United States to study continued to increase through the rest of the century. From 1975 to 1989, more than 84,000 Taiwanese students enrolled in their degree programs in the American universities and colleges in the fourteen years, about 6,000 students a year. Then, from 1990 to 2001, about 200,000 students went to America to study, about 20,000 Taiwanese students every year.

According to governmental statistics in 1997, in higher education there were seventy-eight universities and upper normal institutes with 420,000 students, and 231 colleges for continuing education with 509,000 students. In general education, there were 228 junior high schools with 291,000 students, 719 high schools with 1,074,500 students, 2,540 elementary schools with 1,905,700 students, and 2,770 preschools. In continuing education, there were 204 upper professional schools with 197,000 students, 61 middle schools of specialization with 433,800 students, 295 high schools, and 385 elementary schools. In special education, there were seventeen schools with 88,600 students. In adult education, there were 231 in-service training colleges and 27 distance-learning universities with 189,000 students. The number of students of which each teacher was in charge was decreased from twenty-seven in 1987 to twenty in 1997.

After an uncertain 1970s, Taiwan had developed into a more optimistic 1990s through the major changes in the 1980s, which became the turning point in the island's history. The political, economic, and social changes have set up a new stage and provided more space for Taiwan's reforms and transformation in the new century. Taiwan's transition seems both possible and inevitable because of a simultaneous end of the global Cold War and a coincident power transition through three leaderships in China.

NOTES

1. For more discussions from Chinese perspective, see Gong Li, *Kuayue honggou: 1969–1979 nian zhongmei guanxi de yanbian* [Bridging the chasm: The evolution of Sino-American relations, 1969–1979] (Zhengzhou: Henan renmin chubanshe [Henan People's Press], 1992), 106–8; Wang Taiping, ed., *Zhonghua renmin gongheguo waijiaoshi, 1970–1978* [Diplomatic history of the PRC, 1970–1978] (Beijing: Shijie zhishi chubanshe [World Knowledge Publishing], 1999), 345, 346–48.

2. Nancy Bernkopt Tucker, *Strait Talk: United States-Taiwan Relations and the Crisis with China* (Cambridge, MA: Harvard University Press, 2009), 118–19.

3. Wei-Chin Lee, "U.S. Arms Transfer Policy to Taiwan: From Carter to Clinton," *Journal of Contemporary China* 9, no. 23 (2000), 58.

4. Deng Xiaoping made a historic speech, "Emancipate the Mind, Seek Truth from Facts, and Unite as One in Looking to the Future," at the Third Plenary Session of the CCP Eleventh Party Central Committee in 1978, in *Selected Works of Deng Xiaoping, 1975–1982* (Beijing: Foreign Languages Press, 1995), 150–63.

5. The TRA provides the basis of U.S. policy regarding the security of Taiwan. According to this law, the United States should "provide Taiwan with arms of a defensive character; and [to] maintain the capacity of the United States to resist any resort to force or other forms of coercion that would jeopardize the security, or the social or economic system, of the people on Taiwan." For more details, please see Winston Lord, "The United States and the Security of Taiwan," *U.S. Department of State Dispatch 7*, no. 6 (February 5, 1996), 30.

6. In 1982, the Reagan government informed Congress of its six policy pledges toward the Taiwan issue. The last policy pledge was that the United States did not acknowledge China had sovereignty over Taiwan.

7. Tucker, *Strait Talk*, 121, 122.

8. See Michel Oksenberg, "Taiwan, Tibet, and Hong Kong in Sino-American Relations," in *Living with China: U.S.-China Relations in the Twenty-First Century*, ed. Ezra F. Vogel (New York: W.W. Norton, 1997), 53–96; Xingwei Hu, "The International Responses to and after the Military

Conflicts between the Taiwan Strait," in *The PLA Attacks Taiwan*, ed. Ping He (Mississauga, Canada: Mirror Books, 1995), 346–52.

9. The NPC Standing Committee, "Message to Compatriots in Taiwan," *Beijing Review* 22, no. 1 (January 5, 1979), 15–17.

10. According to Beijing, after reunification, Taiwan would enjoy more autonomous power than Hong Kong and Macao. For instance, Taiwan would maintain its armed forces, and leaders of Taiwan would hold important positions in the national government, such as vice president of the state.

11. Currently, both PRC and ROC have their own anthems and national flags. Beijing has asserted that Taiwan is a province of China and refused to recognize ROC as a sovereign government. But Taiwan's leaders have proclaimed, since the 1990s, that both ROC and PRC should be recognized by the international community and Taiwan should have a seat in the international organizations whose members are sovereign nations, such as the United Nations. Beijing rejected this position of Taiwan and successfully blocked Taiwan's effort to join the United Nations.

12. John F. Copper, *Taiwan: Nation-State or Province?* 4th edition (Boulder, CO: Westview, 2003), 53.

13. For more information on Jiang Jieshi's purge, see Xiaobing Li, *A History of the Modern Chinese Army* (Lexington: University Press of Kentucky, 2007), 42–44.

14. A retired KMT army general met with the author and other scholars at Rongzong [Glory's General] Hospital in Taipei, Taiwan, during May 25–27, 1994.

15. Chen Shichang, *Zhanhuo 70 nian Taiwan shi* [Post-war Taiwan in 70 years] (Taipei: Shibao wenhua, 2015), 100.

16. Odd Arne Westad, *Decisive Encounters: The Chinese Civil War, 1946-1950* (Stanford, CA: Stanford University Press, 2003), 184.

17. Wang Zhangling, *Jiang Jingguo Shanghai dahu ji: Shanghai jingji guanzhi shimo* [Jiang Jingguo's great tiger hunt in Shanghai: A full record of the Shanghai economic reform] (Taipei: Zhizhong chubanshe, 1999).

18. Chen, *Zhanhuo 70 nian Taiwan shi* [Post-war Taiwan in 70 years], 137–38.

19. Wang Yufeng, *Taiwan shi* [History of Taiwan], 3rd edition (Taizhong, Taiwan: Haodu chuban [How-Do Publishing], 2017), 194.

20. Chen, *Zhanhuo 70 nian Taiwan shi* [Post-war Taiwan in 70 years], 288.

21. Gao Mingshi, *Taiwan shi* [History of Taiwan], 2nd edition (Taipei: Wunan tushu, 2015), 280–281.

22. Chen, *Zhanhuo 70 nian Taiwan shi* [Post-war Taiwan in 70 years], 289.

23. Jonathan Manthorpe, *Forbidden Nation: A History of Taiwan* (New York: Palgrave Macmillan, 2005), 209.

24. Copper, *Taiwan: Nation-State or Province*, 53.

25. Qi Jialin, *Taiwan's New History* (Taipei: Intercontinental Press, 2000), 222–23.

26. Manthorpe, *Forbidden Nation*, 216–17.

27. Foreign Minister Mark Chen (Chen Tang-shan), interview by the author at the DPP Campaign Headquarters in Taipei, Taiwan, March 15, 2000. Chen received his MS from the University of Oklahoma in 1966.

28. Wang, *Taiwan shi* [History of Taiwan], 193.

29. "Dang Wai," literally translated as "outside the party," are those opposition politicians who used to run elections as independents and were tolerated by the government since the ruling KMT changed its policy toward the political competition in the 1960s. See Ge Yongguang, *Taiwan Stories: Politics* (Taipei: News Bureau of ROC Executive Yuan, 1998), 14.

30. Steven J. Hood, *The Kuomintang and the Democratization of Taiwan* (Boulder, CO: Westview Press, 1997), 31, 175.

31. Andrew Nathan and Helena Ho, "Chiang Ching-Kuo's Decision for Political Reform," in *Chiang Ching-kuo's Leadership in the Development of the Republic of China on Taiwan*, ed. Shao-chuan Leng (Lanham, MD: University Press of America, 1993), 62–91.

32. Harvey J. Feldman, ed., *Constitutional Reform and the Future of the Republic of China* (New York: M. E. Sharpe, 1991), 12. Also see Cooper, *Taiwan: Nation-State or Province*, 102–109.

33. Shelly Rigger, *From Opposition to Power: Taiwan's Democratic Progressive Party* (Boulder, CO: Lynne Rienner, 2001), 175–76, 201–3.

34. This new phase was broken into three stages in Linda Chao and Ramon H. Myers, *The First Chinese Democracy: Political Life in the Republic of China on Taiwan* (Baltimore, DE: The Johns Hopkins University Press, 1998).

35. Wang, *Taiwan shi* [History of Taiwan], 202.

36. Lee Teng-hui joined the Chinese Communist Party (CCP) in 1946 when he was a student at the National University of Taiwan. He participated in some of the organized students activities. But he left the CCP in 1947.

37. Manthorpe, *Forbidden Nation*, 28.

38. Wang, *Taiwan shi* [History of Taiwan], 202–3.

39. Copper, *Taiwan: Nation-State or Province*, 54.

40. Chen, *Zhanhuo 70 nian Taiwan shi* [Post-war Taiwan in 70 years], 257–58.

41. Gao, *Taiwan shi* [History of Taiwan], 283.

42. Qi, *The Development of Constitutionalism for the ROC*, 87–89.

43. Copper, *Taiwan: Nation-State or Province*, 88; Ge, *Taiwan Stories*, 46.

44. Ge, *Taiwan Stories*, 48.

45. Copper, *Taiwan: Nation-State or Province*, 55, 165–69.

46. Department of Education, Taiwan Provincial Government, *Educational Statistics in Taiwan Province, 1994* (Taipei: Taiwan Provincial Government Printing, 1996), 32–33.

47. ROC Ministry of Education, *Annual Educational Statistics in the Republic of China* (Taipei, Taiwan: Ministry of Education Publishing, 1997), 29–31.

10

Democratization and Independence Movement, 1996–2004

One of the most dramatic socio-political changes in East Asia at the end of the twentieth century was a full-scale democratic transition in Taiwan. Into the dawn of the twenty-first century, Taiwan appears to have an entirely new socio-political landscape characterized by contesting a multiparty system along with an effective mechanism of direct elections. The highlight of this transition was marked by the triumph of Democratic Progressive Party (DPP) in the 2000 presidential election that peacefully put to an end the rule of the Kuomintang (KMT) Nationalist Party over Taiwan in the past fifty years or so. At that time, a new bipartisan system had emerged with a lively participatory national political culture in Taiwan. Most evident was the surge of voter participation in county and city elections as basic patterns of political behavior were changing. The parties had taken shape the democratic process and reflected the growing society of a changing state.

After martial law was abolished in 1987, Taiwan ended its authoritarian period of thirty-eight years and entered a new era. The political changes and economic growth affected this society through the creation of new culture, new goals, and new opportunities. Now, a more democratic and open society prevailed. As a result of political democratization, the freedom of speech, political expression, the press, association, assembly, peaceful demonstration, and political dissent became normal and realistic in Taiwan. Mass media eventually got rid of government control and began to express different opinion, social concerns, and public interest. TV stations increased from previous three official networks to more than one hundred channels. The digital revolution had had a strong and positive impact on the public arena and civil society. As the Taiwanese people became better informed and connected, the impact of the digital transformation on the evolution of both democratic and civil rights had a strong influence on the flexibility of government policy in the context of this major social and political transition.[1]

The economic, social, and cultural changes brought about ideological liberation leading to the amendments of the constitution, free press, and free electoral system. It became a successful story about how an East Asian society built on traditional Confucian paradigm is receptive rather than resistant to Western-style democracy.

Nevertheless, Taiwan's democratization has obscured the dimension of the potential risk that Taiwanese may face down the road in the new century. This dimension of uncertainty manifests itself in the tendency that Taiwanization—an ethno-nationalistic movement toward independence—has been increasingly immersed with democratization. The symbiotic relation of the two reveals that democracy in Taiwan is not merely a process of institutional reforms toward political liberty, but more of a political mobilization toward seeking an international recognition of an independent sovereign state. This hybrid nature of politics makes Taiwan's democracy a complex subject that we cannot fully comprehend with reference to the checklist of democratic characteristics. The subject that deserves more research attention is not the legitimate ideal of democracy itself, but rather under what conditions democracy could work well to bring to people the peace and prosperity.

TAIWANIZATION AND ITS POLITICAL IMPACT

By most accounts, Taiwanization is an unintended consequence of political restructuring initiated by the KMT regime beginning in the mid-1980s. Many scholars have agreed that that was the time when Taiwan took the concrete steps toward democratization.[2] In 1986, the then Republic of China (ROC) president Chiang Ching-kuo, also the KMT chairman, decided to exterminate the long-imposed martial law and lifted the ban on oppositional parties. At the same time, Chiang Ching-kuo selected native-Taiwanese with the intention of diversifying Taiwan's leadership image.[3] His selection and promotion of Lee Teng-hui was one of the best examples.

With Lee Teng-hui succeeding Chiang in power in 1988, tension and conflict inside the KMT ruling circle intensified, often in dispute over issues more on Taiwanization than on democratization itself.[4] Lee's indigenization campaign inside the KMT by forming the clique of Taiwanese in the power center had a strong backlash from the so-called mainlanders who felt that they were increasingly alienated from Lee's policies. Factional conflict inside the KMT severely weakened party's solidarity while facilitating the growth of the DPP. The split within the KMT started in 1993 when a group of dissident KMT members favoring reunification with the mainland China quit the KMT and formed a new political party called New Party. By the end of the 1990s, internal conflict within the KMT became more intensified over the issue of *Feisheng* (elimination of Taiwan's provincial status). On the surface, it was meant to increase the island's administrative efficiency. Its real motive, as everyone privately acknowledges, was to redefine Taiwan's legal status to pave the way for Taiwan's eventual declaration of independent sovereignty vis-à-vis China. *Feisheng* directly triggered the resignation of the then Taiwan provincial governor James C. Y. Soong, who quit the KMT and, then with his followers, formed People's First Party (PFP).

Having been closely entwined, however, Taiwan's democratization is prone to the potential risk contained in Taiwanization. As John Markoff argues, any indigenization movements to purify national culture, though having powerful appeal, can easily connect themselves to political visions that are ferociously antidemocratic.[5] As we have noticed, early signs of ethnocentric-driven prejudice and discrimination revolving around the issue of identity have already shown up. For example, some old citizens with mainland background are called "Chinese pigs" and told "go home." If someone shows his or her pro-unification opinion, he or she would be accused of not loving Taiwan, a step short of denouncing him or her as a "traitor." The New Party, with its pro-unification stance, is often accused of deliberately destroying consensus in Taiwan to sabotage its future, and they have been labeled as "supporters of totalitarianism" because they obstructed democratic transition. Even the former Taiwan provincial governor James Soong felt the pressure of being non-Taiwanese. In his resignation statement, he sadly claims: "Chu-yu (the given name in Chinese) may not have been born here, but grew up eating Taiwanese rice, drinking Taiwanese water. . . . As its first (democratically elected) governor, how can I accept request to 'freeze' provincial status?"[6] His anger toward being labeled as non-Taiwanese is obvious in his tone.

The bigger risk posed by Taiwanization to sustainable democratization is that it touches upon the very sensitive issue of China's reunification. Taiwan's current political status is the outcome of China's Civil War half a century ago when the KMT lost the war and was forced to retreat to Taiwan. Yet until late 1980s, the KMT regime in Taiwan never openly gave up its goal of "taking back the mainland" and remained firm on one-China stance, even after it lost its permanent seat at the United Nations in the early 1970s. Similarly, unification with Taiwan has always been Beijing's top policy concern since Mao times. However, since the early 1990s, President Lee Teng-hui began to move away from one-China policy by emphasizing "two governments," "two reciprocal political entities," and "Taiwan is already a state with independent sovereignty." He also stated, "At the present stage, the Republic of China is on Taiwan and the People's Republic of China is on the mainland." Beijing believed that the Lee government had adopted a series of measures toward actual separation. In 1993, Lee Teng-hui began an effort to put Taiwan back into the United Nations.

After 1979, when the United States and the People's Republic of China (PRC) normalized their relationship, Beijing had established diplomatic relations with more than 170 countries in the world. All of them had to acknowledge the "One-China" policy and promise to handle their relations with Taiwan within the "One-China" framework. This one-China status adopted by both sides of the Taiwan Strait has also gained the long-term recognition of the United States since 1972 when Nixon visited China. This shared reality came to be challenged and shattered by the growing Taiwanization throughout the 1990s, and the trend has been reinforced since pro-independence DPP became the ruling party in 2000. Since 1979, the six-term U.S. government, from President Jimmy Carter to George W. Bush, had all pursued one-China policy. Consequently the U.S. decision makers treat the Taiwan issue based on the one-China framework. They acknowledge publicly that there is only one China and Taiwan is part of it. However, on the other hand, since China does not rule out using force to reunify Taiwan, this would not be in the interest of the U.S. side. To restrict China's using force to attack Taiwan, Washington passed the Taiwan Relations Act of 1979.

In terms of the Taiwan Relations Act, the United States plays the role of a guardian of Taiwan. In addition to the official policy, there are loud voices in the U.S. Congress, the media, and the academy regarding the China and Taiwan issue. They have argued for containing the rising China in the post–Cold War era.[7] Under the pressure of these forces, Washington seems to have deviated somewhat away from its one-China policy. In 1992, U.S. trade representative Carla Hill made a groundbreaking visit to Taiwan. She was the first cabinet-level U.S. official to travel to Taiwan since Washington and Beijing normalized their relations in 1979. At almost the same time President George Bush announced that the United States had made a deal to sell 150 F-16 fighter airplanes to Taiwan. This obviously violated the August 17, 1982, U.S.-China Joint Communiqué. In 1995, the Clinton administration even granted a visa to Taiwan's President Lee Teng-hui to visit his alma mater Cornell University, which resulted in the 1996 Taiwan Strait Crisis.[8]

THE MISSILE CRISIS: GAME CHANGE

Yet the fully mobilized pro-independence "Taiwanization" stirred a strong reaction from mainland China and reached its climax in the 1996 missile crisis across the strait. The tension also mounted in the Taiwan Strait and led to the "Third Taiwan Strait Crisis" during 1995–1996. The crisis began when President Lee Teng-hui made a trip to Cornell University in the United States in June 1995. Jiang Zemin in Beijing had tried to isolate Taiwan and oppose a U.S. State Department's approval for Lee's visit. General Chi Haotian, China's defense minister, convinced Jiang that a show of force was necessary to condemn the United States for ruining Sino-American relations.[9] From July 21 to 26, the People's Liberation Army (PLA) conducted its first missile test in an area only thirty-six miles north of a ROC-held island. At the same time, the Central Military Commission (CMC) also concentrated a large force in Fujian. In mid-August, the PLA conducted another set of missile firings, accompanied by live ammunition exercises. The CMC also ordered the naval exercises in the same month. In the fall, the high command launched one wave after another of military exercises, including firing a joint amphibious landing exercise in November.[10] Even though there were military activities along the strait in the past, this was the first time in many years that they were announced publicly. Beijing's military aggression not only reversed what some observers had called a period of significant rapprochement across the Taiwan Strait but also created the most serious international crisis since Beijing and Taipei engaged in a military conflict over the islands of Jinmen and Mazu in the 1950s.

During the short period of crisis, cross-strait tensions rose drastically, as if war were imminent. Taibei was on high alert and declared that it had made all necessary preparations to deal with a possible invasion. To respond to the PLA activities, the United States sent its aircraft carrier, the *Nimitz*, to pass through the Taiwan Strait in December 1995. Between January and February, the PLA concentrated 100,000 troops along the coast across the strait from Taiwan in order to send a stronger signal to both Taibei and Washington. The tension mounted in the Taiwan Strait even though the Clinton administration and Pentagon believed that Beijing would not attack Taiwan and other offshore islands in the winter of 1995–1996.[11]

In March, the ROC was preparing its first presidential election in Taiwan since 1949, and Lee ran on the KMT ticket. Beijing intended to discourage the Taiwanese to vote for Lee because he had tried to separate Taiwan from China through the independence movement. Jiang again employed the military to threaten the Taiwanese voters. On March 8, the PLA conducted its third set of missile test by firing three M-9 surface-to-surface missiles just twelve miles off Taiwan's major seaport cities, Keelung and Kaohsiung.[12]

On March 8, the United States announced that it was deploying the *Independence* carrier battle group to international waters near Taiwan. To respond to the U.S. naval deployment, China announced more live-fire exercises to be conducted near Penghu during March 12–20, deploying 150,000 troops, 300 airplanes, guided missile destroyers, and submarines. On March 11, the United States deployed the *Nimitz* carrier battle group to the Taiwan area. The *Nimitz* steamed at high speed from the Persian Gulf to the Taiwan Strait to join *Independence* carrier battle group to monitor Chinese military actions. This was the largest U.S. naval movement in the Asia-Pacific region since the Vietnam War, and the first transit by U.S. warships in the area since 1976. China and the United States seemed at the brink of war again in the Taiwan Strait. By sending two carrier battle groups to the Taiwan Strait, the United States showed its readiness to fight over Taiwan.[13]

Fortunately, the Third Taiwan Strait Crisis did not evolve into a war between China and the United States when Lee Teng-hui was elected as Taiwan's president on March 23, 1996. Actually China's intimidation was counterproductive and aroused more anger than fear in Taiwan. According to the Taiwanese survey, China's missile test in March boosted Lee Teng-hui 5 percent in the polls, earning him a majority of the voters. The PLA offensive activities in the 1995–1996 Taiwan Strait Crisis also strengthened the argument for further U.S. arms sales to Taiwan and led to the strengthening of military ties between the United States and Japan.[14] Nonetheless, Robert Ross points out that Beijing and Washington tried to protect their strategic positions through the crisis, and both had reached their goals with certain strategic benefits.[15]

In the early 1990s, when the Soviet Union collapsed and the Cold War ended, the value of China as Washington's strategic partner in containing the Soviet Union disappeared. On the contrary, Washington was not happy to see that Beijing's Communist regime survived and that the fast-growing Chinese economy in the 1990s indicated that with its increasing economic and military power, China might be a potential rival of the United States.[16] Based on such perceptions, Taiwan seemed to be useful for U.S. containment of China. As a result, the United States dramatically increased, both in quality and in quantity, its arms sales to Taiwan.[17] The United States became, in fact, the major source of Taiwan's arms supply. As such, the United States has been an important

Taiwan's defense ministry spokesman Liou Chih-jein shows a map across the Taiwan Strait as the ministry releases satellite photos and data on the 1996 missile crisis, when China tried to influence Taiwan's first presidential election. (Sam Yeh/ AFP/Getty Images)

player in the Taiwan issue game. When Beijing appealed to the Taiwan authorities for a peaceful reunification referring to the Hong Kong
model, Taiwan's Lee Teng-hui regime discarded the one-China principle and sought for Taiwan's eventual independence from China.[18]

On March 23, 1996, the first national election for president and vice
president was successfully held. That election brought into office Lee
Teng-hui and Lien Chan (Lian Zhan) as president and premier, respectively. The election marked a culmination in the long path of Taiwan's
democratization process. The National Development Conference held
in December 1996 attracted more than 170 representatives from different political parties as well as scholars. This conference was the direct
result of Lee Teng-hui's call for such kind of meetings in his 1996 presidential inauguration. In the speech, he declared that "with people's
will in mind" he would push the government to invite representatives
from all around the society to "discuss major topics of national interests and reach consensus so that they can promote national development."[19] The direct impact of the meeting is the 1997 fourth revision of
the constitution.

Beijing continued to criticize Lee as "the general representative of
Taiwan's separatist forces, a saboteur of the stability of the Taiwan
Strait, a stumbling-block preventing the development of relations between China and the United States, and a troublemaker for the peace
and stability of the Asian-Pacific region."[20] However, after Lee Teng-
hui published his "two states" theory, the Chinese government still
believed the "compatriots in Taiwan" and remained in its previous
position "in adhering to 'peaceful reunification' and 'one country, two
system,'" because the cross-strait exchange and trade had developed
rapidly.[21] From 1988 to 1999, the Taiwanese who came to the mainland
for visiting their relatives, sightseeing, or exchanges totaled 16 million turnstile count. The total cross-strait trade volume had reached
$160 billion. And Taiwanese businesses had invested $44 billion in
China, the second-largest direct foreign investor in China only after
Japan. Beijing certainly did not want to slow down the much-needed
foreign investment and trade by any aggressive policy or military
action.

INDEPENDENCE MOVEMENT AND ITS ECONOMIC
AND SOCIAL IMPACTS

In 1999, President Lee Teng-hui surprised the world by announcing
that Taiwan and China have a "state-to state relationship." In May, he
published the book *The Road to Democracy*, which again emphasizes

Taiwan's full autonomy and independence. According to the president, the search for "national identity" was part of Taiwan's democratization. This Taiwanization emphasized shifting away from mainland Chinese affiliations to respecting local ethnic identity and culture, and constructing and honoring Taiwan as the new political and cultural identity of its people. Under the encouragement of Lee, pro-independence forces in Taiwan gained power dramatically. As a result, the pro-independence forces occupied a large number of public offices.

Taiwan's move toward independence may be constrained geoeconomically by its closer economic ties with mainland China. In the past two decades, Taiwan's economy has become more dependent on a vast market of the mainland. Taiwan's exports to mainland China has gained a huge trade surplus for Taiwan. In addition, Taiwanese businesses invested heavily in mainland China with a total of $ 60 billion by 2002, and $107 billion by 2012. There are now about 40,000 Taiwanese-owned businesses or joint ventures in the mainland. The ever stronger economic interdependence apparently is another major constraint on Taiwan's any radical move to independence. After the mainland's missile firing tests in 1996, public opinion poll in Taiwan indicated that those surveyed did not favor any provocative policies to worsen the relations with the mainland, and such public opinion remains consistent in the recent poll that shows that only fewer than 20 percent of the respondents agreed with the government's drastic step to challenge China by declaring "state-to-state" relations as essential to reunification negotiation.[22]

Although Taiwan is disfavored geopolitically on its road toward breaking away from China, it still holds a geo-positional edge in contending with China, and its potential power influence cannot be underestimated by any means. Taiwan's geopolitical edge, however, does not lie with its drive toward independence, but rather with its unique position as a de facto independent territorial entity in relation to China. First, unlike Hong Kong, Taiwan is not a colony to be negotiated between China and a third-party country, and it has its own military and still keeps official diplomatic relations with twenty-nine countries in the world. Second, Taiwan is one of the strong free-market economies in Asia, for it is not only highly modernized but also has an advanced industrial/manufacturing base, and its trading economy is the world's fourteenth largest. Third, perhaps the most important, the democratization, if not mingled with independence movement, would put Taiwan in a better position to negotiate with Beijing for its own future, and because of this status, Taiwan has more maneuvering space than Hong Kong on the international stage to dance with mainland

China over many issues of its own concerns. It would be hard to im-
agine that China could get away with the world condemnation if it
attacks Taiwan without any legitimate reasons to justify the war.

On the other hand, by engaging in negotiation with China over
reunification, Taiwan may be well positioned to join the democratic
force of change in Hong Kong Special Administrative Region (SAR)
to increase pressure on Beijing for a more open society. This becomes
possible because the two regions are not only in geographical prox-
imity but also have much in common now in democratic transition.
While the issue of Hong Kong has apparently made Beijing more flexible in mapping out its unification policy toward Taiwan, Hong Kong
SAR may further benefit from the issue of Taiwan to keep its own system less vulnerable to direct interference from Beijing. Together, the
two regions would likely play a critical role for the future political and
economic changes in mainland China.

As the president through the first general election in Taiwan in 1996,
Lee Teng-hui also tried to abolish the provincial government of Taiwan to complete the state independence. He utilized his native status
and broke through the political dominance of the KMT in Taiwan since
1950. His promotion of Taiwanization and independence movement
undermined the political base of the KMT in Taiwan during his tenure
in office.

A second milestone was set in Taiwan's political history in 2000
when the opposing party DPP successfully defeated the ruling party
KMT in the second national election for president and vice president.
For the first time the transition of political regimes and the power rota-
tion among political parties were completed in a peaceful manner. The
process of democratization in Taiwan is the result of many movements
whose impacts are still not clear to the researchers.

CHEN SHUI-BIAN AND HIS FIRST TERM

On March 18, 2000, history was made when Chen Shui-bian, the
presidential candidate of the opposition DPP of Taiwan, was elected
the tenth president of the ROC. It was the first time that the DPP, a
party with pro-Taiwan's independence from China in the party platform, had won the presidency. And it was also the first time the KMT
had lost its rule that had extended over the whole of China from 1927
to 1949 and the Taiwan region from 1949 to 2000.

Chen Shui-bian was born into a poor peasant family at Guantian,
Tainan County, on October 12, 1950. After graduated from high school
in 1969, he enrolled in the National Taiwan University (NTU) and

majored in business and administration. A year later, Chen rejoined in the Law Department at NTU. In 1974, he became an attorney after his graduation with a law degree from NTU and passed the bar exams.[23] He became involved in the politics after he took the case of the "*Neo-Formosa* Incident" (or Kaohsiung Incident) and defended one of the leaders of antigovernment movement in a military court in 1979. Although his client, Huang Xinjie (Huang Hsin-jieh), and other leading opposition dissidents were found guilty, Chen Shui-bian became popular among the Taiwanese who opposed Chiang's authoritarian regime and asked for political reforms.[24]

In 1981, Chen Shui-bian won his first election as a member in the Taipei City Council. In 1984, he served as the director of the *Neo-Formosa* magazine. After the founding of the DPP in 1986, Chen joined the DPP and soon was elected as a member of the Standing Committee of the DPP Central Committee.[25] In 1989, he won another election for a seat in the Legislative Yuan, and he won the reelection in 1992. During his years in the legislative branch, Chen served as the chairman of the National Defense Committee, drafting the "National Defense Organization Act" and visiting Beijing in July 1991.[26] He became well known as an opposition leader in the KMT-controlled Legislative Yuan, and was selected by *Newsweek Magazine* in the United States as one of the "influential people" in the world in July 1993.

Chen Shui-bian won the mayor election of Taipei in 1994. During his term, Chen launched a campaign against government corruption, illegal prostitution, and gambling in the capital city and gained popular support from the residents. He also set up new targets for the city reforms, including environmental protection, public health, and social works. As the DPP mayor, Chen targeted longtime KMT leaders' squatters on municipal land and ordered Chiang Ching-kuo's estate demolished.[27] All of the reform efforts had prepared him well for the general election in 2000 when he defeated the KMT presidential candidate and became the first non-KMT president in Taiwan since 1949.

The election of 2000 illustrated the new style of political cultural in Taiwan. Before 2000, Taiwan's politics was primarily the business of the political or the KMT elite. The 2000 presidential election started a mass participation in the national politics when the two parties organized themselves statewide. Both parties tried to remark their state politically and morally when Taiwan underwent a great economic and social change.

It should be no surprise that in the 2000 presidential election the KMT lost its ruling power to the DPP. The truth is that what really defeated the KMT was not the oppositional DPP, but its own split-up.

When KMT chairman and ROC president Lee Teng-hui arranged Lien Chan, his vice president, as the presidential candidate, many KMT party members were not happy since they believed more popular reformer James Soong (Song Chuyu) had a better chance to win the election against Chen Shui-bian.[28] Then, Soong left the KMT and organized a new party, the People First Party, to run as the independent, third-party candidate. As a result, James Soong received 36.8 percent of the votes (4.66 million votes), Lien Chan 23.1 percent votes (2.93 million votes), and Chen Shui-bian 39.3 percent votes (4.97 million votes).[29] Chen won the election by a small margin with less than 40 percent of votes because the KMT split. Many KMT members were angry over Lee Teng-hui and believed that he intentionally split the KMT to end the one party's control of Taiwan in fifty years. After the 2000 election, Lee was expelled from the KMT.

The DPP became the ruling party after 2000. However, polls showed that most people of Taiwan did not support either Taiwan's independence or immediate reunification under Beijing's terms of "one country, two systems." The residents in Taiwan knew that Taiwan's independence would result in a war with mainland China. But they were not ready to accept Taiwan's becoming a special administrative region of the PRC, even though China had promised to allow Taiwan to enjoy a high degree of autonomy including allowing Taiwan to retain its military force. Most of the residents in Taiwan favored maintaining the status quo and hoped to keep peace with the mainland, still, a small portion of the residents was for immediate unification, and yet another small percentage of the residents, including part of the DPP members, were in favor of independence.[30] The two major opposition political parties were the KMT and the newly established Pro-People Party. They opposed independence, even though they might disagree, in different degrees, with Beijing's terms of reunification. The two parties together won about 60 percent of the votes in Taiwan's 2000 presidential election. Unfortunately, due to the dispersion of the votes by the two party's candidates, they lost the vote to the pro-independent DPP candidate Chen Shui-bian.

During the campaign, Chen Shui-bian declared that Taiwan was not part of China and it had been an independent nation. After winning the election, Chen tried to moderate his position toward China. Though in his inaugural speech Chen did not proclaim the one-China principle as required by Beijing, he did announce that his government would not seek Taiwan's independence if Beijing would not use military force against Taiwan.[31] However, for Beijing, the one-China principle was the foundation for peaceful relations with Taiwan. Therefore Beijing continued to press Chen's government to accept the one-China principle. Beijing made it clear that China would use military force to defend its territorial integrity if the Taiwan authorities chose independence or if they refused indefinitely to discuss reunification.[32] The tension on the Taiwan Strait continued, and both China and Taiwan prepared for the likely coming war between them.[33]

The 2000 election was a watershed in Taiwan transitional politics. Since then, with the DPP in governing power, Taiwan's democratization had been openly manipulated to justify Taiwanization. After his victory of the 2000 presidential election, Chen Shui-bian was called the "Son of Taiwan." After taking over the office, President Chen began to purge the KMT office-holders from the government and replaced them with the DPP members. For instance, he appointed Tang Fei as the premier of the Executive Yuan in May 2000. Then, in October, Chen appointed Chang Chun-hsiung (Zhang Junxiong) as the new premier to organize the new DPP cabinet. When Chang resigned, Chen appointed another DPP leader Yu Shyi-kun (You Xikuan) as the new premier in January 2002 to keep the executive branch in the hands of the DPP.

Since 2000, Chen Shui-bian continued Lee Teng-hui's policy of independence. After he came to his office, his government refused to accept the one-China principle. Chen and some of his leading officials even refused to identify themselves as "Chinese." Under the pressure from Beijing and Taiwan's internal politics, Chen asserted that the possibility of one-China in the future should not be ruled out. However, the pursuit of Taiwan's independence continued to be the goal of Chen and the DPP. In 2001, Chen flew to Los Angeles, Houston, and New York City, as a first for the president from Taiwan to visit the United States. In 2002, his government began to take away the statues and images of Chiang Kai-shek and Chiang Ching-kuo from public buildings, schools, city centers, and parks. In 2003, Chen flew to New York City again and met Colin Powell, U.S. secretary of state. Then, the word "Taiwan" was printed on the new ROC passports. His approval rating reached around 70 percent.

Under the DPP regime, Taiwanization was set in full-speed motion aimed at severing all traditional ties with mainland China. Two unprecedented moves were (1) to revise the textbooks distinguishing Taiwanese culture from Chinese culture and (2) to define the identity of Taiwanese as genetically different from that of Chinese in the first place. Some extremists even started calling themselves Taiwanese instead of Chinese.

Beijing continued its policy goal on Taiwan issue, that was, to reunify with Taiwan peacefully for territorial integrity of the nation. In the *White Paper*, "The One-China Principle and the Taiwan Issue," issued by the Chinese government in March 2000, Beijing also reserved its right of using force as a last resort of settlement if necessary.[34] Reunification with Taiwan has always been the top goal in Beijing's agenda. The three key tasks of the country in the twenty-first century, proposed by the Beijing government in October 2000, are "to continue the modernization drive, fulfill national reunification with Taiwan, and maintain world peace and promote the development of all nations."[35] For Beijing, the Taiwan issue is related to China's sovereignty, territorial integrity, and national dignity. Beijing's Taiwan policy has been strongly supported by the Chinese people.[36] Since the 1990s, China's nationalism has reemerged and greatly influenced the Chinese people's view on the Taiwan issue.[37]

In addition, Beijing's leaders have important strategic reasons for reunifying with Taiwan because of Taiwan's economic power and its geographical location. As one of the "four Asian little dragons," Taiwan is important for mainland China's modernization. Taiwan's investment in the mainland and mainland-Taiwan-Hong Kong commercial trade are important factors in China's economic growth.[38] Geographically, Taiwan is located as front door of China. If Taiwan were controlled by a regime hostile to China or occupied by a foreign nation, China's "door" to the world would be sealed. A hostile nation that occupies Taiwan will use Taiwan to contain China. Currently, Beijing fears that the U.S.–Japan alliance may use Taiwan to contain the increasing growth of Chinese power. Therefore, Beijing will not allow Taiwan to be independent, and it will not tolerate Taiwan's being taken by any foreign nation.

During Chen's first term as the president from 2000 to 2004, Beijing encouraged Taiwanese residents to visit the mainland to increase mutual understanding. Beijing also encouraged commercial trade between the two sides and Taiwanese direct investment in the mainland. However, fearing the increasing economic exchanges between the mainland and Taiwan, Chen Shui-bian's Taipei government issued various policies to cool down the social and economic exchanges across the Taiwan Strait. But it is clear that Beijing also was prepared to resort to the use of force against Taiwan if necessary. To warn those who had advocated Taiwan's independence, Beijing stated, in the white paper "The One-China Principle and the Taiwan Issue," that mainland China may use military force if Taiwan declares independence, foreign forces were involved, or Taiwan refused indefinitely to hold talks on reunification.[39] This was the first time that Beijing has threatened to use force against Taiwan if Taiwan refused to hold talks on reunification. It has been seen that as Taiwan's social forces for independence have increased in strength, Beijing has begun to reexamine the "peaceful reunification" policy and to prepare for possible use of force as the alternative strategy to achieve its goal of reunification. Frequent military exercises targeted on Taiwan have demonstrated that Beijing has paid increasing attention to the means of military force.

NOTES

1. C. Yu and H. L. Pan, "Educational Reforms with Their Impacts on School Effectiveness and School Improvement in Taiwan," *School Effectiveness and School Improvement* 10 (no. 1, March 1999), 72–86.

2. Xiaobing Li, "Taiwan's Experience, Challenge, and Future," in *Taiwan in the Twenty-First Century*, eds. Xiaobing Li and Zuohong Pan (Lanham, MD: University Press of America, 2003), 3.

3. Steven J. Hood, *The Kuomintang and the Democratization of Taiwan* (Boulder, CO: Westview Press, 1997), 41–43.

4. Jaushieh J. Wu, *Taiwan's Democratization: Forces behind the New Momentum* (Hong Kong: Oxford University Press, 1995), 137–42.

5. John Markoff, *Waves of Democracy: Social Movement and Political Change* (Thousand Oaks, CA: Pine Forge Press, 1996), 29, 87, 186–89.

6. L. H. M. Ling and Chih-yu Shih, "Confucianism with a Liberal Face: The Meaning of Democratic Politics in Postcolonial Taiwan," *Review of Politics* 60 (no. 1, winter 1998), 28.

7. For instance, the Heritage Foundation published a series of pro-Taiwan and anti-China Papers. For example, Richard D. Fisher explained "why the Republic of China deserves steadfast American support." The reasons include, Fisher suggested, that "Taiwan is America's seventh largest trading partner"; Taiwan's "transition to full democracy reflects America's own commitment to democracy"; "Taiwan's democracy could have a positive influence on China." Stephen J. Yates, a pro-Taiwan scholar, finished a dozen papers on the Taiwan issue. His recent papers include "Why Taiwan's Security Needs to Be Enhanced" (October 25, 1999), "China's Taiwan White Paper Power Play" (February 29, 2000), "Taiwan: A Celebration of Democracy" (March 17, 2000), and "Better U.S. Treatment of Taiwan" (September 11, 2000). Yates appealed for Washington to reject Beijing's "one-China" policy. For the texts of these papers, see Heritage Foundation homepage.

8. In March 1996, in an effort to warn Taiwan not to continue its independence movement and the United States not to swerve from its "one-China" policy, the PRC fired two short-range ballistic missiles into splash zones within fifty miles of Kaohsiung, Taiwan's principal port, and two more within thirty miles of the second port, Keelung.

9. For more discussions on General Chi Haotian's hardline position, see John F. Copper, "The Origins of Conflict across the Taiwan Strait; The Problem of Differences in Perceptions"; You Ji, "Changing Leadership Consensus; the Domestic Context of War Game," in *Across the Taiwan*

Strait: Mainland China, Taiwan, and the 1995–1996 Crisis, ed. Suisheng Zhao (London: Routledge, 1999), 43, 91–93.

10. For a detailed overview of the 1995–1996 Taiwan Strait crisis, see Qimao Chen, "The Taiwan Strait Crisis: Causes, Scenarios, and Solutions," in *Across the Taiwan Strait: Mainland China, Taiwan, and the 1995–1996 Crisis*, ed. Suisheng Zhao (London: Routledge, 1999), 127–62.

11. William Perry and Ashton Carter, *Preventive Defense: A New Security for America* (Washington, DC: Brookings Institute, 1999), 92–93.

12. Patric Tyler, *A Great Wall: Six Presidents and China* (New York: Public Affairs, 1999), 33, 195.

13. William Perry, defense secretary, made a public statement on March 11, 1996, about the large U.S. naval maneuver near the Taiwan Strait. For Perry's statement, see *American Forces Press Service*, March 11; and the Department of Defense, *News Briefings*, March 12, 14, and 16, 1996.

14. Robert Ross, "The 1995–96 Taiwan Strait Confrontation: Coercion, Credibility, and the Use of Force," *International Security* 25, no.2 (Fall 2000), 120–23.

15. Ibid., 122.

16. See Richard Berntein and H. Ross Munro, *The Coming Conflict with China* (New York: Alfred A. Knopf, 1997); also, a large number of conservative politicians perceive China as a potential enemy of the United States, and their view can be found in the sensational *Cox Report*. See *U.S. National Security and Military/Commercial Concerns with the People's Republic of China*, Select Committee, U.S. House of Representatives, Christopher Cox, Chairman (the U.S. Government Printing Office, Washington, DC 1999).

17. Wei-Chin Lee, "U.S. Arms Transfer Policy to Taiwan: From Carter to Clinton," *Journal of Contemporary China* (Princeton University) 9, no. 23 (March 2000), 53–75.

18. China assumed sovereignty over the former British colony Hong Kong under the "one country, two systems" principle—after reunification with China, Hong Kong maintained its current capitalism while mainland China continued socialism; Hong Kong became a special region of China with high degree of autonomy.

19. Lee Teng-hui, *The Road to Democracy* (New York: Dell Publishing, 1999), 70–75, 91–94.

20. Taiwan Affairs Office and the Information Office, PRC State Council, "The One-China Principle and the Taiwan Issue, February 2000," in *White Papers of the Chinese Government, 2000–2001*, comp. Information Office, RRC State Council (Beijing: Foreign Languages Press, 2003), 29.

21. *Ibid.*, 31.

22. *Time Magazine*, July 26, 1999, 62–63.

23. Mark Magnier and Ting-I Tsai, "Taiwan's Chief under a Cloud," *Los Angeles Times*, June 23, 2006.

24. Chen, *Zhanhuo 70 nian Taiwan shi* [Post-war Taiwan in 70 years], 289.

25. Manthorpe, *Forbidden Nation*, 209.

26. Wang, *Taiwan shi* [History of Taiwan], 217.

27. General Chiang Wei-kuo, interview by the author at Rongzong [Glory's General] Hospital in Taipei, Taiwan, during May 25–27, 1994.

28. Jieli Li, "Democratic Transition in Taiwan: The Paradox of 'Taiwanization,'" in *Taiwan in the Twenty-First Century*, eds. Xiaobing Li and Zuohong Pan (Lanham, MD: University Press of America, 2003), 221.

29. Copper, *Taiwan: Nation-State or Province*, 59.

30. Taiwan's polls on questions such as relations with China, reunification, independence were always controversial. But consistently, the majority of Taiwan people have wished to maintain peace with the mainland.

31. Beijing's current one-China principle is defined as that there is only one China; both Taiwan and the Chinese mainland are part of Chinese territories; and Chinese territories are not allowed to split.

32. See the Taiwan Affairs Office and the Information Office of the State Council, People's Republic of China "The One-China Principle and the Taiwan Issue," *Beijing Review*, March 6, 2000, 16–24. This is Beijing's latest official position on the Taiwan issue. This paper provides the "three conditions" on which Beijing may use force on Taiwan "if a grave turn of events occurs leading to the separation of Taiwan from China in any name, or if Taiwan is invaded and occupied by foreign countries, or if the Taiwan authorities refuse, sine die, the peaceful settlement of cross-Straits reunification through negotiations, then the Chinese government will only be forced to adopt all drastic measures possible, including the use of force, to safeguard China's sovereignty and territorial integrity and fulfill the great course of reunification. The Chinese government and the people absolutely have the determination and ability to safeguard China's sovereignty and territorial integrity, and will never tolerate, condone or remain indifferent to the realization of any scheme to divide China. Any such scheme is doomed to failure."

33. Susan V. Lawrence, "Breathing Space," *Far Eastern Economic Review* (June 1, 2000), 16–17.

34. "The One-China Principle and the Taiwan Issue," *Beijing Review*, March 6, 2000. Beijing's official policy toward Taiwan is usually summarized as eight Chinese characters: *heping tongyi, yiguo liangzhi* [one country, two systems, and peaceful reunification].

35. Taiwan Affairs Office and the Information Office, PRC State Council, "The One-China Principle and the Taiwan Issue, February 2000," in *White Papers of the Chinese Government, 2000–2001*, comp. Information Office, RRC State Council (Beijing: Foreign Languages Press, 2003), 28.

36. Since 1995, a variety of polls conducted in China have shown that over 95 percent of the mainland Chinese supported using military force to solve the Taiwan issue if necessary. For an instance, a poll conducted in March 2000 showed that over 95 percent of the people preferred the use of force to settle the Taiwan issue. See *Jiefang Ribao* March 17, 2000 (electronic edition).

37. Regarding growing Chinese nationalism since the 1990s, see Song Qiang and others, *Zhongguo keyi shuo bu* [China can say no] (Beijing: Zhonghua gongshang lianhe chubanshe [China Industrial and Commercial Publishing], 1996); Fang Ning, Wang Xiaodong, and Song Qiang, *Quanqiuhua yinying xia de zhongguo zhilu* [China's road under the shadow of globalization] (Beijing: Zhongguo shehui kexue chubanshe [China Social Sciences Press], 1999); Han Deqiang, *Penzhuang: Quanqiuhua xianjing yu zhongguo xianshi xuanze* [The pitfall of globalization and a realistic choice for China] (Beijing: Jingji guanli chubanshe [Economics and Administration Publishing, 2000). For the best theoretical discussion of Chinese nationalism, see Suisheng Zhao, "Chinese Nationalism and Its International Orientation," *Political Science Quarterly* 115, no. 1 (Spring 2000), 1–33.

38. See Suisheng Zhao, "Economic Interdependence and Political Divergence," in *Across the Taiwan Strait: Mainland China, Taiwan, and the 1995–1996 Crisis*, ed. Suisheng Zhao (New York: Rutledge, 1999); Enbao Wang, "The Economic Relationship between Taiwan and Mainland China," in *The Asian Economic Crisis and Taiwan's Economy*, Baizhu Chen and Shaomin Huang (Beijing: Jinji chubanshe [Economics Press], 2000); David Shambaugh, *Greater China: The Next Superpower?* (New York: Oxford University Press, 1995). The Chinese worldwide believe that economic cooperation of the Greater China (the mainland, Hong Kong, Macao, and Taiwan) is the key for China's revival.

39. Beijing's white paper "The One-China Principle and the Taiwan Issue," *Beijing Review*, March 6, 2000, 16–24.

11

Taiwan in the New Century

Since the beginning of the new millennium, Taiwan has witnessed tremendous political, economic, and social changes, which seem quite different from its past experience. In the spring of 2000, a two-party system and bipartisan politics began. Tensions have mounted across the strait since President Chen Shui-bian was elected. The "miracle economy" ended in 2010, and Taiwan began an economic recession. Its gross domestic product (GDP) grew 10.7 percent in 2010, but its growth slowed down to 4 percent in 2011, and fell to 1.3 percent in 2012, when its GDP totaled $918.3 billion and per capita GDP was $39,400. Its export and natural resources became more dependent on China, its largest trading partner, with 27.1 percent of Taiwan's total exports in 2012, although their political differences and territorial conflicts continue.

Taiwan's presidential election in 2008 had once again put its future in the spotlight when the KMT returned to power with Ma Ying-jeou as its president from 2008 to 2016. Then, the Democratic Progressive Party (DPP) came back with Tsai Ing-wen's victory of the 2016 general election. Some scholars argue that few places in the world face a future "more fraught with uncertainty" than Taiwan in the 2010s.[1] Taiwan had reached a crossroad in its development and confronts some new challenges. Its new problems demand a re-assessment of the major issues and need more intellectual engagement. Scholars agree that Taiwan's future in the twenty-first century depends on its social and political transition from a traditional society to a modern, democratic society.[2]

Under the current DPP government, Taiwan's move toward independence may be constrained geo-economically by its closer economic ties with mainland China. In the past two decades, Taiwan's economy became more dependent on a vast market of the mainland. Taiwan's exports to mainland China has gained a huge trade surplus for Taiwan. In addition, Taiwanese businesses invested heavily in mainland China with a total of $68 billion by 2015, and also there were about 50,000 Taiwanese-owned businesses or joint ventures in the mainland in the mid-2010s. The ever stronger economic interdependence apparently present as another major constraint on Taiwan's any radical move to independence. In the meantime, however, Taiwan is still troubled by complex and sensitive issues from the past. Historical factors and present disputes appear to be mutually reinforcing. Currently, therefore, this traditional hotspot remains active, and the escalation of sovereign or maritime disputes has clear signs in the South China Sea and East China Sea, all posing new security challenges to Taiwan, China, and other East Asian countries. It is a region where historical unsettlement and current disagreement interweave.

CHEN'S SECOND TERM: ISSUES AND SCANDALS

In 2003, President Chen Shui-bian declared his intention to run for the reelection on the DPP ticket with Annette Lu (Lu Xiulian), one of the famous "Kaohsiung Eight" in the *Formosa* Incident, as his campaign partner in 2014. The KMT had learned a hard lesson in the 2000 election when the party split, and they lost the election to DPP. Therefore, the KMT, the People First Party (PFP), and several other opposition parties joined force under a political umbrella as the "Pan-Blue Coalition" against the DPP. (Blue is the color of the KMT.) To prevent splitting the vote, Lien Chen of the KMT ran for president and James Soong of the PFP ran as his partner for vice president. Although they had different agenda, the Pan-Blue Coalition as a conservative group emphasized traditional policy to maintain the status quo in the Taiwan Strait and a Chinese nationalist identity. In the meantime, the DPP and other associated parties came together as the "Pan-Green Coalition" and called for political reforms and social changes by supporting a stronger Taiwanization, or Taiwan localization, with Taiwanese identity. (Green is the color of the DPP.)[3]

During his campaign tour, Chen was shot when his motor parade went through the street of Tainan on March 19, 2004. Both President Chen Shui-bian and Vice President Lu Xiulian (Annette Lu) were slightly wounded. The 3/19 shooting actually increased Chen's popularity because of the public anger and sympathy. Nevertheless, the opponents suspected the shooting was staged by Chen's campaign one day before the election, even though the investigation committee did not find any evidence to prove the connection between the DPP and the shooter, who died a few days after the shooting.[4]

In the election of March 20, 2004, Chen Shui-bian won his reelection by a very narrow margin about 0.22 percent of the vote. Chen/Lu received 6.47 million votes while Lian/Soong 6.44 million votes. In his inauguration speech on May 20, Chen Shui-bian called for "believe Taiwan and continue the reform." During his second term (2004–2008), Chen continued his effort to promote Taiwanization, look for more international support and recognition, and push the independence movement forward. In 2004, for example, Chen pushed the Legislative Yuan to pass a referendum to demand the People's Liberation Army (PLA) to remove the missiles along the Taiwan Strait. In 2005, Chen attended the funeral of Pope John Paul II as the first Republic of China (ROC) president who had ever visited Europe since 1949 because very few European countries had diplomatic relationships with the ROC after the 1970s. Later that year, Chen traveled to Miami, Florida, and met members from U.S. Congress. He was selected as one of the world most influential people for *Time 100* in 2005.[5] In January 2006, he appointed the former DPP chairman Su Zhuochang as the premier of the Executive Yuan.

In the meantime, President Chen also tried to push his U.S. arms purchase proposal through the Legislative Yuan without success since both legislative and executive branches have been divided between the "Pan-Green Coalition" and "Pan-Blue Coalition."[6] Beijing was firmly against his effort and continued to attack Chen's "one Taiwan, one-China" policy. The Hu Jintao government in Beijing warned that Chen's action had seriously damaged the basis for peaceful reunification of the two sides and jeopardized peace and stability in the East Asia-Pacific region. China had also increased its criticism against the U.S. arms sale to Taiwan as "gross interference" in China's internal affairs and "a grave threat to China's security." The People's Republic of China (PRC) president Hu Jintao tried to remind the Bush administration and Congress that the United States had promised to adhere to a one-China policy, which has brought to the development of Sino-U.S. relations and the relative stability of the Taiwan situation. Any future

U.S. arms sale to Taiwan, including advanced weapons and equipment, might jeopardize the peace and stability of the Asia-Pacific region and the world at large.

During his second term, Chen's approving rate declined since many Taiwanese people, including the DPP members, became disappointed by Chen's family scandals during 2005–2007. The continuing scandals brought political turmoil to Chen's administration and tremendously undermined Chen's political support and the DPP's popularity. His approval rating dropped from 79 percent during his first term to 21 percent in the later second term. Chen had to change six different premiers within seven years during his tenure. The DPP also elected and reelected seven different party chairmen in seven years (2000–2006).

Among his major scandal cases, his family was accused for its involvement in the labor contract for high-speed train development, which had been explored by the media in August 2005. Then, his son-in-law Chao Chien-ming (Zhao Jianming) was convicted for insider trading and sentenced to prison by the Taipei Court. In 2006, his wife Wu Shu-chen (Wu Shuzhen) was charged of misuse of governmental funds about $450,000. Although the prosecutor also believed Chen Shui-bian provided her with fake receipts to claim expenses, they could not prosecute the sitting president. But the increasing demands for his impeachment became popular across the island, including from the former chairman of the DPP Shih Ming-teh (Shi Mingde). In 2006, Shi launched "anti-corruption campaign" and mobilized several hundreds of thousands of protesters to join the mass demonstrations and public rallies to bring down Chen. In June 2006, President Chen agreed to pass over the government power to Premier Su Tseng-chang, and announced he would not be involved in any political campaigning.[7] In the mid-term election of 2007, the "Pan-Blue Coalition" defeated most candidates from the "Pan-Green Coalition" and controlled both the Legislative Yuan and Executive Yang. In January 2008, Chen resigned as the chairman of the DPP.

Nevertheless, his scandals continued to be explored and reported by the media. In May 2008, there was another administration's crisis when Deputy Premier Qiu Yiren, Foreign Minister Huang Zhifang, Deputy Minister of Defense Ke Chengheng, and several other government officials resigned from their positions in Chen's government. President Chen Shui-bian had caused serious political damage to the DPP, which suffered a defeat in the 2008 presidential election. DPP candidate Frank Hsieh (Hsieh Chang-ting) lost to the KMT presidential candidate Ma Ying-jeou (Ma Yingjiu), former mayor of Taipei.

After he left office in 2008, Chen Shui-bian was charged guilty of corruption and abuse of authority by the court. On September 11, 2009, the Taipei District Court sentenced both Chen and his wife life in prison and a fine of NT$200 million (about $6.13 million) for their embezzlement, bribery, and money laundering of NT$490 million (more than $15 million) when he served as ROC president from 2000 to 2008.[8] He is the first president of the ROC to receive a prison sentence. On June 11, 2010, the Taiwan High Court reduced Chen's life sentence to 20 years in prison. On December 2, Chen Shui-bian was sent to the Taipei Prison and began to serve his sentence. He tried to commit suicide on June 2, 2013, but was unsuccessful.

THE KMT RETURNS: MA AS THE PRESIDENT

Ma Ying-jeou was born in Hong Kong on July 13, 1950. His family moved to Taiwan in 1952. Ma joined the KMT in 1967 and enrolled in the Law School of the National Taiwan University in 1968. After graduation with his Bachelor of Laws (LLB) degree in 1972, Ying-jeou served in the marine corps and navy of the ROC from 1972 to 1974. Then, he went to the United States for his graduate studies on a scholarship. He received his Master of Laws (LLM) degree from New York University in 1976, and Scientiae Juridicae Doctor or Juridicae Scientiae Doctor (SJD) degree from Harvard University in 1981. After his graduation from Harvard, Dr. Ma worked as a research advisor at Law School of the University of Maryland in 1981, and then legal consultant for the Boston First Bank in Massachusetts.[9] Dr. Ma married Christine Chow in 1981, and they had their first daughter Lesley (Ma Wei-chung) in New York City. Ma Ying-jeou published his thesis, *Legal Problems of Seabed Boundary Determination in the East China Sea*, in the United States in 1984.

After his return to Taiwan in 1981, Ma Ying-jeou was introduced by Qian Fu to President Chiang Ching-kuo and served as Chiang's English secretary and interpreter. Having earned trust and political experience, Ma began to serve in the KMT Party Center after 1984. For example, he was appointed as the director of the Mainland Tasks Committee in 1988, deputy secretary general of the KMT Central Committee in 1990, deputy director of the KMT National Unification Committee in 1991, and KMT representative to the National Assembly.

Ma Ying-jeou became a national leader in 1993 when he was appointed as the minister of justice by Lien Chan, then premier of the Executive Yuan. Nevertheless, his hardliner policy and strong law enforcement against corruption, local power abuse, and political scandals brought him sharp criticism from the KMT, which had been heavily involved in the illegal activities and historically depended on the local groups. Without the party support, Ma resigned from the post of minister of justice in 1996, and accepted a teaching position at Law School of the National Political University. He tried to avoid political conflict and make no enemy. In the local election of 1997, the KMT lost more than half of the counties and cities to the DPP because Taipei mayor Chen Shui-bian led the DPP support group and traveled from county to county and from city to city to help the DPP candidates' campaigns.[10] The KMT faced a political crisis and badly needed a strong candidate to defeat Chen Shui-bian, who was planning for his reelection of Taipei's mayor in 1998. Ma Ying-jeou became the party's star candidate for the 1998 Taipei mayor election.

In December 1998, Ma Ying-jeou defeated Chen Shui-bian by receiving 51.13 percent votes. Mayor Chen lost his reelection with only 45.91 percent votes.[11] During his first term from 1998 to 2002, Ma Ying-jeou tried to establish a transparent, honest, and upright mayor's office. He worked with mass media, civil groups, and private sector to improve city transportation, utility services, and public facilities. During his tenure, Taipei created six additional speed train routes and increased public train commuting capacity by more than six times.[12] The capital city also built six more bridges to improve the highway system to ease the heavy traffic in and out Taipei. Ma Ying-jeou soon became a popular mayor since his city government invested heavily in public health, environmental protection, public education, and infrastructural improvement. In 2001, Ma was elected a member of the Standing Committee of the KMT Central Committee and entered the Party Center. In 2002, he won his reelection with 64 percent votes and served his second term as the mayor of Taipei. Then, Ma was elected vice chairman of the KMT in 2003 and the KMT chairman in 2005 with 72.36 percent votes. In July 2009, Ma was reelected the chairman of the KMT with 93.87 percent votes.[13] Nevertheless, he faced some political and social issues during his two terms as Taipei's mayor, including health insurance rates, government control of water supply during the drought, and a scandal of Taipei Bank. The case against him was dismissed later after an investigation by the Taipei prosecutor.

In the general election of 2008, Ma ran as presidential candidate on the KMT ticket. He won the presidential election with 58.45 percent votes and defeated DPP candidate Frank Hsieh. After he took over office in May, President Ma Ying-jeou made a major shift in Taiwan's policy toward China from calling for Taiwan's independence by Chen's government during 2000–2008 to maintaining the status quo in

In the general election of 2008, Ma Ying-jeou, former mayor of Taipei (1998–2006), won the presidential election by defeating DPP candidate Frank Hsieh. President Ma made a major shift of Taiwan's policy toward China from calling for independence to maintaining the status quo during his tenure from 2008–2016. (Fang Chun Che / Dreamstime.com)

the Taiwan Strait. Ma had expressed his opposition to Taiwan independence during his campaign.

In his inauguration speech, President Ma emphasized his cross-strait policy with six words, "no reunification, no independence, and no war." However, some critics pointed out that Ma's long-term goal was for eventual unification. During his terms, Ma developed a neutral policy to avoid tension and crisis, while Taiwan was capable of cooperating with China. He refused to allow the Dalai Lama to visit Taiwan to avoid provoking Beijing. Ma did the same to a Chinese political dissent and student leader of the democracy and human rights movement Wang Dan by postponing his visit for three times and eventually canceling Wang's visit. In the meantime, Taipei and Beijing resumed the high-level meetings on a regular basis between Taiwan Affairs Office of the PRC State Council in Beijing and the Mainland Affairs Council (MAC) of the ROC Legislative Yuan in Taipei. On April 12, 2008, his vice president Vincent Siew formally met Hu Jintao, president of the PRC, at the Boao International Forum in Hainan.

On September 7, 2008, President Ma publicly stated that the relations between Taiwan and China were a "special relationship not between two nations."[14] The concept of the "special relationship between two nations" had been an official position from Lee Teng-hui between 1996 and 2000 to Chen Shui-bian between 2000 and 2008. President Ma believed in one that the two sides could be handled according to the "1992 Consensus." Through these meetings, both sides had signed twenty-three agreements on trade, transportation and communication, technology, financial, and educational exchanges. One of these agreements led to the direct sea, air, and mail links across the strait after more than fifty years of division, separation, and total ban of any communication between China and Taiwan. By the end of 2008, the commercial flights had increased from zero to seventy-five regularly scheduled passenger flights every day, and zero to forty-six cargo flights daily.[15] By 2010, the passenger flights increased to 120 flights daily and cargo flights up to 80 flights every day. According to Taiwan's statistics, more than eighteen million visitors came from China and visited Taiwan, and more than 35,000 Chinese students had enrolled in Taiwan's universities, colleges, and grade schools during this period.

The improved relationship has also heralded a closer energy cooperation between the two sides. Taiwan has very limited domestic energy resources and relies on imports for most of its energy requirements, especially oil, about 44 percent of primary energy demand. In 2008, China Petroleum Corporation (CPC), Taiwanese state oil and gas firm, began a closer cooperation with mainland Chinese oil and gas companies in the exploration and refining segments. In 2009, the CPC president visited Beijing and negotiated with the China National Offshore Oil Corporation over the joint exploration of the Taiwan Strait and outlined plans to process more crude oil for the China National Petroleum Corporation (CNPC) in Taiwanese refineries.[16]

In the general election of 2012, Ma ran for his reelection with Wu Den-yih as his partner. Ma/Wu won the reelection by 51.6 percent votes and defeated the DPP candidate Tsai Ing-wen (Cai Yingwen), who received 45.6 percent votes. During his second term from 2012 to 2016, Ma continued his anti-independence and pro-reunification policy and retained the status quo. In the spring of 2012, Beijing invited Taipei to work together to resolve the territorial dispute in the East China Sea with Japan. On November 7, 2015, President Ma Ying-jeou met Xi Jinping, president of the PRC, at Singapore. Both made important speeches about their historic meeting. Ma maintained his status quo policy and made five points on how to reduce the tension and improve the cross-strait economic, social, and culture relations. Xi welcomed Ma's positive policy and made the same promise to improve the relationship with Taiwan. Tsai Ing-wen, chair of the DPP, criticized Ma's pro-Beijing policy while his government did not do enough about Taiwan's sovereignty and national security. Ma responded by calling Tsai a Taiwan independence extremist. However, there were also some sharp criticisms against Ma's close relationship with China inside the KMT. In December 2014, Ma resigned from the position of the KMT chairman.

MA AND THE DISPUTED ISLANDS IN SOUTH AND EAST CHINA SEAS

On January 28, 2016, President Ma Ying-jeou led an official delegation of the Taiwanese government to visit the ROC-controlled Taiping Island (also known as Itu Aba Island), the largest island (about 110 acres) in the Spratly Island Group, in the South China Sea. It is one of the disputed islands among several nations around the South China Sea. The South China Sea as part of the Pacific Ocean is located south of mainland China; west of the Philippines; north of Indonesia, Malaysia, and Brunei; and east of Singapore and Vietnam. It covers an oval area from the Taiwan Strait in the northeast to the Malacca Strait in the southwest, totaling 1.4 million square miles.

The South China Sea is strategically important because it is the second most used sea lane in the world, with one-third of the world's shipping transit passing through its waters. Beneath its seabed were proved crude oil reserves of 7.7 billion barrels in 2013, about 20 percent of the total in the Asia-Pacific region. It is estimated to have natural gas reserves of 266 trillion cubic feet, about 45 percent of the total in the Asia-Pacific region. In the 1980s, as oil and gas shifted to deep water explorations, international tensions rose among some of the surrounding countries over the sovereignty of the islands in the South China Sea. Several states and territories have borders on the sea: the PRC, the ROC, Taiwan, the Philippines, Malaysia, Brunei, Indonesia, Singapore, and Vietnam. Some of them claim the sovereignty of the South China Sea by occupying some of its islands.[17]

The South China Sea has more than 250 islands with shoals, reefs, and sandbars, which are grouped into several archipelagos. The Spratly Islands, as the largest group, also called "Nansha" by both the PRC and ROC, covers a water area of 61,800 square miles, including about 100 small islands. Of these the PRC controls seven islands, Vietnam twenty-nine, the Philippines nine, Malaysia nine, and Taiwan (or the ROC) one, the Taiping Island.[18]

During World War II, the Allied powers decided at Cairo and Potsdam that the ROC government would accept the surrender of the Japanese troops in Taiwan and some Pacific islands, including both the Spratly and Paracel Islands. In November 1946, the ROC sent marine troops of the KMT navy to occupy the island in 1946. Then, the ROC government published the postwar administrative atlas, including all the 102 islands of the Spratly Island Group in the ROC's map of 1948. The Taiwanese established a permanent presence on the Spratly Island in 1956. In December 2007, the Taiping Island Airport was completed.[19] On February 2, 2008, President Chen Shui-bian accompanied by a large naval force visited the island. Thereafter, President Ma Ying-jeou continued to claim the ROC sovereignty of the Spratly Island Group during his two terms in office. He visited Taiwan's garrison at the Taiping Island in January before the 2016 Chinese Luna New Year. Ma also rejected the classification made by the international court of arbitration in July 2016 to consider the Taiping Island as a rock so it may not be entitled to a 200 nautical mile exclusive economic zone and continental shelf. He believes that all these islands in the South China Sea belong to the ROC.[20]

On April 9, 2016, President Ma Ying-jeou visited Taiwanese coast guard personnel at the Pengjia Island in the East China Sea. The island under the control of the ROC is one of the disputed islands among China, Japan, and Taiwan in the East China Sea. The East China Sea is a marginal sea in the Western Pacific Ocean, west of the Kyushu and Ryukyu Islands of Japan, north of the South China Sea, east of China, and south of the Yellow Sea. Taiwan is surrounded by the East China Sea in the north. In 1969, UNECAFE (United Nations Economic Commission for Asia and the Far East) indicated potential oil and gas reserves in the East China Sea. Soon thereafter, oil and gas explorations began. The area is estimated to contain approximately seven trillion cubic feet of natural gas and up to 100 billion barrels of oil.[21] With its subtropic climate with high salinity, its water holds a top place in the country's marine productivity. It is strategically important for the surrounding states, including South Korea, Japan, the ROC, and the PRC. The ROC government asserted sovereignty of the Diaoyu/Senkaku (or *Diaoyutai* in Taiwanese). Its Executive Yuan announced in December 1971 that these islands belonged to Yilan County of Taiwan. Beijing blamed Taipei's failure to protest America's "return" of the islands to Japan in 1972, since Chiang Kai-shek needed the United States for support.[22]

After the 1990s, public protests and political propaganda, as well as civilian conflict, increased between China, Japan, and Taiwan in the East China Sea. Among the Sino-Japanese sovereign disputes are at least two major sovereign issues: the Diaoyu/Senkaku Islands and the median line between the two countries. China claims the territorial sovereignty and associated maritime jurisdiction over the disputed areas in the East China Sea. The Japanese government maintains its position that the Senkaku Islands are an inherent territory of Japan and that "there exists no issue of territorial sovereignty to be resolved concerning the Senkaku Islands."[23] Since 2010, military tensions have mounted between China and Japan in the East China Sea. Both have deployed naval or coast guard vessels to the disputed waters and sent aircraft to patrol the areas.

In early 2012, Beijing invited Taipei to work together to resolve the territorial dispute in the East China Sea with Japan. In April, Lai Shin-yuan, minister of the ROC MAC, declined the invitation, announcing that "the ROC and Mainland China will not deal together with the disputes."[24] Nevertheless, President Ma Ying-jeou continued to claim the ROC's sovereignty of the Senkaku Island. He has published three books on the legal status of the disputed islands in the East China Sea from international maritime law perspective.

In November 2013, Beijing began using the definition of "China's East Sea" (*Zhongguo Donghai*), where Beijing had announced to establish the Air Defense Identification Zone (ADIZ).[25] In early 2014, the Chinese air force, or the PLA air force (PLAAF), began dispatching aircraft to patrol the ADIZ to identify foreign aircraft, to shadow planes to "collect evidence," and to administer warnings. In 2015, the Chinese navy, or the PLA navy (PLAN), conducted three large-scale military exercises in the East China Sea. The third live-fire exercise during August 24–28 involved more than 100 naval vessels, dozens of aircraft, and information regarding warfare units. Chinese warships fired nearly 100 various missiles.[26] In 2016, the territorial conflict escalated to military confrontation involving naval vessels, coast guard gunboats, and fighters in the disputed areas. The recent confrontation between Chinese and Japanese navies in the East China Sea has aroused serious concerns in the international community regarding security and stability in the Asia-Pacific region. The East China Sea has become one of the most worrisome flash points in Asia, an important source of insecurity in the Western Pacific, and a possible place to involve U.S. armed forces against the PLA in East Asia. The U.S. Air Force continues to fly military aircraft in the ADIZ without informing China, defying China's declaration that the region falls into Chinese airspace defense zone. Public debates and strategic research in America focus on what these events may mean to the United States, and how to best deal with the PLAN in case of crisis or even a war in the Pacific. Moreover, President Donald Trump has promised to commit U.S. forces for the defense of both Japan and South Korea.

TSAI ING-WEN AND THE 2016 ELECTION

The DPP regained some popularity during 2014–2016 when Tsai Ing-wen served as the party chair and the party won local elections in 2014. In the general election of 2016, the DPP nominated Tsai again for the party's presidential candidate. Tsai Ing-wen won the election and became the first female president in the history of the ROC and Taiwan. Ing-wen was born into a rich businessman family in the city of Taipei, on August 31, 1956. Her father left Taiwan for Northeast China during the Pacific War to avoid the Japanese draft. He learned mechanical skills through the war and opened auto repair shops in Taipei after Japan surrendered.[27] Soon her father began to invest in real estate, construction, restaurants, and coffee shops. Ing-wen grew up in her parents' large mansion. After her graduation from the National Taiwan University with a law degree in 1978, Tsai Ing-wen traveled overseas for her graduate studies in law and international trade. In 1980, she received her master's degree from the Law School of Cornell University in America. In 1984, she obtained her PhD degree in law from the London School of Economics in England.[28] During her years at Cornell in New York, Tsai Ing-wen had a boyfriend. He, however, was killed in an accident. Then, she met another boyfriend in London, and both fell in love. They could not continue their relationship since Tsai's father was against their engagement or marriage.[29] Tsai Ing-wen remains single today.

After her return to Taiwan, Tsai Ing-wen took a teaching position as associate professor at the School of Law of the National Political University from 1984 to 1990, and professor at the Institute of Law of Soochow University from 1991 to 1993. Then, she returned to the National Political University and taught at the Department of International Trade from 1993 to 2000.[30] During these years, Tsai began her involvement in the national policy planning and Taiwan's politics.

In 1993, Tsai Ing-wen was invited to serve as an advisor for the International Economic Organization and an independent member (no party affiliation) of the Trade Investigation Committee of the Economic Ministry. She served as one of the negotiators for Taiwan's WTO (World Trade Organization) affairs. In 1994, she was appointed the planning coordinator of the "Research Group for Drafting the Regulations on Hong Kong and Macao." In the same year, Tsai became a consulting member of the MAC of the Legislative Yuan. In 1999, she was one of the consulting members for the National Security Council.[31] Hardworking and skillful, she got her nickname *Xiao Ing* (Little Hero).

Tsai Ing-wen and her stories began to hit the headline and the front-page of Taiwan's media in 1998, when President Lee Teng-hui appointed her as his spokesperson in the Taiwanese government delegation headed by Koo Chen-fu (Gu Zhenfu) to visit Beijing. Soon she became part of the decision-making organ for Taiwan's policy toward the mainland. In 1998, she served in the "Tasks Team to Strengthen the National Status of the ROC Sovereignty," which drafted the "special state-to-state relations" doctrine for President Lee Teng-hui. Media described their close working relations and identical opinion as a political "father-daughter" relationship.[32] Before the end of his term, President Lee recommended Tsai to Chen Shui-bian, who won the election of 2000 and became the first DPP president after fifty years of the KMT authoritarian control of Taiwan.

Tsai Ing-wen became a high-ranking government official in May 2000 when President Chen appointed her as the minister of the MAC in the Legislative Yuan. As one of the few independent (nonpartisan) ministers in Chen's government, Tsai continued the "two

states" doctrine and then promoted Chen's interpretation of "each side has a state" during 2000–2004 when she was the MAC minister. In 2004, she joined the DPP. In 2005, Tsai was nominated by the DPP and then elected as a legislator-at-large of the Legislative Yuan. She served as the deputy chair of the Executive Administration Division and chair for the Consumer Protection Commission in the legislative body. In 2006, Tsai became the vice chair of the Legislative Yuan, a post referred to as vice premier.[33]

She began her political leadership in 2007 and soon made three "firsts" in the political history of Taiwan. In May 2008, Tsai Ing-wen defeated Koo

In 2016, Tsai Ing-wen, chair of the Democratic Progressive Party (DPP), won the general election against KMT and PFP and became the first female president of the Republic of China (ROC) in both China and Taiwan. (Sam Yeh/AFP/Getty Images)

Kwang-ming and was elected chair of the DPP at its Twelfth National Congress. She was the first female politician who had ever served as the leader of a major political party in the ROC. After her first term during 2008–2010, Tsai was reelected at the Thirteenth National Congress and continued to serve as the DPP chair from 2010 to 2012. During her second term as the party chair, she designed in January 2010 and passed in August the "DPP Political Agenda for the Next Years," starting a party reform in the DPP. In 2011, Tsai called the party to engage in the social reform under her five major tasks to improve Taiwanese people's lifestyle such as closing the gap between the rich and poor, improving the public education, and establishing a complete social welfare system.

In the general election of 2012, she won the DPP primary and ran for president against sitting KMT president Ma Ying-jeou. Then, Tsai Ing-wen became the first female presidential candidate in the political history of Taiwan. She received 6.1 million votes (about 45.6 percent), and her opponent Ma Ying-jeou won his reelection with 6.8 million votes (51.6 percent). Tsai sharply criticized President Ma's pro-China policy during his second term and continued her independence movement in and outside the DPP. In May 2014, Tsai Ing-wen was again elected the chair of the DPP for 2014–2016. She visited the United States in 2015 and met congressional leaders such as Senators John McCain and Jack Reed.[34]

In the general election of 2016, Tsai ran again for president on the DPP ticket with Chen Jian-ren as her partner against the opponents from the KMT and PFP. During her presidential campaign, she described the KMT policies "disastrous" and "unstable" as "black-box operations." She promised the voters her political transparency and "Taiwanese people first" policy. On January 16, 2016, Tsai Ing-wen won the election with 6.9 million votes, more than 56.1 percent, while KMT candidate Eric Chu received 3.8 million votes (only 31 percent) and PFP candidate James Soong 1.6 million votes (12.8 percent). Now Tsai Ing-wen became the first female president of the ROC both in China and in Taiwan.

THE TSAI'S GOVERNMENT AND TAIWAN–CHINA RELATIONS

After taking over the office in May 2016, President Tsai Ing-wen has modified her party's push for the independence of Taiwan and maintained the status quo with China as the "centerpiece of party policy." She said there was no "green or blue" in Taiwan's diplomacy. The DPP president continued the progress made in cross-strait relations by previous KMT governments and emphasizes the importance of economic and trade links with mainland China. Nevertheless, she continues to criticize the KMT pro-China policy and calls for reducing, if not ending, Taiwan's economic dependency on China.

President Tsai supported President Barack Obama's East Asia policy, which was to highlight the new Trans-Pacific Partnership removing trade barriers between the United States, Taiwan, and several other Pacific Rim countries, as well as continuing the sale of most military equipment to Taiwan.[35] Tsai met Marcus Jadotte, assistant secretary of U.S Commerce Department on May 24, 2016. In early December, Tsai Ing-wen called president-elect Donald Trump and congratulated him on his campaign victory. Trump talked to Tsai Ing-wen on the phone, and made her the first Taiwanese president who had ever talked to the U.S. president since 1979.[36] She also tried to depart from the "Southward Policy" under both Lee Teng-hui and Chen Shui-bian governments with a focus on the Pacific island countries. President Tsai emphasizes a "New Southward Policy" with a focus on India and Southeast Asia. She believes that India will become an economic and technology center in Asia soon. Taiwan should strengthen its business ties with India.

In 2017, President Tsai faced the new challenges with uncertainty and unstable factors in East Asia. The destabilizing factors in the region that first came from China's political situation and reform have produced uncertainties and un-stability. The PRC today has little in common with the Cold War China. The government has brought back Confucianism and nationalism—subjects that had been destroyed during the revolution of the Chinese Communist Party (CCP)—as ruling philosophies and ideologies. Randall Peerenboom considers this development as China's path forward rather than as a problem, "or at least that it is too early to tell."[37] He believes that "China is now following the path of other East Asian countries that have achieved sustained economic growth, established the rule of law, and developed constitutional or rights-based democracies, albeit not necessarily liberal rights-based democracies."[38] Many strategic calculations and predictions depend on the CCP's current agenda to maintain an economic growth and social stability.

Xi Jinping has made it clear that China is a superpower and that it wants to be treated as a global power. The new leader made some important policy changes to fit nationalist ideas and popular social movements. He therefore continues to employ nationalism as an ideology to unite China and to fight for its superpower status, perhaps resulting in one more source of legitimacy for the CCP as the country's ruling party. Xi has been taking tougher positions on political control, anti-corruption movement, national defense, and military modernization, as well as territorial issues such as the disputed islands in the South China Sea.[39]

The pragmatic nationalism is dictated by the Xi government through the 2010s to pursue China's unity, strength, prosperity, and dignity rather than choosing civil and human rights as its core. This brand of nationalism emphasizes a common goal rather than holding individual rights as its fundamental value or democracy as its desired result. The government frequently calls on individuals to sacrifice personal rights for the national interest. The country has its own normative principles, which have been described as the "Chinese characteristics." As a new member of the global community, moreover, the PRC has not always followed all international standards, but has adopted regulations selectively. Beijing considers many matters, including human rights, as domestic problems, and believes no foreign government or organization should interfere in its internal affairs.

In conclusion, the 2020s will be the turning point in the history of Taiwan. The recent changes and the new development have set up a new stage and provided more space for Taiwan's reforms and transformation in the years to come. Taiwan's transition seems possible and inevitable because of a simultaneous regionalization in East Asia. Although East Asia faces many challenges, the integration of national interests among all countries keeps deepening, and most countries have steadily passed their economic transformation and social transition. While the center of world economies is moving toward the East Asia-Pacific, stability and prosperity of the region are of great significance to maintaining world peace and development, and are in the best interests of all East Asian countries as well. Taiwanese government and people treasure the favorable and hard-won environment and momentum for growth, establish a new concept of common security, and on the basis of mutual trust, work to build a new type of East Asian security relationship featuring mutual trust, cooperation, mutual benefit, democracy, and equality. The building of strategic mutual trust should follow Taiwan's unique characteristics and its own rules of development, adhere to innovation, and actively learn from the experience of other regions. Then, based on the mutual trust, Taiwan and China may develop their own security organizations or mechanisms in the Asia-Pacific to build and maintain the regional peace and stability. Taiwanese people have been historically able to grasp the opportunities, solve the problems, and achieve sound and sustainable developments.

NOTES

1. For examples, see Richard Louis Edmonds and Steven M. Gold-stein, *Taiwan in the Twentieth Century: A Retrospective View* (Oxford, UK: Cambridge University Press, 2001); John F. Copper, *Taiwan: Nation-State or Province?* (Boulder, CO: Westview Press, 2003).

2. Xiaobing Li, "Taiwan's Experience, Challenge, and Future," in *Taiwan in the Twenty-first Century*, eds. Xiaobing Li and Zuohong Pan (Lanham, MD: University Press of America, 2003), 1.

3. Chen Shichang, *Zhanhuo 70 nian Taiwan shi* [Post-war Taiwan in 70 years] (Taipei: Shibao wenhua, 2015), 288.

4. Gao Mingshi, *Taiwan shi* [History of Taiwan], 2nd edition (Taipei: Wunan tushu, 2015), 284.

5. *The 2005 Time 100*, http://time.com/time/subscribe/2005/time100/leaders/100shui-bian.html. Assessed on January 20, 2017.

6. Wang Yufeng, *Taiwan shi* [History of Taiwan], 3rd edition (Taizhong, Taiwan: Haodu chuban [How-Do Publishing], 2017), 217.

7. BBC, "Taiwan Leader Surrenders Powers," *BBC News*, June 1, 2016. http://news.bbc.co.uk/2/hi/asia-pacific/5035838.stm. Assessed on February 10, 2017.

8. Wang, *Taiwan shi* [History of Taiwan], 219.

9. Office of the President, ROC (Taiwan), "Biography of President Ma Ying-jeou," http://english.president.gov.tw/Default.aspx?tablid=454 Assessed on October 8, 2017.

10. Wang, *Taiwan shi* [History of Taiwan], 216–17.

11. Ho Szu-yin, Director of Institute of International Relations, National Chengchi University, interview by the author on March 16, 2000, Taipei, Taiwan.

12. President Ma Ying-jeou, interview by the author in Ma's office on June 8, 2017. Ma served as the Mayor of Taipei during 1998–2008.

13. Ho Szu-yin, director of Institute of International Relations, National Chengchi University, interview by the author on March 16, 2000, Taipei, Taiwan.

14. Ma Ying-jeou, "Special Non-State-to-State Relationship and Lee's Treason," *ziyou shibao [Liberty Times]*, September 7, 2008.

15. Mark McDonald, "Direct Flights between China and Taiwan Begin," *The New York Times*, December 15, 2008. http://www.nytimes.com/200/8/12/15/news/15iht-15TAIWAN.18675854.html.

16. Xiaobing Li and Michael Molina, "Taiwan (The Republic of China)," in *Oil: A Cultural and Geographic Encyclopedia of Black Gold*, eds. Xiaobing Li and Michael Molina (Santa Barbara, CA: ABC-CLIO, 2014), 2: 671–74.

17. Xiaobing Li, "South China Sea," in *Modern China: Understanding Modern Nation*, ed. Li (Santa Barbara, CA: ABC-CLIO, 2016), 20–22.

18. Sarah Raine and Christian Miere, *Regional Disorder: The South China Sea Disputes* (London: Routledge, 2013), 17–19, 42–43.

19. Ministry of National Defense, ROC, "MND Admits Strategic Value of Spratly Airstrip," *Taipei Times*, January 6, 2006.

20. A former president of the ROC meeting with the author and other scholars in Taipei, Taiwan, on June 8, 2017.

21. BBC, "Questions and Answers: China-Japan Islands Row," *BBC Chinese (UK)*, September 11, 2012. http://www.bbc.co.uk/news/world-asia-pacific-11341139. Assessed on August 24, 2017.

22. Ibid.

23. Reuters, "Japan Refuses China Demand for Apology in Boat Row," *Reuters*, September 25, 2010. http://www.reuters.com/articles/us-japan-china-defense-idUSKCN. Assessed on November 10, 2017.

24. Radio Taiwan International, "Taipei Declines Beijing's Invitation to Solve Disputed Territory Issues Together," *Radio Taiwan International*, April 26, 2012.

25. Ji You, *China's Military Transformation: Politics and War Preparation* (Cambridge, UK: Polity Press, 2016), 10, 72, 77–78.

26. M. Pajagopalan, "China Conducts Air, Sea Drills in East China Sea," Reuters, August 27, 2015. http://www.retuers.com/articles/us-china-defense-idUSKCN0QW1EX20150827. Assessed November 20, 2017.

27. Chen Hsin-yi, "A Woman of Many Parts: Tsai Ing-wen," *Taiwan Panorama*, July 2012. http://www.taiwan-panorama.com/en/show_issue. Assessed September 20, 2017.

28. Tom Phillips, "Taiwan Elections: The British Educated Scholar Soon to Be the Most Powerful Woman in the Chinese-Speaking world," *Guardian*, January 15, 2016. http://www.theguardian.com/world/2016/jan/15.

29. "Cai Yingwen" (Tsai Ing-wen), https://baike.baidu.com/item/caiyingwen/353?fr=aladdin. Assessed January 17, 2018.

30. "Profile: Tsai Ing-wen," *BBC*, January 12, 2012. http://www.bbc.co.uk/news/world-asia-16464515 Assessed on November 3, 2017.

31. "Ing-wen Tsai: Executive Profile and Biography," *Bloomberg Business*. https://www.bloomberg.com/research/stocks/people/person.asp?personId=100145584.

32. Chris Wang, "2012 Elections: Yu Chang Papers Altered Twice: DPP," *Taipei Times*, December 22, 2011. http://www.taipeitimes.com/News/front/archives/2011/12/22/20035212327. Assessed September 25, 2017.

33. "Taiwan's New Premier Picks Tough Strategist as Deputy in Limited Cabinet Reshuffle," *The China Post*, May 17, 2007. http://www.chinapost.com.tw/news/archives/front/2007517/109921.htm. Assessed August 12, 2017.

34. Chris Fuchs, "Contributing Reports," *Taipei Times*, June 7, 2015. http://www.taipeitimes.com/News/taiwan/archives/2015/06/07/2003620128. Assessed September 18, 2017.

35. Gardiner Harris, "Vietnam Arms Embargo to Be Fully Lifted, Obama Says in Hanoi," *New York Times* (May 23, 2016). http://www.ny times.com/2016/05/24/world/asia/vietnam-us-arms-embargo-obama. html?_r=0. Assessed August 28, 2017.

36. The Reuters reports. https://www.reuters.com/article/us-usa -trump-china-tsai-idUSKBN13V1T7. Assessed October 2, 2017.

37. Randall Peerenboom, "Law and Development of Constitutional Democracy: Is China a Problem Case?" *The Annals of the American Academy, AAPSS*, 603 (January 2006), 192.

38. Peerenboom, *ibid.*, 193.

39. Xiaoxiao Li, "Unity and Stability: Xi Jinping's Promise and the CCP's Future," in *Evolution of Power: China's Struggle, Survival, and Success*, eds. Xiaobing Li and Xiansheng Tian (Lanham, MD: Lexington Books, 2014), 351–66.

Notable People in the History of Taiwan

Chen Shui-bian (1950–), president of the Republic of China (ROC) from 2000 to 2008. On March 18, 2000, history was made when Chen, the presidential candidate of the opposition Democratic Progressive Party (DPP) of Taiwan, was elected the tenth president. It was the first time the DPP, a party with pro-Taiwan's independence from China in the party platform, had won the presidency. The KMT had lost its rule that had extended over the whole of China from 1927 to 1949 and the Taiwan region from 1949 to 2000. After taking over the office, President Chen began to purge the KMT office-holders from the government and replaced them with the DPP members. In 2001, Chen flew to Los Angeles, Houston, and New York City, as a first for the president from Taiwan to visit the United States. In 2002, his government began to take away the statues and images of Chiang Kai-shek and Chiang Ching-kuo from public buildings, schools, city centers, and parks. In 2003, Chen flew to New York City again and met Colin Powell, U.S. secretary of state. His approval rating reached around 70 percent. In the election of 2004, Chen won his re-election. He was selected as one of the world most influential people for *Time 100* in 2005. During his second term (2004–2008), Chen continued his effort to promote Taiwanization, look for more international support and recognition, and push the independence movement forward. Chen's approving rate declined since many Taiwanese people, including the DPP members, became disappointed by Chen's family scandals during 2005–2007. The continuing scandals brought political turmoil to the Chen administration and tremendously undermined Chen's political support and the DPP's popularity. Then, his son-in-law Chao Chien-ming (Zhao Jianming) was convicted for insider trading in 2005 and sentenced for prison. In 2006, his wife Wu Shu-chen (Wu Shuzhen) was indicted of corruption. After he left office in 2008, Chen Shuibian was charged guilty of corruption and abuse of authority by the court. On September 11, 2009, the Taipei District Court sentenced both Chen and his wife life in prison and a fine of NT$200 million (about $6.13 million) for their embezzlement, bribery, and money laundering of NT$490 million (more than $15 million) when he served as ROC president.

Chen Yi (Ch'en Yi, 1883–1950), the first Chinese governor (1945–1947) in Taiwan after World War II and crushed an armed uprising during February–March 1947 known as the "2–28 Incident." On October 25, 1945, Governor Ch'en Yi arrived at Taipei with 12,000 KMT troops to receive the Japanese surrender. By 1946, the KMT garrison increased to 48,000 troops in Taiwan. Taiwanese people began to lose their confidence and trust in the KMT government when it seemed to them that public resources and even private properties had been transferred to serve certain individual interests. On February 28, in the capital city, many workers joined in a strike, students walked out of their classrooms, and shops were closed to protest the killing and demand the prosecution of the agents. In the afternoon, several thousand protesters marched to the governor's administrative office building. The soldiers opened fire, killed three, and wounded several more. Many rebels became organized and armed themselves. Some local politicians, intellectual elites, celebrities, and scholars joined the uprising, and played leadership roles with different political orientations. Governor Ch'en declared martial law and ordered the military to fire on the armed residents. On March 8, the Twenty-first Infantry Division from Shanghai arrived at Keelung and Kaohsiung, totaling 13,000 troops. The military suppression campaign began from March 9 to 13 by attacking, shooting, looting, and arresting massive numbers of people. By the end of March, an estimated 28,000 Taiwanese were killed, while 120 officials, soldiers, and mainlanders were killed during the riots. In April, Governor Ch'en Yi was dismissed.

Chiang Ching-kuo (Jiang Jingguo, 1910–1988), son of Chiang Kai-shek and president of the ROC from 1978 to 1988. Chiang Kai-shek appointed his son as the chairman of the KMT Taiwan Committee in 1951. After his arrival at Taiwan, Chiang Kai-shek created the General Department of Political Tasks in the Defense Ministry and appointed Chiang Ching-kuo as the first director. In July 1950, Chiang Ching-kuo opened the Political Officers Academy to train the party's officers for the services needed to maintain the party's control over the military. In 1972, President Chiang made his son Ching-kuo chairman of the Executive Yuan as the premier. Thereafter, Chiang Kai-shek began to pass political power to Ching-kuo since his health dramatically declined after an earlier car accident. After Chiang Kai-shek died in 1975, Taiwan began a new period as the "Chiang Ching-kuo Era" (1978–1989). The KMT government under Chiang Ching-kuo's new leadership initiated a democratic breakthrough, replacing martial law with new laws and promised political reform. The opposing political forces established a political party DPP in 1986 after the *Formosa Incident* (or Kaohsiung Incident) in 1979. During the era, Chiang Ching-kuo accomplished the Ten Major Constructions and Twelve New Development Projects, including the creation of the China Steel Corporation, Kaohsiung Super-sized Ship Building Yard, Petro-chemical Park, Chong-shan (Sun Yat-sen) Highway, Chong-cheng (Chiang Kai-shek) International Airport, and nuclear power plants. All of these major construction projects contributed to the "Taiwan Miracle" and helped its economy during and after the Nixon Shock and Middle East Oil Crises in the 1970s. He successfully transformed Taiwan's economic focus from export-oriented manufacturing to domestic needs-based productivity. Chiang Ching-kuo died on January 13, 1988.

Chiang Kai-shek (Jiang Jieshi, 1887–1975), the most important political and military leaders of the KMT in the twentieth century and president of the ROC in Taiwan from 1950 to 1975. After the Northern Expedition, Chiang re-established the ROC under KMT control with himself as president in 1927. During World War II of 1937–1945, he suffered heavy losses as the Japanese increased their territory in China, and he had to move his government several times. In the civil war of 1946–1949, the KMT lost several million troops as well as its control of mainland China to the Communists. On December 8, 1949, President Chiang moved the seat of his ROC government to Taiwan and officially announced martial law in Taiwan on March 14, 1950. Between 1949 and 1970, more than 140,000 people were arrested for 30,000 political crime charges. More than 4,000 of them were executed, and 9,000 were sentenced to life in prison. Then, Chiang focused his efforts on three areas as his priority to consolidate his control of Taiwan, including party reform; local democratization through village, township, and county elections; and land reform. All of the three policy efforts worked and laid a solid foundation for the survival and success of the Chiang's regime for thirty-nine years, when he served as the ROC president for five terms from 1950 to 1975 in Taiwan. With U.S. help, Taiwan shifted to a manufacturing economy. Through 1972, Taiwan significantly grew both its GNP and its per capita GNP significantly. Although Taiwan lagged behind Japan, Chiang ensured a faster growth rate than his counterparts in Beijing. Chiang Kai-shek held on to power until his death on April 5, 1975.

Eisenhower, Dwight D. (1890–1969), president of the United States from 1953 to 1961. After he entered the White House in January 1953, President Eisenhower continued Truman's policy to disengage the Chinese in the Taiwan Strait. America's increasing involvement dashed Beijing's hopes for a possible end to the Chinese Civil War. Chinese leaders in Beijing suspected that the United States was carrying out a policy of "unleashing Chiang." In September 1954, the People's Liberation Army (PLA) batteries heavily bombed KMT-held offshore islands and the First Taiwan Strait Crisis began. The Eisenhower administration signed the Washington-Taiwan Mutual Defense Treaty on December 2 to strengthen the defense of Taiwan. In January 1955, the PLA troops landed at Yijiangshan Island. To stop the further PLA attack, Eisenhower requested authorization from Congress for the United States to participate in the defense of Taiwan and some of the offshore islands in the Taiwan Strait. On January 29, Congress passed the Formosa Resolution, which authorized Eisenhower to employ U.S. armed forces to protect Taiwan from a possible PLA invasion. The Second Taiwan Strait Crisis erupted over the offshore islands of Jinmen and Mazu on August 23, 1958, when the PLA heavily bombarded the islands. In response to the rapidly escalating PLA threat, the Eisenhower administration reinforced U.S. naval forces in East Asia and directed U.S. warships to help the KMT protect Jinmen supply lines.

Goto Shimpei (1857–1929), Japanese politician, cabinet minister of the Taisho government, and the chief civil administrator (1898–1906) under the fourth colonial governor in Taiwan. Goto's new deal policy included bringing foreign loans, respecting Taiwanese tradition, and improving local economy. Japanese capital was not only allowed to enter Taiwan but also encouraged to overwhelm the backward

Taiwanese economy. His policy proved successful and laid solid foundation for Japan's colonial rule in Taiwan. After his years, Taiwan changed from depending on Japanese assistance to benefitting Japan. In 1902, Taiwan began the construction of the cross-island railroad from north to south and completed it in 1908. During his tenure, Taiwan started the construction of two modern harbors in Keelung and Kaohsiung and a hydroelectric power plant.

Kangxi (K'ang-hsi, r. 1662–1722), the second Manchu emperor of the Qing dynasty (1662–1722). He dispatched a large force of 20,000 troops and 300 war junks commanded by Shi Lang to attack Penghu and Taiwan in 1683. General Shi defeated Zheng's defense forces and occupied Taiwan. Thereafter, Qing began its 211-year administration and garrison on the islands.

Lee Teng-hui (Li Denghui, 1923–), president of the ROC in Taiwan from 1989 to 2000. He received his PhD in agricultural economics from Cornell University in 1968. He was a Taiwan-born local official who was handpicked by Chiang and promoted to the KMT Party Center as vice president and then Chiang's successor. Chiang Ching-kuo announced in December 1985 that the next president would not come from the Chiang family. Lifting martial law (Emergency Decree) in 1988 initiated a new stage of transition to democracy, which also went through several sub-stages of its own thereafter. Constitutional reform was a very important part of Taiwan's democratization during 1989–1996. In the 1990s, President Lee began to move away from one-China policy by emphasizing "two governments," "two reciprocal political entities," and "Taiwan is already a state with independent sovereignty." In 1999, Present Lee surprised the world by announcing that Taiwan and China had a "state-to state relationship." In the meantime, from 1988 to 1999, the Taiwanese who came to the mainland for visiting their relatives, sightseeing, or exchanges totaled 16 million turnstile count. The total cross-strait trade volume had reached $160 billion. In addition, Taiwanese businesses had invested $44 billion in China, the second-largest direct foreign investor in China only after Japan.

Li Dan (Li Tan, ?–1625), also known as Yan Siqi (Yen Ssu-chi), the leader of a Chinese pirate army. Li established his merchant-pirate empire on Taiwan in the 1620s and controlled trade along the Fujian coast. He became a Christian in Manila and a major supplier to the Dutch-China trade. "Captain China," as Europeans referred to him, became popular among Westerners. Li brought many Chinese immigrants to

Taiwan by going around the Ming's sea bans. A monument of "Yan Siqi's Exploration of Taiwan" stands in the city center of present-day Peikang.

Li Hongzhang (Li Hung-chang, 1823–1901), Chinese politician, general of the Qing army, and minister of the Manchu government. After he lost his fleet to Japanese Navy in the Sino-Japanese War of 1894, Li had to sign the Treaty of Shimonoseki on April 17, 1895. Under this treaty, the Qing government recognized the entire independence of Korea and surrendered the Liaodong Peninsula, Taiwan, and the Penghu Islands to Japan. China also paid Japan 200 million taels of silver as war reparation.

Lin Xiantang (Lin Hsien-t'ang, 1881–1956), Taiwanese activist and leader of the Chinese cultural movement against Japanese colonization of Taiwan. In 1915, Lin opened his private schools to teach Chinese language and culture at Taipei. In 1920, Lin Xiantang and many Taiwanese intellectuals in Japan sent their petition to Japanese Diet for a Taiwanese legislative branch in Tokyo. After their petition was rejected, they founded the Taiwan Cultural Association in 1921. The association published its newsletters, newspapers, and a magazine, *Taiwan Youth Magazine*. It organized local associations, book clubs, and youth society, and sponsored summer schools, cultural seminars, and foreign film translations. These new cultural movements played an important role in shaping a new Taiwanese nationalism.

Liu Mingchuan (Liu Ming-chuan, 1836–1896), Chinese general and the first governor of Taiwan Province. During the Sino-French War, Liu was sent by Beijing to defend Taiwan in 1885. After the war, the Qing court proclaimed the founding of the Province of Taiwan, and Liu Mingchuan was appointed as the first provincial governor of Taiwan (1886–1892). Governor Liu continued the Self-Strengthening Movement by establishing new administrative branches and carrying out reform policies for modernization. In 1886, he founded the general office of telegram in Taipei and began to construct the telegram lines of more than 1,300 miles. Taiwan became the first province in China to use telephone. In 1887, he began to build the railway line between Taipei and Keelung, which was completed in 1891. It became the first railway operated in China.

Ma Ying-jeou (Ma Yingjiu, 1950–), president of the ROC in Taiwan from 2000 to 2008. He received his Master of Laws (LLM) degree from New York University in 1976 and Scientiae Juridicae Doctor or Juridicae Scientiae Doctor (SJD) degree from Harvard University in 1981. Ma Ying-jeou became a leader in 1993 when he was appointed as the minister of the Justice Ministry by Lien Chen, then premier of the Executive Yuan. In December 1998, Ma Ying-jeou defeated Chen Shui-bian in Taipei mayor election. In the general election of 2008, Ma ran as presidential candidate on the KMT ticket. After he took over office in May, President Ma Ying-jeou made a major shift of Taiwan's policy toward China from calling an independence by Chen's government during 2000–2008 to maintain the status quo in the Taiwan Strait. Through the improved relationship, both sides had signed twenty-three agreements on trade, transportation and communication, technology, financial, and educational exchanges. One of these agreements led to the direct sea, air, and mail links across the strait after more than fifty years of division, separation, and total ban of any communication between China and Taiwan. By the end of 2008, the commercial flights had increased from zero to seventy-five regularly scheduled passenger flights every day, and zero to forty-six cargo flights daily. More than eighteen million visitors came from China and visited Taiwan, and more than 35,000 Chinese students had enrolled in Taiwan's universities, colleges, and grade schools during this period. In the general election of 2012, Ma defeated the DPP candidate Tsai Ing-wen and served his second term from 2012 to 2016. On November 7, 2015, President Ma Ying-jeou met Xi Jinping, president of the People's Republic of China (PRC), at Singapore. However, there were also some sharp critics against Ma's close relationship with China inside the KMT. In December 2014, Ma resigned as chairman from the KMT.

Mackay, George L., Canadian Christian priest and dentist. After he arrived at Taiwan in 1871, Rev. Mackay began to help the Taiwanese with their oral cavities and opened the first dentist clinic at Taipei in 1879. He established Oxford College in 1882 as the first higher education institute in Taiwan and later became today's Seminary of Taiwan. In 1884, he opened the Tamsui Girls Academy, which became the Tamsui Middle School later.

Mao Zedong (Mao Tse-tung, 1893–1976), the most important Chinese Communist leader in the twentieth century, cofounder and chairman of the Chinese Communist Party (CCP), and the founder and first president of the PRC. In 1937, the KMT government came to an agreement with Mao to jointly resist the Japanese invasion of China (1937–1945). The CCP's regular army had grown from 56,000 in

1937 to 1.27 million in 1945, supported by militias numbering another 2.68 million. China's full-scale civil war resumed between the KMT and the CCP in June 1946. By September 1949, the CCP forces, or the PLA, occupied most of the country except for Tibet, Taiwan, and various offshore islands. Chiang moved the seat of his KMT government from the mainland to Taiwan later that year. On October 1, 1949, Mao declared the birth of the PRC and of the new republic's alliance with Moscow. China began to move into the center stage of the global Cold War between the Soviet Union and the United States, two contending camps headed by two superpowers. In 1954 and 1958, Mao launched two attacks on the KMT-held offshore islands known as the First and Second Taiwan Strait Crisis. In 1972, Mao met U.S. president Richard Nixon in Beijing and normalized the diplomatic relations between the PRC and the United States. Mao died in Beijing on September 9, 1976.

Meiji (r. 1868–1912), emperor of Japan and the leader of the Meiji Restoration. During the Meiji Restoration, Japan transformed from a divided state to an industrialized and Westernized country and became the most powerful state in Asia by the end of the nineteenth century. As a new rising power, Japan began to adopt an aggressive foreign policy, promoting overseas territorial expansion to protect its own interests and security as well as to expand its overseas trade. Japan defeated Qing China in the Sino-Japanese War of 1894. Qing government signed the Treaty of Shimonoseki in 1895, recognizing the entire independence of Korea and surrendering Taiwan and the Penghu Islands to Japan. Then, Japan defeated Russia in the Russo-Japanese War of 1904.

Nixon, Richard (1913–1994), U.S. president from 1969 to 1974. In the early 1970s, President Nixon and his national security advisor Henry Kissinger initiated a new U.S. foreign policy, détente, to replace the containment policy of the previous decades, which had involved the United States in the Vietnam War since 1965. Consequently, Washington's China policy also changed dramatically and sought to extend rapprochement with Beijing. Nixon met Mao Zedong in Beijing in February 1972, the first U.S. leader who had ever visited Communist China since it was founded in 1949. The Shanghai Communiqué, issued during Nixon's visit to the PRC, signaled a major shift in America's policy toward Taiwan. The United States officially abandoned its long-standing position that Taiwan's regime was the legitimate government of the Chinese people. Nevertheless, the United States reserved the right to provide Taiwan with the arms necessary to defend itself against any aggression by the PRC.

Nuyts, Pieter, the first Dutch governor appointed by the Dutch East India Company to Taiwan. Governor Nuyts built Fort Zeelandia (present-day Anping Castle) at Tayown in 1624 and sent the Dutch forces to crush the aboriginal resistances against the Dutch colonization.

Qi Jiguang (Ch'i Ji-guang, 1528–1587), Chinese general of the Ming army and national hero in the war against the Japanese pirates. During the 1550s–1560s, Emperor Jiajing (Chia-ching, r. 1522–1566) reinforced anti-piracy efforts and appointed General Qi in charge of the war against Japanese pirates. With the support of the local authorities and coastal villagers, Qi repeatedly defeated these pirates in Zhejiang, Fujian, and Guangdong during 1561–1565 and improved the coastal defense situation.

Rudao, Mona (Mouna Rudao, 1880–1930), chief of Mahebo village, Seediq tribe of Atayal aboriginal Taiwanese, and leader of the anti-Japanese resistance known as the "Wushe (Masha) Revolt" in 1930. On October 27, Rudao organized several aboriginal villages to attack Japanese police stations and administrative offices in the surrounding towns. They captured 180 rifles and more than 23,000 rounds of ammunition. Around the noon, they launched a general attack on the Wushe School, which hosted the annual community event, and killed 197 Japanese. The Japanese governor-general sent 4,000 troops and police to stop the armed rebellion. It took three weeks for the Japanese troops to stop the aboriginal rebels. Chief Rudao committed suicide, and his body was never found. During the rebellion, the aborigines lost 644 people. Rudao became a Taiwanese hero in popular culture, and his story was made into the 2003 TV drama *Dana Sakura* and the 2011 Taiwanese film *Seediq Bale*.

Shen Baozhen (Shen Bao-ch'en, 1820–1879), Chinese minister of the Qing dynasty and the emperor's envoy to Taiwan. In 1874, Emperor Tongzhi (T'ung-chih, r. 1862–1874) sent Minister Shen to Taiwan with 10,000 Qing troops to negotiate with Japan after the Mudan Incident. Shen accepted Japanese demand of the Penghu Islands and paid Japan 500,000 oz. of silver. Then, Shen launched political and economic reforms and the Self-strengthening Movement on Taiwan by lifting the immigration ban and opening the mountainous region of the aborigines. He built new roads, schools, and other facilities in the remote mountainous areas. Shen left Taiwan after his promotion to the governor-general of South China.

Sui Yangdi (Yang-ti, r. 605–617), the second emperor of the Sui dynasty (581–618). Sui Yangdi sent his fleet to Taiwan twice in 607 and 610. After the expeditionary forces of more than 10,000 strong suffered heavy casualties, Sui generals convinced the emperor that controlling a backward island was not worth another large-scale landing.

Sun Li-jen (Sun Liren, 1900–1990), army chief and commander of the Taiwan Defense. In 1950, Chiang purged different factions from the army and established his personal control of the military. In 1955, Chiang detained General Sun Li-jen by charging him with failure to report Communist spies in his staff. General Sun was detained for thirty years before his death in 1990. In the year of 1955, more than 300 generals and officers were accused and purged with charges of conspiracy under Sun. Some of them died of torture or were executed.

Sun Quan (Sun Chuan, 182–252), emperor of the State of Wu during the Three Kingdoms period (220–280) in China. Wu emperor Sun sent an expeditionary force of 10,000 men to attack *Yizhou* (Taiwan) in 230. Although his generals brought back several thousand Taiwanese, the Wu army lost more than half of their troops as mainland Han soldiers were susceptible to tropical diseases like malaria and small pox.

Sun Yat-sen (Sun Zhongshan, 1866–1925), the most important revolutionary leader in modern Chinese history and the founder of the ROC. On October 10, 1911, under Sun's influence and anti-Manchu organization, some new army officers revolted (October 10, or "Double Tens," celebrated as the National Day for the ROC at Taiwan) against the Qing dynasty. The success of the Wuchang uprising led many more army officers to join the revolution. In the next two months, fifteen provinces proclaimed their independence from the Qing Empire. The provisional government of the ROC elected Sun president, and he inaugurated in Nanjing on January 1, 1912. As a great breakthrough in Chinese history, it ended 2,000 years of monarchy and built the first republic in Asian history. In August, Sun organized the KMT as modern political party in China and opened the Whampoa (Huangpu) Military Academy (the West Point of China) in 1924. He appointed Chiang Kai-shek as its first commandant. Sun Yat-sen died on March 12, 1925, of cancer.

Tang Jingsong (Tang Ching-sung, 1841–1903), Qing governor of Taiwan (1892–1895) and the president of the Taiwan Republic in 1895. During the Sino-Japanese negotiations, Taiwanese were panic about Qing's position to sacrifice Taiwan in exchange for Japanese military withdrawal from China. After the treaty was signed in April, Governor Tang Jingsong decided to save Taiwan from Japanese colonization by founding the "Taiwan Republic," and by securing independence from the Qing government, on May 25, 1895. Tang proclaimed himself as the president of the Taiwan Republic. The purpose of Tang's action was to stop Japan's taking-over rather than leaving the Qing dynasty. After Japanese defeated the defensive troops, the Taiwan Republic collapsed on October 21. During the resistance, more than 14,000 Taiwanese were killed.

Truman, Harry S. (1884–1972), U.S. president from 1945 to 1953. On June 27, two days after the Korean War broke out, President Truman announced that the U.S. Seventh Fleet would be deployed to the Taiwan Strait to prevent a Chinese Communist attack on KMT-held Taiwan. Truman's order became the turning point in the U.S. Taiwan policy and had a strong impact on the future of Taiwan. Under the Presidential Directive, the United States for the first time committed its armed forces to the defense and security of the ROC government. The Truman administration shifted its strategy on Taiwan from the hands-off policy to a military commitment. On August 4, 1950, the first combat group of American fighters and bombers from the U.S. Thirteenth Air Force arrived at the Taibei air base. Before the end of August, the Truman administration sent $140 million in military aid to Taiwan. On May 1, 1951, the U.S. "Military Advisory Assistant Group" was established in Taiwan. To ensure the island's safety, the new policy was a reflection of the president's view on East Asia that Taiwan could survive the Chinese Civil War by joining the "free world" in the global Cold War.

Tsai Ing-wen (Cai Yingwen, 1956–), president of the ROC since 2016. She received her Master of Laws (LLM) degree from the Law School of Cornell University in 1980, and obtained her PhD degree in law from the London School of Economics in England in 1984. Tsai became a consulting member of the Mainland Affairs Council (MAC) of the Legislative Yuan in 1994 and one of the consulting members of the National Security Council in 1999. She became a high-ranking government official in May 2000 when President Chen appointed her as the minister of MAC. In 2004, she joined the DPP. In 2005, Tsai was nominated by the DPP and then elected as a legislator-at-large of the Legislative Yuan. In 2006, she became the vice chair of the Legislative Yuan, a post referred to as vice premier. In 2008, Tsai defeated Koo Kwang-ming and was elected chair of the DPP at its Twelfth National Congress. She was the first female politician who had ever served as the leader of a major political party in Taiwan. After her first term during 2008–2010, Tsai was reelected at the Thirteenth National Congress and continued to serve as the DPP Chair from 2010 to 2012. In the general election of 2012, she won the DPP primary and ran for president against the sitting KMT president Ma Ying-jeou. Tsai became the first female presidential candidate in the political history of Taiwan. In the general election of 2016, Tsai ran again for president on the DPP ticket with Chen Jian-ren as her partner against the opponents from the KMT and People First Party (PFP). On January 16, 2016, Tsai Ing-wen won the election with 6.9 million votes, more than 56.1 percent, and became the first female president of the ROC both in China and in Taiwan. After taking over the office in May, President Tsai has modified her party's push for the independence of Taiwan and maintained the status quo with China as the "centerpiece of party policy." She said there was no "green or blue" in Taiwan's diplomacy. In early December, Tsai had an unprecedented telephone call with President-elect Donald Trump. It was the first time that the ROC president had ever talked to the U.S. president since 1979. She continued the progress made in cross-strait relations by previous KMT governments with an emphasis on the importance of economic and trade links with mainland China. Nevertheless, she criticized the KMT pro-China policy and calls for reducing, if not ending, Taiwan's economic dependency on China.

Xiaozong (Hsiao-tsung, r. 1163–1189), emperor of the Song dynasty. Song Xiaozong established administration and garrison at the Penghu Islands in 1171. Under the Quanzhou district government of Fujian Province, the Penghu office and Song troops collected taxes and protected Chinese fishermen and settlers, about 1,300 people at that time, from Japanese *Wakou* pirates and Taiwanese attacks.

Zheng Chenggong (Cheng Cheng-kung, or Koxinga, 1624–1662), Ming general and national hero in the anti-Dutch colonization war. General Zheng led a resistance war against the Qing dynasty in southern China from 1646 to 1662. When Longwu was crowned in Nanjing in 1644, his father Zheng Zhilong presented him to the emperor, who bestowed upon him a new name, "Chenggong" (success). He was also granted the honor to use the imperial surname Zhu (Chu). Then,

Zheng Chenggong became *Kuoxingye* (Koxinga in Fujian dialect), "Lord of the Imperial Surnam." In 1662, he defeated the Dutch garrison on Taiwan and ended the thirty-eight-year Dutch colonization. Thereafter, he became a national hero both in China and in Taiwan. He and his family controlled the island from 1662 to 1683.

Zheng He (Cheng Ho, 1371–1435), an imperial official, naval admiral, diplomat, and eunuch of the Ming dynasty (1368–1644). Zheng He became famous after he made seven voyages to the Western seas (Indian Ocean) between 1405 and 1433. Over 2,000 vessels were built under his command during 1404–1419, including a hundred big "treasure ships". Some of his ships reached Taiwan during the voyages.

Zheng Jing (Cheng Ching, 1642–1681), the ruler of Taiwan from 1662 to 1680. After his father Zhang Chenggong died, Zheng Jing continued the resistance movement at Taiwan by launching northern expeditions against Qing's China. To make Taiwan his political and military base, Zheng terminated Dutch colonial system and replaced it with a Ming-style administration. He and his ministers brought more Chinese immigrants to Taiwan and developed military farms, trade, handcraft shops, and road construction. Two years after his death, Taiwan surrendered to the Qing regime in 1683.

Zheng Zhilong (Cheng Chih-lung, 1602–1661), the head of a pirate army in Taiwan and later an admiral of the Ming navy. Zheng had a fleet of more than one thousand war junks and more than ten pirate bases in northern Taiwan. He dominated the Taiwan Strait and controlled European trade with China. In 1629, the Ming emperor commissioned Zheng as a naval commodore and promoted him an admiral a year later. His fleet helped 20,000 Chinese immigrants from Fujian to Taiwan. Zheng surrendered to the Qing dynasty in 1646 after Beijing offered him the governorship of two provinces, Guangdong and Fujian. The Qing court, however, did not trust him and arrested him after his arrival at Beijing. He was executed in 1661 when he refused to ask his son Zheng Chenggong to surrender to the Qing regime.

Bibliographic Essay

The history of Taiwan has changed over times from its indigenous origins to colonization by the Dutch in the seventeenth century and by the Japanese in the nineteenth century. Then the country entered a complex relationship with China after World War II and the Chinese Civil War that would come to define modern identity. Historians from various nations have made a claim to Taiwan, and it can be difficult to distinguish what exactly Taiwanese was/is and what being Taiwanese means. This essay attempts to provide a balanced historiography, including published materials from the United States, Europe, Taiwan, and China, for appreciating the significant historical development of Taiwan in a global history.

GENERAL HISTORY

For general coverage of Taiwanese history, there are several good titles in English published in recent years, including John F. Copper's sixth edition of his book, *Taiwan: Nation-State or Province?* (London: Routledge, 2018). Murray A. Rubinstein edited a collection of essays, *Taiwan: A New History* (London: Routledge, 2015). His expanded edition includes seventeen essays covering from aboriginal origins to democratic reforms in the 2000s. Among other titles is Shelley Rigger's

Why Taiwan Matters: Small Island, Global Powerhouse, updated edition (Lanham, MD: Rowman & Littlefield, 2014). A few survey books on Chinese history provide good coverage of the history of Taiwan, including Scott L. Kastner's *Political Conflict and Economic Interdependence across the Taiwan Strait and Beyond* (Stanford, CA: Stanford University Press, 2009) and Albert M. Craig's *The Heritage of Chinese Civilization* (Upper Saddle, NJ: Pearson Education, 2007). As a classic history text on East Asia, John K. Fairbank, Edwin O. Reischauer, and Albert M. Craig outline the history of Taiwan in their *East Asian: Transition and Transformation*, revised edition (Boston, MA: Houghton Mifflin, 1989).

Among recent publications in Chinese by Taiwanese historians are Wang Yufeng, *Taiwan shi* [History of Taiwan], third edition (Taichung, Taiwan: Haodu chuban [How-to Publishing], 2017) and Gao Min-shi, ed., *Taiwan shi* [History of Taiwan], second edition (Taipei: Wunan tushu [Wunan Books], 2015). In Taiwan, Lian Heng's book, *Taiwan tongzhi* [A comprehensive history of Taiwan] (Beijing: Shangwu yinshuguan [Commercial Publishing], 1983), remains its scholarly authority in the historiography of Taiwan after many years. Lian Heng is the father of Lian Zhan, premier of Taiwan from 1993 to 1997, vice president of the ROC from 1996 to 2000, and the chairman of the KMT from 2000 to 2006.

In China, most history books include Taiwan's history for political reasons. Among the recent texts are History Research Institute, China Academy of Social Sciences, *Jianming zhongguo lishi duben* [Concise history of China] (Beijing: Zhongguo shehui kexueyuan chubanshe [China Academy of Social Sciences Press], 2012) and China National Military Museum, comp., *Zhongguo zhanzheng fazhanshi* [History of Chinese warfare] (Beijing: Renmin chubanshe [People's Press], 2001). There were earlier publications on Taiwan, for example, Zhao Rushi, *Zhufan Zhi* [Records of offshore territories] (Shanghai: Zhonghua shuju [China Books], 1985) and Chen Bisheng, *Taiwan difang shi* [A local history of Taiwan] (Beijing: Zhongguo shehui kexue chubanshe [China Social Science Press], 1982).

ANCIENT TIME

For the early civilization and aboriginal cultures, there are quite few books covering prehistory, indigenous tradition, ethnic minorities, and their early experience in Taiwan. For example, Morgan Deane, *Decisive Battles in Chinese History* (Yardley, PA: Westholme Publishing, 2018) and Xiaobing Li and Patrick Fuliang Shan, eds., *Ethnic China: Identity, Assimilation, and Resistance* (Lanham, MD: Lexington Books,

2015). During the ancient age between 200 BC and AD 1400, there are more readings available. David C. Kang, *East Asia before the West: Five Centuries of Trade and Tribute* (New York: Columbia University Press, 2012); Peter Lorge, *War, Politics and Society in Early Modern China, 900–1795* (London: Routledge, 2005); and Jonathan Manthorpe, *Forbidden Nation: A History of Taiwan* (New York: Palgrave Macmillan, 2005) are on the list. Other books of the world and Chinese histories are also helpful for a better understanding of Taiwan's past. They are authored by Michael S. Neiberg, *Warfare in World History* (London: Routledge, 2001); John K. Fairbank and Merle Goldman, *China: A New History*, enlarged edition (Cambridge, MA: Harvard University Press, 1998); W. G. Goddard, *Formosa: A Study in Chinese History* (London: Macmillan, 1996); and Frederic Wakeman, Jr., *The Fall of Imperial China* (New York: Free Press, 1975). This shared ancient history with China is important because it is one of the foremost reasons China has used to make a claim that Taiwan belongs to the People's Republic of China (PRC).

More titles are available both in Taiwan and in China about the ancient history of Taiwan. For example, *Shang Shu* [Book of pre-history documents] (Beijing: Qinghua University Collection, 1997); Qi Jialin, *Xin Taiwan shi* [Taiwan's new history] (Taipei: Taiwan Publishing, 2000); Cen Zhongmian, *Sui Tang shi* [History of Sui and Tang dynasties] (Beijing: Zhonghua shuju [China Books], 1985); and Compilation Committee, National Palace Museum, ROC, *A Chronological Table of Chinese and World Cultures* (Taipei: National Palace Museum, 1985).

COLONIAL PERIODS

Taiwan experienced two major colonial periods. The first one is known as the Dutch colonization from 1624 to 1662; the second is the Japanese colonization from 1895 to 1945. There are several books on the early European influence and the Dutch colonization. Xiaobing Li, Yi Sun, and Wynn Gadkar-Wilcox, *East Asia and the West: An Entangled History* (San Diego: Cognella, 2019); Gavin Menzies, *1421: The Year China Discovered America* (New York: Perennial, 2003); and Chiao-min Hsieh, *Taiwan-Ilha Formosa: A Geographical Perspective* (Washington, DC: Butterworths, 1964).

For the Japanese colonization of Taiwan, several Japanese history books provide some background information such as Milton W. Meyer, *Japan: A Concise History*, fourth edition (Lanham, MD: Rowman & Littlefield, 2013) and James L. McClain, *Japan: A Modern History* (New York: Norton, 2002). Other books focus on Japan's intention, strategy, and war-fighting experience. They are by Kenneth M. Swope,

A Dragon's Head and a Serpent's Tail: Ming China and the First Great East Asian War, 1592–1598 (Norman: University of Oklahoma Press, 2009); Samuel Hawley, *The Imjin War: Japan's Sixteenth-Century Invasion of Korea and Attempt to Conquer China* (Seoul, Korea: Royal Asiatic Society, 2005); and Conlan, *In Little Need of Divine Intervention: Scrolls of the Mongol Invasions of Japan* (Ithaca, NY: Cornell University Press, 2001). Among the books and primary sources on the war of 1894 are S.C.M. Paine, *The Sino-Japanese War of 1894–1895: Perceptions, Power and Primacy* (Cambridge, UK: Cambridge University Press, 2005) and Munemitsu Mutsu and Mark Berger Gordon, *Kenkenroku: A Diplomatic Record of the Sino-Japanese War: 1894–1895* (Princeton, NJ: Princeton University Press, 1982).

MODERN AGE

Taiwan entered early modern age in the 1600s. Many general history books cover the unique experience of the Taiwanese who had to deal with Europeans, Japanese, Chinese Ming and Qing dynasties for their modernization. Among the modern history books are Xiaobing Li, *Modern China: Understanding the Modern Nation* (Santa Barbara, CA: ABC-CLIO, 2015); Jonathan D. Spence, *The Search for Modern China*, third edition (New York: W. W. Norton, 2013); Keith R. Schoppa, *Revolution and Its Past: Identities and Change in Modern Chinese History*, second edition (Upper Saddle River, NJ: Prentice Hall, 2006); Immanuel C. Y. Hsu, *The Rise of Modern China*, sixth edition (Oxford, UK: Oxford University Press, 2000); and Simon Long, *Taiwan: China's Last Frontier* (New York: St. Martin's, 1991). Many titles focus on some specific topics such as Edward L. Dreyer's *Zheng He: China and the Oceans in the Early Ming Dynasty, 1405–1433* (New York: Pearson/Longman, 2007) and Michael S. Neiberg's *Warfare in World History* (London: Routledge, 2001).

In Taiwan and China, historians also focus on some specific themes like nationalism, transnationalism, industrialization, globalization, and geopolitics for their political agenda and security concerns. Some popular textbooks and primary sources are Jiang Renjie, *Jiegou Cheng Chenggong* [Revisit Cheng Chenggong] (Taipei: Sanmin chubanshe [Three Peoples Publishing], 2006); Shen Fuwei, *Zhongxi wenhua jiaoliushi* [History of the cultural exchanges between the East and West] (Shanghai: Shanghai renmin chubanshe [Shanghai People's Press], 1985); Compilation Committee, *Kangxi tongyi Taiwan dang'an shiliao xuanji* [Selected archival history materials on Kangxi's unification of Taiwan] (Fuzhou: Fujian renmin chubanshe [Fujian People's Press], 1983); and History Department, Tianjin Normal College, comp., *Zhongguo jianshi* [A concise history of China] (Beijing: Renmin jiaoyu chubanshe [People's Education Press], 1980).

WORLD WARS AND CIVIL WAR

The two world wars and the Chinese Civil War of 1946–1949 had strong impacts on Taiwan. Although World War II ended the Japanese colonization, the civil war brought about a new authoritarian government in Taiwan for the next thirty-eight years. The books providing some significant interpretations on these big events include Milton W. Meyer, *Japan: A Concise History*, fourth edition (Lanham, MD: Rowman & Littlefield, 2013); Franco David Macri, *Clash of Empires in South China: The Allied Nations' Proxy War with Japan, 1935–1941* (Lawrence: University Press of Kansas, 2012); Peter Zarrow, *China in War and Revolution, 1895–1949* (New York: Routledge, 2005); and Jack Gray, *Rebellions and Revolutions: China from the 1800s to 2000* (Oxford, UK: Oxford University Press, 2002).

Several distinguished titles focus on the Chinese Civil War. Some historians in the West agree that the Chinese Communist Party's (CCP's) victory over the KMT was politically predestined, including the conflicts between two parties, influences of American involvements, intellectuals' critiques, student movements, and land reforms. Some, however, have questioned the emphasis on particular scenes or relations. Joseph Esherick, for example, observes that early works on the civil war and land reforms had a partial analysis with rosy descriptions. Esherick suggests not to think the Chinese revolution explainable by "anti-pole" structures, as "China and the West, state and society, urban-rural or class contradictions" in his work. Suzanne Pepper stresses in her book, *Civil War in China: The Political Struggle, 1945–1949* (Berkeley: University of California Press, 1978), that although the CCP land reform succeeded in gaining support to match the GMD, people's attitudes toward the two were not totally either advantageous or disadvantageous for either party during the war. Nevertheless, the CCP was one of the minority parties and was not accused of being responsible for the war, which the GMD, already powerful, could not escape. Odd Arne Westad and Edward L. Dreyer explain the outcome of the civil war in conventional military-historical terms in their works: Westad, *Decisive Encounters: The Chinese Civil War, 1946–1950* (Stanford, CA: Stanford University Press, 2003) and Dreyer, *China at War, 1901–1949* (New York: Longman, 1995).

Taiwanese and Chinese historians explored the government archives and official documents and tried to reconstruct what happened to Taiwan during the first half of the twentieth century. Among the major books are Chen Shichang, *Zhanhuo 70 nian Taiwan shi* [Post-war Taiwan in 70 years] (Taipei: Shibao wenhua, 2015); Wang Zhangling, *Jiang Jingguo Shanghai dahu ji: Shanghai jingji guanzhi shimo* [Jiang Jingguo's Great Tiger Hunt in Shanghai: A Full Record of the Shanghai Economic Reform] (Taipei: Zhizhong chubanshe, 1999); Military History Research Division, China Academy of Military Sciences (CAMS), *Zhongguo renmin jiefangjun zhanshi* [War history of the PLA] (Beijing: Junshi kexue chubanshe [Military Science Press, 1987); Yang Guoyu, *Dangdai Zhongguo haijun* [Contemporary Chinese navy] (Beijing: Zhongguo shehui kexue chubanshe [China Social Sciences Press], 1987); and Ma Ying-jeou, *Cong xin haiyangfa lun Diaoyutai lieyu yu Donghai huajie wenti* [New oceanic regulations: Issues of the Diaoyu Islands and border of the East China Sea] (Taipei: Zhengzhong Books, 1986).

THE COLD WAR

Taiwan survived through the Cold War. For historical background of the Cold War in East Asia, Xiaobing Li, *The Cold War in East Asia* (London: Routledge, 2018); Michael Szonyi, *Cold War Island: Quemoy on the Front Line* (New York: Cambridge University Press, 2008); and Malcolm Muir, Jr., ed., *The Cold War: From Détente to the Soviet Collapse* (Lexington: Virginia Military Institute Press, 2006) provide global background of the Cold War between the United States and the Soviet Union and two contending camps headed by the two superpowers.

The major reason for Taiwan's success during the 1950s–1970s is the change of U.S. policy toward Taiwan from a "hand-off," nonintervention to "hand-on" involvement. For U.S. military commitment and economic aid, the Cold War historians provide a wide range of coverage. Among the research monographs and primary sources are James I. Matray, ed., *Northeast Asia and the Legacy of Harry S. Truman: Japan, China, and the Two Koreas* (Kirksville, MO: Truman State University, 2012); Robert G. Sutter, *U.S.-Chinese Relations: Perilous Past, Pragmatic Present* (New York: Rowman & Littlefield Publishers, 2010); Nancy Bernkopt Tucker, *Strait Talk: United States-Taiwan Relations and the Crisis with China* (Cambridge, MA: Harvard University Press, 2009); Patrick Tyler, *A Great Wall: Six Presidents and China* (New York: Public Affairs, 1999); Xiaoyuan Liu, *A Partnership for Disorder: China, the United States, and Their Policies for the Postwar Disposition of the Japanese Empire, 1941–1945* (Cambridge, UK: Cambridge University Press, 1996); Thomas J. Christensen, *Useful Adversaries: Grand Strategy,*

Domestic Mobilization, and Sino-American Conflict, 1947–1958 (Princeton, NJ: Princeton University Press, 1996); Lanxin Xiang, *Recasting the Imperial Far East: Britain and America in China, 1945–1950* (Armonk, NY: M. E. Sharpe, 1995); Nancy Bernkopf Tucker, *Taiwan, Hong Kong, and the United States, 1945–1992: Uncertain Friendships* (New York: Twayne Publishers, 1994); David Finkelstein, *Washington's Taiwan Dilemma, 1949–1950: From Abandonment to Salvation* (Fairfax, VA: George Mason University Press, 1993); Richard M. Fried, *Nightmare in Red* (New York: Oxford University Press, 1990); Doak Barnett, *China and the Major Powers in East Asia* (Washington, DC: Brookings Institute, 1977); and U.S. State Department, *Area Handbook for the Republic of China* (Washington, DC: U.S. Government Printing Office, 1969).

There are more titles on Taiwan's political, economic, and social reforms, for example, Baizhu Chen and Shaomin Huang, *The Asian Economic Crisis and Taiwan's Economy* (Beijing: Jinji chubanshe [Economics Press], 2000); Ge Yong-guang, *Taiwan Stories: Politics* (Taipei: Government Information Bureau, ROC Executive Yuan, 1999); Qi Guang-yu, *The Development of Constitutionalism for the ROC: The Constitutional Evolution since 1949* (Taipei: Yangzhi Cultural Publishing, 1998); Linda Chao and Ramon H. Myers, *The First Chinese Democracy: Political Life in the Republic of China on Taiwan* (Baltimore, MD: John Hopkins University Press, 1998); Steven J. Hood, *The Kuomintang and the Democratization of Taiwan* (Boulder, CO: Westview Press, 1997); John Markoff, *Waves of Democracy: Social Movement and Political Change* (Thousand Oaks, CA: Pine Forge Press, 1996); Jaushieh J. Wu, *Taiwan's Democratization: Forces behind the New Momentum* (Hong Kong: Oxford University Press, 1995); Tun-jen Cheng, Chi Huang, and Samuel S. G. Wu, *Inherited Rivalry: Conflict across the Taiwan Straits* (Boulder, CO: Lynne Rienner, 1995); Shao-chuan Leng, ed., *Chiang Ching-kuo's Leadership in the Development of the Republic of China on Taiwan* (Lanham, MD: University Press of America, 1993); and Harvey J. Feldman, ed., *Constitutional Reform and the Future of the Republic of China* (New York: M. E. Sharpe, 1991).

Since the late 1980s, significant progress toward the study of Cold War history has occurred. The flowering of the "reform and opening" era in China resulted in a more flexible political and academic environment compared to the time of Mao Zedong's reign, leading to a relaxation of the extremely rigid criteria for releasing party and military documents. Consequently, some fresh and meaningful historical materials, including papers of the former leaders, party and government documents, and local archives, are now available to historians. Among the Chinese titles on Cold War diplomacy are Wang Taiping, ed., *Zhonghua renmin gongheguo waijiaoshi, 1970–1978* [Diplomatic history of the PRC, 1970–1978] (Beijing: Shijie zhishi chubanshe [World Knowledge Publishing], 1999); Su Ge, *Meiguo duihua zhengce yu Taiwan wenti* [U.S. China policy and the issue of Taiwan] (Beijing: Shijie zhishi chubanshe [World Knowledge Publishing], 1998); and Gong Li, *Kuayue honggou: 1969–1979 nian zhongmei guanxi de yanbian* [Bridging the chasm: The evolution of Sino-American relations, 1969–1979] (Zhengzhou: Henan renmin chubanshe [Henan People's Press], 1992).

Among the Cold War military history and Taiwan are Shen Weiping, *8–23 Paoji Jinmen* [8–23 bombardment of Jinmen] (Beijing: Huayi chubanshe [Huayi Publishers], 1999); Di Jiu and Ke Feng, *Chaozhang chaoluo; guogong jiaozhu Taiwan haixia jishi* [Record of the CCP-GMD confrontation in the Taiwan Straits] (Beijing: Zhongguo gongshang chubanshe [China Industrial and Commercial Publishing], 1996]; and History Compilation and Translation Bureau, ROC Defense Ministry, *8–23 Paozhan shengli 30 zhounian jinian wenji* [Recollection for the 30th anniversary of the Victorious August 23 Artillery Battle] (Taipei: Guofangbu yinzhichang [Defense Ministry Printing Office], 1989); Han Huaizhi, *Dangdai Zhongguo jundui de junshi gongzuo* [Military affairs of contemporary China] (Beijing: Zhongguo shehui kexue chubanshe [China's Social Science Press], 1989); and Wang Dinglie, *Dongdai Zhongguo kongjun* [Contemporary Chinese air force] (Beijing: Zhongguo shehui kexue chubanshe [China's Social Sciences Press], 1989). Certainly, the Chinese government still has a long way to go before "free academic inquiry" becomes reality, but the value of the opening of documentary materials for the study of military history cannot be underestimated.

CONTEMPORARY TAIWAN

Taiwan faces a long road ahead for its independence or its unification with China. Nevertheless, the Taiwanese democratic government has allowed its people to voice their interests, concerns, and ideas. U.S. president Donald Trump has started to reach out to Taiwan when many people in the world believe that Taiwan faces a historical movement in history. Many new books attempt to reinterpret the history of Taiwan such as Y. R. Gong Ben and G. B. Wei, *Native Ethnic Groups in Taiwan* (Taiwan: Cheng Xin Publishing Company, 2001) and Xiaobing Li and Zuohong Pan, eds., *Taiwan in the Twenty-first Century* (New York: University Press of America, 2003). Some of the authors focus on some specific issues, including Sarah Raine and Christian Miere, *Regional Disorder: The South China Sea Disputes* (London: Routledge,

2013); Syaru Shirley Lin, *Taiwan's China Dilemma: Contested Identities and Multiple Interests in Taiwan's Cross-Strait Economic Policy* (Stanford, CA: Stanford University Press, 2016); and Suisheng Zhao, ed., *Across the Taiwan Strait: Mainland China, Taiwan, and the 1995–1996 Crisis* (London: Routledge, 1999). There are some important primary sources on Taiwan, including *U.S. National Security and Military/Commercial Concerns with the People's Republic of China*, Select Committee, U.S. House of Representatives, Christopher Cox, Chairman (the U.S. Government Printing Office, Washington, D.C. 1999); Richard Berntein and H. Ross Munro, *The Coming Conflict with China* (New York: Alfred A. Knopf, 1997); Ezra F. Vogel, ed., *Living with China: U.S.-China Relations in the Twenty-First Century* (New York: W.W. Norton, 1997).

More Chinese sources for history study on Taiwan. For example, Committee of Aborigines in Taiwan, Executive Yuan, *Taiwan yuanzhu minzu gezu renkou tongji* [Statistics of all ethnic minorities in Taiwan] (Taipei: Government Printing Office, 2008); ROC Government Information Office, *The Republic of China Year Book: Taiwan 2002* (Taipei: Government Information Office, 2002) ROC Directorate General of Budget, *Statistical Yearbook of the Republic of China 2001* (Taipei: Accounting and Statistics, Executive Yuan, 2001); Government Information Bureau, ROC Executive Yuan, *A Glance at ROC* (Taipei: ROC Government Printing Office, 2000); ROC Ministry of Education, *Annual Educational Statistics in the Republic of China* (Taipei: Ministry of Education Publishing, 1997); B. H. Huang, *Education Reform: Concepts, Strategies and Measures* (Taipei, 1996); Council on Education Reform. *The Concluding Report* (Taipei: ROC Government Printing Office, 1996); Department of Education, Taiwan Provincial Government, *Educational Statistics in Taiwan Province, 1994* (Taipei: Taiwan Provincial Government Printing, 1996); W. S. Fu, *Critical Heritage and Creative Development* (Taipei: Dongda Publishing, 1991); and Compilation Committee of ROC History, *A Pictorial History of the Republic of China* (Taipei: Modern China Press, 1981).

The list of literature includes publications, academy textbooks, and educational materials about Taiwan's history. These sources add a viable view of the global perspective, which reinterpreted a series of fundamental issues crucial to understanding the history of Taiwan. Having covered many issues on the Taiwanese history and published in recent years, they provide a useful research bibliography for students who are interested in the history of modern Taiwan, but do not read Chinese.

Index

About the Author

XIAOBING LI, PhD, is professor of the Department of History and Geography and director of the Western Pacific Institute at the University of Central Oklahoma. He is author, editor, or coeditor of ABC-CLIO's *Modern China; Oil: A Cultural and Geographic Encyclopedia of Black Gold; China at War: An Encyclopedia,* and *Civil Liberties in China.* His other recent works include *East Asia and the West: An Entangled History; The Cold War in East Asia; Power versus Law in Modern China; Corruption and Anti-corruption in Modern China; Ethnic China: Identity, Assimilation, and Resistance; Urbanization and Party Survival in China: People vs. Power; China's Battle for Korea: The 1951 Spring Offensive; Evolution of Power: China's Struggle, Survival, and Success; Modern Chinese Legal Reform: New Perspectives,* and *Taiwan in the Twenty-first Century.*

The History of Ukraine
Paul Kubicek

The History of Venezuela, Second
Edition
H. Micheal Tarver

The History of Vietnam
Justin Corfield